NONFICTION FOR YOUNG ADULTS

FROM

DELIGHT

▶ TO ◀

WISDOM

by
Betty Carter
and
Richard F. Abrahamson

ORYX PRESS
1990

The rare Arabian Oryx is believed to have inspired the myth of the unicorn. This desert antelope became virtually extinct in the early 1960s. At that time several groups of international conservationists arranged to have 9 animals sent to the Phoenix Zoo to be the nucleus of a captive breeding herd. Today the Oryx population is nearly 800, and over 400 have been returned to reserves in the Middle East.

Copyright © 1990 by
The Oryx Press
4041 North Central at Indian School Rd.
Phoenix, AZ 85012-3397

Published simultaneously in Canada

Printed and Bound in the United States of America

∞ The paper used in this publication meets the minimum requirements of American National Standard for Information Science—Permanence of Paper for Printed Library Materials, ANSI Z39.48, 1984.

Library of Congress Cataloging-in-Publication Data

Carter, Betty, 1944–
    Nonfiction for young adults: from delight to wisdom / by Betty Carter and Richard F. Abrahamson.
    p. cm.
Includes bibliographical references.
ISBN 0-89774-555-8
1. Young adults—Books and reading 2. Young adult literature—Bibliography. I. Abrahamson, Richard F. II. Title.
Z1037.A1C345 1990   90-7046
011.62'5—dc20   CIP

To our dads:

Bill Brogdon, who played the ninth inning with the same grace and style he showed in the other eight.

BC

For Stan the Man and his field of dreams.

RFA

Contents

Acknowledgments

When we first planned this book, we naively assumed that any pleasure in the production of it would come through our reading, our work with young adults, and the hammering out of ideas between ourselves. How wrong we were! The sense of joy has instead stemmed from our contact with the librarians and teachers who shared their programs and ideas for their classrooms; the editors who freely gave of their time and expertise; the publicists who patiently endured our many queries; and our colleagues, who listened to endless problems we generated, and patiently offered advice. We can thank only a few: Jim Thomas, who believed in this project from the moment of inception; Karen Harris, whose humor and insights got us out of innumerable theoretical traps; and Bill Morris, who generously extended professionalism into the realm of friendship.

Special thanks must go to the authors who consented to be interviewed. We believed in the concept of these interviews from the moment we began putting the book together, but two factors made them a reality. First of all, the College of Education at the University of Houston provided grant money to underwrite some of the costs of obtaining them. Second, the authors themselves turned this process from a dry journalistic routine into an exciting learning experience. Lee J. Ames, Brent Ashabranner, Daniel and Susan Cohen, James Cross Giblin, Milton Meltzer, and Laurence Pringle not only donated their time, but did so graciously.

Our respective families deserve special mention. Neta Carter not only gave moral support, but she also typed a portion of the manuscript. Beth and Meg Abrahamson filled our houses with pictures drawn from the Lee J. Ames books. Our spouses, Don and Margaret, endured a hot Texas summer even though they wanted the four of us to go to Hawaii. Now we can. We couldn't have done this book without you.

Introduction

When you opened this book, you became part of an impressive national statistic concerning adult reading patterns: You began reading nonfiction. Your reasons for doing so may have been a personal desire to add to your knowledge of young adult literature or from a more immediate need to fulfill the requirements for a college course, but nonetheless you are now—like the majority of literate adult Americans—reading nonfiction. Although we may find transitory diversion or cathartic identification through novels or short stories, both book buying and book borrowing statistics confirm that nonfiction makes up the bulk of our reading selections. From magazines to newspapers, cookbooks to textbooks, personal accounts to essays, we are a nation of nonfiction readers.

These patterns do not emerge overnight; instead, they result from a subtle shifting of interests as we grow older. This transition period, like many others, occurs during the teen years. Despite this trend, nonfiction works, particularly informational books, have been neglected in textbooks, in course content for librarians and teachers, and in research studies. Recognizing the low status of nonfiction, Milton Meltzer, a highly regarded author of informational books for young adults, quotes English critic Aidan Chambers's views on the place of nonfiction in children's literature:

> While it has not been completely ignored, . . . nonfiction "does get brushed off and pushed to the back . . . as though information books were socially inferior to the upper-crust stuff we call literature." The doyens of children's literature . . . have narrowed its meaning to encompass only stories, poems, and plays—"the holy three. . . . We'd do better by children, and ourselves if we revised its accepted definition to include all that is published . . . every book, no matter what its content and purpose, deserves and demands the respect and treatment—the skill and care—of art."[1]

We hope this book will begin to negate the prejudice against nonfiction. We hope to show the literary qualities of nonfiction as well as to define its importance for young adults. We suggest that the vital element nonfiction lacks is professional attention. Since we know that young adults read nonfiction and that nonfiction volumes make up an average of two-thirds to three-fourths of most library holdings, it's time to take a serious look at the genre. First, though, we need to define it.

Whenever we talk to young adults about nonfiction books, we always begin by asking them to tell us exactly what they think non-fiction is. Invariably, one student will raise a hand and volunteer the clichéd assumption that nonfiction is true and fiction is not true. At such times we realize that this student is repeating a piece of mythology that has been passed down to, and accepted by, young people in much the same way that other educational legends—like George Washington chopping down the cherry tree and Abe Lincoln trudging through a winter storm to return a borrowed book—have become a part of the folklore of classrooms around this country.

Nonfiction books aren't defined by the degree of authenticity or fabrication within their pages but, rather, by whether they belong in one of two subclassifications in the Dewey Decimal system. When Melvil Dewey first designed this scheme, he grouped all books into ten major subject divisions and assigned each a hundreds number.[2]

Figure 1. Major Classifications of the Dewey Decimal System

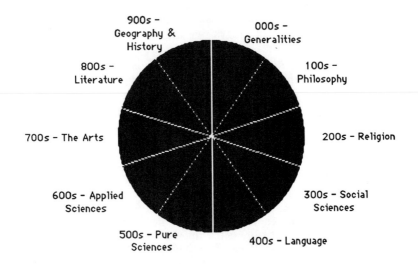

He further divided each of the major classifications into ten distinct subcategories. The 800s, or literature section, including plays, novels, poetry, and short stories, were initially grouped by the author's original language; differences were designated by numbers appearing in the tens place.[3]

Figure 2. Dewey Decimal System–The 800s

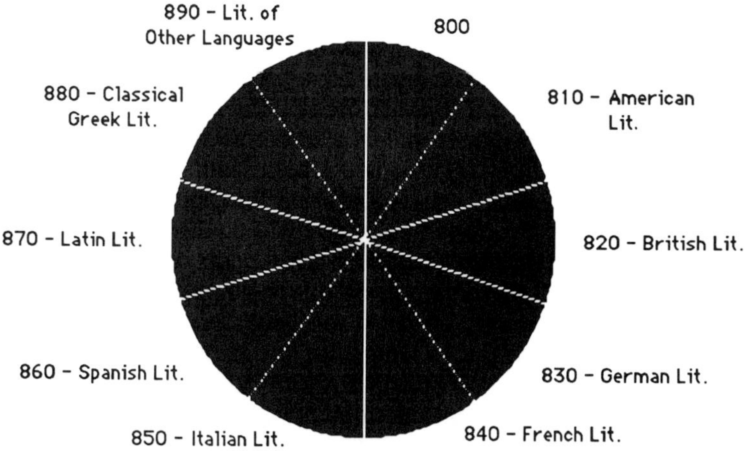

Pie chart with segments:
- 890 – Lit. of Other Languages
- 800
- 880 – Classical Greek Lit.
- 810 – American Lit.
- 870 – Latin Lit.
- 820 – British Lit.
- 860 – Spanish Lit.
- 830 – German Lit.
- 850 – Italian Lit.
- 840 – French Lit.

Each of these ten segments received further divisions by form, designated by the units number.[4]

Figure 3. Division by Form. 810–889: The Dewey Decimal System

	Poetry	Drama	Fiction	Essays	Speeches	Letters	Satire & Humor	Misc. Writing	Other Areas
American Lit.	810	812	813	814	815	816	817	818	819
British Lit.	821	822	823	824	825	826	827	828	829
German Lit.	831	832	833	834	835	836	837	838	839
French Lit.	841	842	843	844	845	846	847	848	849
Italian Lit.	851	852	853	854	855	856	857	858	859
Spanish Lit.	861	862	863	864	865	866	867	868	869
Latin Lit.	871	872	873*	874**	875	876	877	878	879
Classical Greek Lit.	881	882	883*	884**	885	886	887	888	889

* Includes epic poetry and fiction
** Includes lyric poetry

Because books by English, American, French, or Russian authors appeared in their own categories, locating a particular novel or volume of short stories, especially in large collections, quickly became a baffling and tiresome chore. Books by Dickens and Dostoyevsky were shelved far from one another, while those by Agatha Christie and Joseph Conrad appeared in the same section.

To counter the confusion, librarians removed all their novels and short stories from the literature, or 800s section, and placed them in a separate area simply arranged in alphabetical order by the author or editor's last name. Thus fiction was born. And nonfiction, depending on one's orientation toward literature, became either everything but fiction or merely the remainder of the collection. Poetry survived as nonfiction, as did plays, comic books, jokes, riddles, superstitions, and folktales. While within these forms individual volumes may contain truths, none in its entirety is either true or factual. And because these books remain as nonfiction, nonfiction cannot simply be defined as "true."

So what is nonfiction, then? Simply put, it's any book that's not a novel or a short story. Nonfiction includes those books cataloged by subject as well as by form: factual books about topics such as the solar system, automobiles, curiosities and wonders, and cooking. Similar volumes, best known as informational works, represent the bulk of books discussed in the following chapters. A great many of these volumes promise hours of pleasure, stimulation, and contemplation for their young adult readers. Others offer only tedium and boredom. As professionals interested in both young adults and their literature, we must differentiate between the exhilarating and the utilitarian, and separate those books that convey wonder and passion from those that merely deliver data. We hope to dismiss the latter works and concentrate on the former—the ones, that to paraphrase Robert Probst, feed a child's thinking rather than control it.[5] At their best, these informational books are characterized by beautifully written prose, definable themes, unifying structure, and stimulating topics. We'll look at how to evaluate these books, how they came to be, and how to use them in library and classroom settings.

The book you are about to read discusses seven issues related to information books, each one making up a single chapter. The first addresses the reading interests of teenagers, emphasizing the role of nonfiction in young adult book selection. It is the teenage readers who drew us into the field of nonfiction, and we hope they do the same for you.

Equally as important as young adult readers are the books available to them, and next we'll examine these works. Five chapters concern criteria for evaluation: accuracy, content, style, organization, and format. But beware. Evaluation is neither cut and dried nor simple. There is no finite number of items to tally for a book to receive a distinguished rating. Rather, the criteria represent points worthy of consideration, matters that can only be weighed within the context of each book. Don't look for a checklist here, for we don't intend to provide one. Expect instead to find issues raised which you alone will resolve with each individual volume of nonfiction you encounter.

Young adults and books will not automatically find each other; they need a matchmaker to bring them together. That agent is you, the professional librarian or teacher. The final chapter addresses your role in this literary triangle: how to use informational books in promoting recreational reading, supplementing the curriculum, programming, and maintaining a current collection.

Interspersed between each of these chapters are interviews with seven prominent authors of informational books. These writers will share their creative processes from the first moment they identify the concept for a work to researching, writing, designing, and publishing nonfiction for young adults.

In our reading we've come to respect nonfiction. We've encountered authors we've grown to admire, titles deserving to be read, and young adults seeking reading guidance. We hope that through this book we can extend some of these pleasures to you.

NOTES

1. Meltzer, Milton (1976). Where Do All the Prizes Go? The Case for Non-fiction. *The Horn Book, 52*, p. 19.

2. Dewey, Melvil (1979). *Dewey Decimal Classification and Relative Index.* Vol. 1, pp. xxv–xxxvii.

3. Dewey, Melvil (1979). *Dewey Decimal Classification and Relative Index.* Vol. 2, *Schedules.* pp. 1389–1434.

4. Dewey, Melvil (1979). *Dewey Decimal Classification and Relative Index.* Vol. 2, *Schedules.* pp. 1398–1421.

5. Probst, Robert E. Adolescent Literature and the English Curriculum. *English Journal, 75*, pp. 26–30.

CHAPTER 1
Interest

"Tell me a story, daddy," a small boy begs before going off to bed. "A story with magic, excitement, danger, and dragons." With this simple request a nighttime ceremony begins: Once upon a time in a land far away there lived a poor woodcutter with three sons. . . .

The enchantment of another world fills the boy's mind as he listens to the time-honored tale of a brave lad, a beautiful princess, and daring deeds. As the power of the ancient story takes hold, both father and son settle into contentment: the youngster pleased with this special time spent with his dad, and the parent confident that he has delivered just what his child requested.

Or has he? Perhaps the father has substituted his own ideas of magic and excitement for those of his son. Perhaps the youngster finds wonder not in the granting of three wishes but rather in the emergence of a moth from a cocoon, the flowering of a zinnia from seed, or the appearance of a rainbow after a storm. Hasn't the father defined his son's wishes in his own terms? Perhaps a deeper satisfaction for the boy might come from the story of how a cicada sheds its skin, or how a comet follows its orbit around the sun, or how a modern-day dragon, the giant monitor lizard, survives its brutal habitat on the island of Komodo.

Not all children will respond to this realistic definition of story, but neither will they consistently choose fantasy over fact when looking for reading material. Youngsters want both, and teachers and librarians who truly serve them will provide many opportunities for interaction with literature in all its forms.

Such professionals need not remove folktales or fantasy or poetry or realistic fiction from a child's early exposure to literature and story. Nor must they eliminate fiction from a young adult's literary life. What they create instead are expanded experiences with books, which include the wonder of nature, the drama of real people slaying their own dragons, and the excitement of discovery. They choose this course not because they *like* informational books, but because children, teenagers, and adults show strong preferences for such works. This position is clearly supported by the available research on reading interests.

READING RESEARCH

What Young Adults Read

Researchers who want to know what young people like to read typically ask them. Respected investigators must consider and define three major qualifiers when designing their queries: whom to ask, what to ask, and how to ask it.

Whom to ask. Since no one person or research team can question every teenager about what he or she likes to read, scholars must impose some limits to establish their population. They can talk to the neighbor who baby-sits their children; the most widely read students in their favorite literature classes; the volunteers in the school or public library; all high school students from one school, district, or state; just boys or just girls; voracious readers or remedial readers; junior high students or high school students; young adults proficient in English or those learning it as a second language. The possibilities go on and on, and with each, the likelihood increases that investigative results will change.

What to ask. Researchers can record favorite books; books studied in school; books circulated in libraries; or books purchased in supermarkets, malls, or bookstores. They can put a time limit on these choices by asking teenagers to recap their favorite books of all time, of the last year, or the last week. Investigators can also ask for specific titles, genres, subjects, or authors. Again, each focus influences both the results of a study and the perceptions of interest.

How to ask. Researchers can employ one of these methodologies: survey, interview, or an examination of books chosen in popularity polls. They can interview young people in person, realizing that teenagers will naturally return what they think researchers want to hear. Or they can move one step back from the process and ask young adults to check a list of their favorite titles, knowing that such a list will, in effect, narrow their choices. Researchers can submit lists of subjects and genres or brief synopses of imaginary books and direct teenagers to indicate their favorites. Or they can study titles purchased or circulated, as indicated in state polls like that in Iowa or nationwide projects like Young Adult Choices from the International Reading Association. Each interrogative approach yields slightly different results. Therefore, the conclusions from one study can never be completely generalized to a universal population of young adults. Each piece of research constitutes just one more slice in the reading interest pie. Although some wedges may prove more generous than others, they still remain parts of the whole.

With all the permutations available to researchers, and all the subtle influences found in books, it's no wonder that librarians and teachers don't know precisely what all young adults like to read. But by looking at several significant studies, they can still substantiate the following assumptions: Young adults read nonfiction; this interest in nonfiction crosses ability levels; and on the whole, teenage boys tend to read more nonfiction than teenage girls. The following discussion will examine each of these statements in more detail.

Young Adults Read Nonfiction

This interest does not manifest itself suddenly with the onset of puberty, but proceeds developmentally, beginning in the primary grades and increasing through the high school years. To validate the statement that teenagers read more nonfiction than children do, it's necessary to establish that young children read nonfiction.

One problem in accumulating hard data to support this thesis results from the unfortunate, but all too common, educational practice of limiting the library selections of preschool and primary-grade children to those books designated as "E" or Easy Books. The sentiments behind such policies are usually well intentioned. School administrators wish to provide young children with a narrow, appropriate pool from which to choose books, rather than bewilder them by offering free rein within the vast holdings of a particular library. In practice, these restrictions not only violate a child's right to read what he or she wants, but also severely limit the nonfiction choices available. An "E" designation on a book more often than not denotes easy fiction. Nonfiction books, particularly informational ones, receive a Dewey Decimal classification and are shelved in another part of the library. The problem lies not with the designation of "E" or Easy Books, but rather in the informal practice that confines young children to this section. Consequently, many researchers often don't know whether or not young children enjoy nonfiction, for they don't have the opportunities to find out.

Despite this situation, a clean tally of children's reading preferences, including both nonfiction and fiction book selections, exists. In 1984, school librarian Glenda Childress analyzed the reading selections of kindergarten and first-grade children over a period of 18 weeks. Of the 1,184 books circulated during that time, 40% were nonfiction, strongly suggesting that young children do indeed read nonfiction.[1]

(While Childress defines nonfiction as "informational books drawn from the ten Dewey classes, excluding folklore, poetry and plays, and certain other borderline types of literature,"[2] other researchers employ different definitions. For example, some include plays, comics, and riddles as nonfiction. Even though information books are always included in these designations, their frequency of appearance cannot be reported with any degree of exactitude. Therefore, in this chapter the term *nonfiction* will not be used as a synonym for information books but instead as the category encompassing information books.)

Other evidence supports the assumption that nonfiction contributes to part of an elementary child's pleasure reading. In 1974 Judith Blair discovered that about one-fifth of the reading material chosen by the second-, third-, and fourth-grade students she studied consisted of nonfiction.[3]

Figures from the International Reading Association's Children's Choices Program also corroborate these data. Each year over 10,000 U.S. youngsters participate in this project. Provided with several hundred titles published the previous year, the children select the books they want to read, or hear, and rate each book on a graduated preference scale. Pressure, encouragement, and rewards from teachers and librarians to read and evaluate certain titles are strictly forbidden. At the end of each school year, the ballots are tabulated and the approximately 100 titles receiving the most positive votes are designated as Children's Choices. We examined all of the selections from the first ten years of the project (1975–1984) and concluded that out of the 295 books freely selected and favored by children, 43% were nonfiction. By breaking down these selections, we further designated 21% of the preferred nonfiction books as informational works.

In a similar annual venture, teenagers indicate their favorite books through the International Reading Association's Young Adults' Choices project. This latecomer to preference polls was created in 1987, and information on only the first two years is now available. In the first balloting (1987), 10% of the books selected as favorites were nonfiction. The following year that number increased to 20%. These figures may not look like much of a trend when compared with those from the Children's Choices Program, but given the pool—heavily favoring fiction—from which young adults made their choices, they proportionally represent as many nonfiction as fiction titles.

While the figures from the young adults' choices project indicate that young adults will indeed choose some nonfiction for pleasure reading, they don't support the thesis that they read more nonfiction than young children do, nor do they indicate that older teenagers read more nonfiction than younger adolescents. This evidence can be found elsewhere.

George Norvell, in his massive 1973 reading study, used data collected from 2,556,090 students responding to 4,993 reading selections. He concluded that a strong interest in nonfiction emerges at about the fourth grade and that interest grows during adolescence.[4] Similarly, in their 1972 review of the literature concerning interests, Purves and Beach reached the same conclusion: Nonfiction becomes an increasingly important component in overall reading preferences as young adults mature.[5]

This progression first emerged in an early study conducted by Ruth Strang. In 1946 she asked teenagers in grades seven through eleven, "What kind of book or article would you choose to read above all others?"[6] She reports that students in grade eight began showing interest in books on vocational guidance and careers, and that this interest grew until it was greatest among the juniors. Strang asked these adolescents, "Suppose you were going to write a book or article that persons of your age would all want to read, what would be its title?"[7] The older respondents favored informational subjects: selecting an appropriate college, explaining school government, understanding a particular religion, and facing adult situations. Younger students, on the other hand, were more concerned with the fictional topics of adventure, romance, and mystery.

The trend for older teenagers to choose nonfiction more often than younger teenagers also influences book buying. A 1986 Gallup survey of the books young adults purchase revealed that only 19% of the books bought by younger teens were nonfiction. Among older adolescents, that number increased significantly: Approximately 40% of the books they paid for were nonfiction volumes.[8]

It must be noted that not all reading interest studies agree with these results, particularly those that ask teenagers, or their teachers and librarians, to cite their favorite books; invariably these designs produce lists of novels. In 1978 Los Angeles librarians Campbell, Davis, and Quinn asked their young adult patrons for titles of books they would most likely recommend to others. All of the top ten choices were novels.[9] Similarly, in the same year, Julie Alm requested that secondary school youngsters write down their favorite titles. The ten books most often mentioned were works of fiction.[10] When Barbara Samuels polled secondary English teachers in 1981 for the most popular titles with their students, fiction was again returned.[11]

While the above investigations indicate that particular novels are favored by many students, they do not conclude that nonfiction books are not being read or enjoyed. We contend that Norvell's 1973 assertion stands. Young adults read nonfiction, and as they grow older they read more nonfiction. But does this trend hold true for proficient as well as remedial readers? The next section addresses this issue.

Interest in Nonfiction Crosses Ability Levels

The impact of intelligence and reading ability on individual preferences has been examined in numerous studies. In 1968 Jo Stanchfield conducted conferences with 158 boys in grades four through eight as a method for determining their reading interests. She found age-level concerns surprisingly similar for those youngsters "reading above grade level, at grade level, and below grade level."[12] In their 1972 study Purves and Beach also concluded that, generally, adolescents of different ability levels have comparable interests.[13] Just one year later Norvell declared that intelligence was not an important determiner of reading interests.[14] Similarly, Robert Whitehead reported in his 1984 summary of interest studies that there exists little difference in choices across reading abilities.[15]

These findings do not stand undisputed. In 1963 Anthony Soares asked 1,653 students to rate sixty short stories. He concluded that low-ability students prefer works of nonfiction, particularly science, more than high-ability students do. In an expanded discussion of the same project four years later, he further declared that high-ability students do not like nonfiction at all.[16]

By contrast, Carter determined that high-ability students do indeed read nonfiction for pleasure. During the spring semester of 1981, she looked at those books circulated in her school library by intellectually talented junior high students. Their reading selections were compared to a control group matched by age and sex, but otherwise randomly chosen from the rest of the school population. Those young adults identified as gifted read almost twice as many books as did the randomly selected group, their choices reflected a wider range of interests, and included nonfiction. In fact, 34% of the leisure reading of these academically able teenagers came from nonfiction books. It must be noted, however, that while their classmates checked out fewer nonfiction volumes from the school library, these books represented a greater percent of their pleasure reading circulations.[17] The results of that study are summarized in Figure 4. The heading numbers refer to the general Dewey Decimal classification of the books.

Figure 4. Nonfiction-Circulations for Leisure Reading

Student Group	No. Books	Avg. NF vol Circ. per student	% Leisure Circ.	% 000	% 100	% 200	% 300	% 400	% 500	% 600	% 700	% 800	% 900	% B
Identified Gifted	123	5.6	34	7	3	-	12	2	7	9	45	3	5	7
Control	82	3.7	54	4	4	-	10	-	11	22	40	-	6	2

Studies focusing on less proficient young adult readers prominently mention the importance of nonfiction in the book selections of these teenagers. In 1984 Cathleen Nichols examined the reading preferences of remedial high school students. She does not compare their interests with teenagers of differing achievement levels, but does report that for these adolescents nonfiction books were overwhelmingly preferred over fictional works. Moreover, they seemed to prefer nonfiction of an informational nature; when Nichols further asked these 953 students why they read books, they responded "primarily to learn new things." [18]

More recently, in 1986, Michael C. McKenna also surveyed the reading interests of remedial secondary students: 576 junior high and high school students enrolled in special reading classes. The seven most popular topics—cartoon and comic books; weird but true stories; rock stars; ghosts; magic; stories about famous people; and exploring the unknown—were all nonfiction.[19]

Teenage Boys Read More Nonfiction Than Teenage Girls

The reader's sex has been found to dramatically affect reading interests. Sex differences manifest themselves early, with boys and girls exhibiting strong but divergent preferences for either fiction or nonfiction. Even Glenda Childress's kindergarten and first-grade students exhibited dramatic sex differences in their reading selections. Thirty-two percent of the boys' books were nonfiction; only eight percent of the girls' were. Linda Messina's 1979 study, in which she compared interest inventories with library circulation records in her fourth-grade class, revealed that males overwhelmingly preferred nonfiction books. Boys circulated 163 books, and eighty-five percent of those were nonfiction. By contrast, only fifteen percent of the books circulated by girls were nonfiction.[20]

Historically, other researchers have noted similar characteristics among male and female readers. In reviewing the literature for his 1921 interest study, Arthur Jordan observed sex differences in choices of fiction as well as nonfiction. Although he concluded "that boys and girls read more fiction than anything else and like it better," he added that boys "often show a real liking for history,"[21] while girls at any age do not show an interest in history, travel, science, or adventure.

Young adults are quite aware of these distinctions. In talking to her father about her reading habits, one junior high student, who was devouring fictional series at a prodigious rate, confessed that all her friends swapped and re-read each others' books, while the boys in the class just kept reading all "that nonfiction stuff." A twelfth grader responding to the book *Spaceshots*, included in the 1987 *Young Adult Choices* poll, reveals a similar awareness. While she indicated that she liked the book because "it had neat pictures," she also admitted that "for me this kind of stuff is boring mainly because I'm a girl."

At the conclusion of his extensive 1973 interest study, Norvell asserts that a student's gender remains the most powerful determiner of reading interests. These results have been repeated in other studies, like those conducted by Rudman and Stanchfield, and are listed in the bibliography at the end of the book, allowing us to conclude that boys, more often than girls, prefer nonfiction.

This summation does not indicate that librarians and teachers should shy away from offering nonfiction when working with girls and eliminate fiction from boys' reading recommendations. It does indicate though, that when suggesting books, such professionals should be aware of these differences, and possibly use narrative informational books, biography, or personal accounts as bridges between nonfiction and fiction.

Although the findings from all these studies yield mixed results, they nonetheless indicate that nonfiction is an important part of a young adult's reading material. Undoubtedly the required reading and research for school assignments accounts for some of these circulated volumes. But not all of them. Much of the nonfiction read by young adults is read for pleasure, diversion, and entertainment.

Pleasure versus Curriculum

We have discussed the various methods researchers use to determine which books young adults prefer to read. By asking students their purpose in checking out particular volumes from a library, researchers can obtain a different kind of information—their *reasons* for choosing the books they do.

(This particular method brings up an important point. Can librarians and teachers hypothesize that just because young adults circulate a particular book they will actually read it? According to a study designed by Robert Karlin specifically to answer that question, they can make that assumption a little over half of the time. Karlin reached this conclusion by monitoring the reading of students in grades seven through nine. By questioning these teenagers at the time they returned borrowed materials to the library, he found that 59% of the books were completely read, 24% partially read, and 17% not read at all. Correlation studies comparing library circulations to young adults' expressed reading interests reveal that circulation statistics indeed reflect interests; Karlin indicates that these figures also represent much material actually read.[22])

In her 1982 survey of reading habits of gifted junior high students, Betty Carter required students to fill out cards on each book they checked out. These cards asked for the student's name, the book's title and author, and the student's reason for wanting to read that particular volume. Purposes for reading were divided into four options: class assignments, pleasure reading, no real reason, and other. Through this information she determined that 34% of the identified gifted students' pleasure reading consisted of nonfiction and 54% of the control group's leisure reading material was nonfiction. Surprisingly, she also discovered that fiction rather than nonfiction was most often required for school assignments.

At certain times young adults will freely offer their unsolicited opinions concerning books and thus share their motivation from reading specific titles. The ninth grader who ran into his school library, grabbed the librarian by the arm, and stated, "I've just got to have that book *From Ab to Zogg*. You see, I'm really *into* Middle Earth," left little doubt in anyone's mind that he was circulating that particular non-fiction volume for pleasure.

Researchers can also examine the books young adults choose to read and make educated guesses about the purpose of that material. Books selected in the Young Adults Choices project, for example, are freely chosen without any curricular demands or rewards attached to them. So when books like Bernard Edelman's *Dear America: Letters Home from Vietnam*; Timothy Ferris' *Spaceshots*; Don Lawson's *Album of the Vietnam War*; or Kolodny, Kolodny, and Brattner's *Smart Choices* appear as winners, librarians and teachers can confidently assume that they were read for pleasure.

Still another method exists for determining whether books are being read for pleasure. Researchers can also note those books circulated through a school library, examine that institution's curriculum, and determine whether or not any possible correlation exists between the two. The two of us chose that method by studying almost 50,000 circulations from three junior high schools. Those frequently circulated books—particularly the ones popular on all campuses—that lacked any relationship to course content or specific assignments became likely candidates for pleasure reading.[23]

Several popular informational books from our study appeared to complement the curriculum, but on closer observation these assumptions proved false, indicating that these informational books were circulated for pleasure reading. Two such favored books were Milton Meltzer's *The Truth about the Ku Klux Klan* and Fred J. Cook's *The Ku Klux Klan: America's Recurring Nightmare*. In Texas, the social studies curriculum covers American history in the eighth grade, but that coverage stops with the Civil War, before the Klan ever came into existence. Neither civics nor any other comparative government courses are taught at the junior high level. Information about government, the Klan, secret societies, or specific human rights are not a part of the core junior high curriculum. Despite this situation, students on all campuses circulated these books, indicating that their interest came from outside the walls of their classrooms.

But isn't one of the purposes of school, particularly at the middle/junior high level, to spark interests? Shouldn't some of the topics covered in class drive students to their libraries to find out more about them? We hope so. We hope situations, like the following memory recorded by one of G. Robert Carlsen's former students, repeats itself elsewhere:

> In the eighth grade, I thought I had found my life's work when we started to study electricity. I even remember trying to read some engineering books, and especially one on armature winding. I read the biography of Thomas Edison and dug into everything I could find on electricity. That was the first year I asked for books for Christmas.[24]

In only a single incident were we able to confirm such a phenomenon in our study. On one particular campus, the socioeconomic level of the students and their families negated the possibility of large numbers of them owning computers. Computers had also not been previously available at the elementary schools feeding into this junior high. Most students were introduced to computers in their content classes, through a new course in computer literacy, and with an extensive computer laboratory housed within the library. These young adolescents flocked to the library demanding computer books—books on programming, books on artificial intelligence, books on computer crime, and books on the uses of computers in society. That they discovered computers in school remains an educated guess; that they turned to books to feed this interest stands undisputed.

The most important factor to remember when attempting to determine purpose for reading is that readers approach books in one of two ways: They either look for what they can carry away from the text or they look for what they can experience through the text. Many adults assume that nonfiction, with its information and facts, provides the forum for the former, while fiction, with its characters and storyline, the vehicle for the latter. What is often forgotten is that the individual will, depending on his or her own needs and attitudes, look for different things in the same book. The way someone interacts with a book, or that person's "stance," is determined by the individual reader rather than by the author.

It will come as no surprise to those of you presently working with young adults that *The Guinness Book of World Records* emerged as the most popular informational title checked out during our circulation study. Young adults annually gravitate toward this one volume. They buy it, put their names on waiting lists for it, and even surreptitiously "borrow" it from friends and libraries. Some teenage readers will discover many fascinating facts: The largest sundae ever constructed weighed 33,616.75 pounds; the "Trieste" descended to the greatest ocean depths ever recorded, or 35,820 feet; and the longest slow-pitch baseball game lasted 111 hours and two minutes. The black-and-white photographs also receive attention; a particularly common sight in school and public libraries remains one of groups of young adults gathered around *The Guinness Book* examining and exclaiming over those weird and wonderful pictures of the world's longest limousine, the man with tattoos over most of his body, and Imelda Marcos's enormous shoe collection.

Some young adults derive pleasure from these experiences, from just seeing or reading about unusual events and curiosities of their world. Others approach *The Guinness Book* with a different attitude. They pore over the photograph of the man with the world's longest fingernails and wonder what his life is like. How does he change the sheets on his bed, scratch a mosquito bite, or take photographs? Similarly, they fantasize about having a 13-inch waist, or giving birth to a baby at age 57. The distinction here is important: Books don't determine purpose, readers do. Depending on the reader, then, *The Guinness Book of World Records* may well represent a utilitarian tool or an interactive experience. For many young adults, it is the latter.

Other popular titles from our study indicate that readers derive pleasure through still different avenues. The identification that some teens feel with fictional characters parallels the direct involvement others find not in vicariously experiencing but in actually interacting with the text. Books addressed to the reader as doer, or how-to books, were strongly favored by our particular junior high population. Selected works of Lee J. Ames, the most popular author in the study, surpassed individual offerings from such well-known fiction writers as Judy Blume, M. E. Kerr, and S. E. Hinton. Closely following Ames in popularity were Jim Arnosky, Paul Frame, and Don Bolognese, all noted author/illustrators of books about drawing and sketching. Interestingly enough, several of these authors advocate a method of mimicry, in direct contrast to the three schools' art curricula, which prohibit copying as a legitimate artistic technique.

These selections do not represent the only how-to books that received popular attention. Volumes on how to play certain sports, make paper airplanes, tell a joke, care for pets, and program a computer also figured prominently among the monitored circulations. Again, we could find no correlation between these books and either the mandated curriculum or individual teacher assignments. Even required book reports failed to allow these kinds of books and topics.

Pleasure also comes from knowing and confirming. The satisfaction and power in finding out certain information or exploring unknown theories cannot be denied. Frequently, however, young adults don't want to discover new knowledge, they want to verify what they already know. Some adolescents find comfort in the fact that Frank and Joe Hardy will solve their latest mystery or that Jessica Wakefield at Sweet Valley High will continue to scheme her way through school. There's a different kind of knowledge in nonfiction—not about how stories work but about how facts work. There's reassurance in discovering in book after book that Tyrannosaurus Rex is still a meat eater, that Saturn has rings around it, and that birds eat six times their weight in food. At the 1988 International Reading Association convention in Toronto, Seymour Simon, a respected author of nonfiction for children and young adults, alluded to this phenomenon. He recalled that as a child he kept rereading books about the same scientific topic, not because he necessarily wanted to find out new information, but because he felt so smart to already know most of the facts mentioned.

Series nonfiction provides similar reassurances about form rather than content. The pull of series fiction remains strong with young adults because of the very predictability of the plots. Apparently a similar process works with nonfiction. For example, as with fiction, young adolescents know whether or not they are too sophisticated for the introductory material in elementary books, like Franklin Watts' *First Book* series, or if they are prepared for the sophisticated treatment in the *Impact Books* series, from the same publisher. The books all address different topics, but the distinct packaging of both series, coupled with teenagers' familiarity with previous offerings, alerts potential readers to the level and depth of coverage of any given subject. Similarly, the *Eyewitness Books* from Knopf follow an established form, but not a set formula. The stunning visuals and spare text remain consistent, while each subject dictates its own content.

THE ROLE OF TEACHERS AND LIBRARIANS

Teachers and librarians are a powerful force in helping adolescents develop into lifetime readers. Two distinct behaviors tend to characterize these influential professionals. First, they discover what individual readers profess to like, and they help feed those interests through books. Second, they challenge and entice those same readers by introducing new and different kinds of books and topics. They do this in two ways, each as important as the other: They know their books and they know their students and patrons.

Knowing books translates into reading books. There's a strong tendency for librarians and teachers to equate reading books with reading fiction. Textbooks on young adult literature heavily favor fiction, the content of young adult literature courses typically stress fiction, lists of teen-favored books contain fiction, and awards and prizes traditionally go to fictional works. Many teachers and librarians are drawn to their particular professions because they themselves enjoy fiction. Yet, the undisputed fact remains that young adults read nonfiction. And since teachers and librarians accept the charge to help young adults grow into mature readers, they must read widely in all areas of literature—in the multiple genres of fiction as well as in poetry, drama, information books, and biography.

Just knowing which topics young adults may favor will not provide enough information for consistently recommending good books. In our study, for instance, drawing and the decorative arts represented the most heavily circulated division in all three libraries. A total of twenty-seven books received enough circulations to warrant consideration: Nine were classified as comics, sixteen as how-to-draw books, and two as handicrafts. However, these subject labels lacked the specificity necessary to accurately describe the content of the books.

A further examination of these twenty-seven titles revealed that content overlapped from other areas. The three most frequently circulated drawing books were Don Bolognese's *Drawing Horses & Foals* and Lee J. Ames's *Draw 50 Dogs* and *Draw 50 Airplanes, Aircraft and*

Spacecraft. Horses, dogs, and airplanes all appeared independently as popular topics: Three books with twenty-four circulations are about horses, five books with fifty-eight circulations concern dogs, while four books, with a total of fifty-four circulations, describe airplanes. In addition, other frequently circulated, but more general, works on animals and flight mention these subjects. In other words, topics in the books these young adults chose to read transcended standard Dewey Decimal divisions.

These students did not restrict their topical interest exclusively to nonfiction. Fictional stories about dogs, for example, were also widely circulated. In the second edition of *Literature for Today's Young Adults,* Nilsen and Donelson discuss dog stories and suggest thirteen novels. Seven of these titles were housed in the junior high libraries, and the circulation figures for these books provide an interesting comparison to the informational checkouts. Figure 5 lists these seven titles, along with six nonfiction titles concerning dogs, in order of popularity:

Figure 5. Circulations of Dog Books

Book	Number of Circulations	Classification
Old Yeller	53	Fiction
Where the Red Fern Grows	37	Fiction
Draw 50 Dogs	29	Nonfiction
Crescent Color Guide to Dogs	17	Nonfiction
TFH Book of Puppies	16	Nonfiction
The Incredible Journey	16	Fiction
All About Dogs	9	Nonfiction
Crescent Color Guide to Puppies	8	Nonfiction
Wonderful World of Dogs	8	Nonfiction
Dog Days of Arthur Cane	3	Fiction
Bel Ria	0	Fiction
Member of the Family	0	Fiction
Goodbye My Lady	0	Fiction

What these figures show, and show quite clearly, is that out of thirteen books about dogs, two fiction titles were definitely preferred by these students; but informational books were also important components of this subject area reading. Young adults may express an interest in a particular topic, but when recommending books to meet that interest, educators cannot assume book type. A stated interest in dogs, for example, does not predicate a preference for a fiction book, a drawing book, or a pet book.

Conversely, an interest in genre may well be just as nonspecific. All of the how-to-draw books did not receive an equal number of circulations. Students favored this type of book, but they also showed a definite preference for particular topics. The secret of popularity does not lie exclusively in format or in topic.

Knowing students and patrons involves another kind of awareness. It doesn't mean that teachers and librarians need to be familiar with every nuance of a young adult's life. It does require that they understand adolescents and their stages of reading development in general, and have some idea of their interests in particular. This knowledge also extends beyond mere topic to include perceptions concerning what draws a teenager to a particular subject. Does one young adult, for example, read about dinosaurs because of an interest in the prehistoric world, the animal world, or the sensational? Armed with these kinds of insights, teachers and librarians can begin to make appropriate recommendations that will not only satisfy an interest but gradually expand it.

Introducing new ideas, subjects, and books allows young adults to discover fresh interests. When administering the 1981 Children's Choices program at a local junior high school, we noticed this phenomenon. One boy turned in his ballot on David Macaulay's *Unbuilding* with this written response, "I liked the book because I like books on architecture."

"I never knew you were interested in architecture," the librarian said after reading his comments. "I wasn't," he volunteered, "until I read this book. But now I am."

Merely requiring young adults to read widely or forcing books on them will not automatically turn them into lifetime readers. But introducing a variety of books in classrooms, booktalks, and curriculum-related activities will begin to. Of course none of these tools will ever replace that one-to-one relationship between teachers and librarians and the teenagers they work with. Understanding the nuances of their interests and possessing the knowledge to match these with appropriate reading material are the most powerful tools teachers and librarians have for positively influencing a young adult's reading.

NOTES

1. Childress, Glenda (1985). Gender Gap in the Library: Different Choices for Boys and Girls. *Top of the News, 42*, p. 69–73.

2. Childress (1985), p. 70.

3. Blair, Judith R. (1974). The Status of Non-fiction in the Reading Interests of Second, Third and Fourth Graders. Med thesis: Rutgers University, ED 095481.

4. Norvell, George (1973). *The Reading Interests of Young People.* East Lansing, MI: Michigan State University Press.

5. Purves, Alan C. and Beach, Richard (1972). *Literature and the Reader: Research in Response to Literature, Reading Interests, and the Teaching of Literature.* Urbana, IL: National Council of the Teachers of English.

6. Strang, Ruth (1946). Reading Interest, 1946. *English Journal, 35*, p. 477.

7. Strang, Ruth (1946). p. 478.

8. Wood, Leonard A. (1986). How Teenage Book Tastes Change. *Publishers Weekly*, August 22, p. 39.

9. Campbell, Patty, Davis, Pat, and Quinn, Jerry (1978). "We Got There . . . It was Worth the Trip!" In Jana Varlejs, *Young Adult Literature in the Seventies.* Metuchen, NJ: Scarecrow Press, pp. 179–185.

10. Alm, Julie N. (1978). "Young Adult Favorites: Reading Profiles from Nine Hawaii High Schools." In Jana Varlejs, *Young Adult Literature in the Seventies.* Metuchen, NJ: Scarecrow Press.

11. Samuels, Barbara G. (1981). A National Survey to Determine the Status of the Young Adult Novel in the Secondary School English Classroom. Unpublished Doctoral Dissertation, University of Houston.

12. Stanchfield, Jo M. (1962). Boys' Reading Interests as Revealed through Personal Conferences. *The Reading Teacher, 16,* p. 43.

13. Purves, Alan C. and Beach, Richard (1972). *Literature and the Reader: Research in Response to Literature, Reading Interests, and the Teaching of Literature.* Urbana, IL: National Council of the Teachers of English.

14. Norvell, George (1973). *The Reading Interests of Young People.* East Lansing, MI: Michigan State University Press.

15. Whitehead, Robert J. (1984). *A Guide to Selecting Books for Children.* Metuchen, NJ: Scarecrow Press.

16. Soares, Anthony T. (1963). Sailent Elements of Recreational Reading of Junior High Students. *Elementary English, 40,* pp. 843–845.

17. Carter, Betty (1982). Leisure Reading Habits of Gifted Students in a Suburban Junior High School. *Top of the News, 38,* pp. 312–317.

18. Nichols, Cathleen Armstrong (1984). Reading Preferences of Remedial Ninth, Tenth, Eleventh and Twelth Grade Students from California. Unpublished Doctoral Dissertation.

19. McKenna, Michael C. (1986). Reading Interests of Remedial Secondary School Students. *Journal of Reading 29,* pp. 346–351.

20. Messina, Linda E. (1979). The Relationship of the Expressed Reading Interests of Fourth Grade Students to Their Free Selection of Library Book Choices. M.A. Thesis: Kean College of New Jersey, ED 169505.

21. Jordan, Arthur M. (1921). *Children's Interests in Reading.* New York: Teachers College, Columbia University, p. 41.

22. Karlin, Robert (1962). Library Book Borrowing vs. Library Book Reading. *The Reading Teacher, 16,* pp. 77–81.

23. Carter, Betty (1987). A Content Analysis of the Most Frequently Circulated Information Books in Three Junior High Libraries. Unpublished Doctoral Dissertation, University of Houston.

24. Carlsen, G. Robert, and Sherrill, Anne (1988). *Voices of Readers: How We Come to Love Books.* Urbana, IL: National Council of the Teachers of English, p. 80.

CHAPTER 2
A Conversation with
Lee J. Ames

Lee J. Ames is the creator of the successful Draw 50 *books. His step-by-step drawing method has made his work popular with teenagers—in fact, with readers of all ages. His loyal fans have purchased over 1.5 million copies of his drawing books. Ames has illustrated more than 150 books, worked at the Walt Disney Studios, run his own advertising agency, and taught at New York City's School of Visual Arts.*

Lee J. Ames

A&C In a recent study of nonfiction books circulated in junior high libraries, drawing books were the most circulated kind of nonfiction, and your books were the most checked-out of all the drawing titles. We know that you've sold over 1.5 million copies of your books. Who is your audience, and does it surprise you to know how popular you are with junior high readers?

LJA Does it surprise me? It startles me. . . . I'm thrilled with it. As my partner [Murray Zak] put it, even if it is a little late in life that all these good things are happening, we're delighted.

A&C Is it your experience that the books are more popular at the elementary, junior high, or high school level? Or does it seem to go across all those grade levels?

LJA I think my books seem to be most popular with fourth, fifth, and sixth graders primarily. I know the books move down to the lower grades and up to those places where modesty forbids the reader from saying that he's interested, but we know that they do get there. There's even a good deal of circulation among senior citizens like myself.

A&C Why do you think youngsters like the *Draw 50* books so much?

LJA That's the question I've been waiting for. Trying to analyze it, I think what has happened is that I've come up with a product that certainly is more closely related to the visual experience that the kids are accustomed to, television and such, than other books. The threat of having to understand the cryptography of text is eliminated. I think kids find that it's an easy way to get into dealing, as they have been asked to do, with books. I feel delighted that I'm simply opening the door to the world of books through this textless device. I think the visual participation my books offer is probably the prime reason for their popularity.

A&C We're wondering if you think youngsters "read" your books? Is that a word that you would attach to your books? Do they participate in them?

LJA That has been a problem for me. It's difficult for me to even refer to myself as an author. What have I written? I've drawn pictures, but did the Egyptian "read" his hieroglyphics? I do believe my books are being read. The mind is being stimulated.

A&C Would you talk us through the process of creating one of your drawing books from the initial idea straight through to the finished product?

LJA I'll try. The first consideration is to find a subject area which is broadly interesting to people, kids if possible. Having found that, you've got to hold it down to approximately fifty objects or things in that area. Now the next step is to draw the first subject. That will probably require sixty, seventy, or eighty steps to draw. Next I have to whittle down all those steps to get to the simplified approach I use in the *Draw 50* books—that's usually from five to twelve steps. What I do is work backwards. When I've got my finished drawing, I go back through the original steps selecting the essential ones to be used. I then do the drawing again using those simplified steps to make sure I come up with an object that looks like my original sketch. I do that forty-nine more times, and I've got a book. If it sounds a little complicated, that's because it is.

A&C How long does it take you to do a book?

LJA It takes me anywhere from two months to four years. I think the book that really gave me the greatest trouble was *Draw 50 Cars, Trucks, and Motorcycles*. I held off on that book because of the complexity of the subject matter. I fought the battle for a long time, but over the course of years, I gradually began to gather the best possible material that I could find and started to work on it slowly. The actual work, after the research, probably took about six months. But on the whole that book took years to do. On the other hand, some things like the *Draw 50 Monsters* or the more recent *Draw 50 Beasties and Yugglies and Turnover Uglies and Things That Go Bump in the Night* could be pushed through in about two or three months with little problem.

A&C Of the major textbooks now in children's and adolescent literature, all list a set of criteria for what makes a good nonfiction book. You're an artist and a successful author of drawing books. What makes a good drawing book, Lee?

Figure 7. Jacket Cover Illustration from *Draw 50 Cars, Trucks, and Motorcycles.*

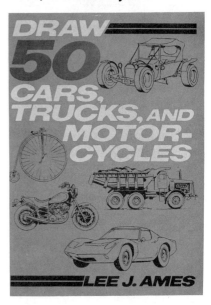

LJA A book that will stimulate the "reader" to want to draw and provide some sort of nonthreatening, simple approach are the two things that I think every successful drawing book ought to have.

A&C How do you answer the critics who say your books encourage mimicry and not real art?

LJA The first book that I did, *Draw, Draw, Draw*, which is a little different from the *Draw 50* series, elicited a letter from an artist. She was very critical of my rote-like approach. That kind of hurt, and it got me thinking about my approach to drawing. I offer a rote procedure to create a specific drawing. I don't pretend to show my students how or why I've developed this particular approach, to start with the eyes or the head, for example. I expected that I might get criticized for using this, but I also remembered that when I was a kid the important thing among my peers was who could come up with the best drawings. It didn't make a damn bit of difference how one did it. Of course, you were not supposed to, don't ask me why, trace, but if you could copy the head of Lincoln from a five-dollar bill, your peers would give you acclaim. They'd say, "Hey, this guy can really draw!" That encouragement would lead, as it did me, to attempt other drawings. I firmly believe that in all artistic endeavors mimicry is prerequisite to creativity. Unless you've learned to speak, you can't tell a story. Unless you've learned to mimic musical tones, you can't produce satisfying musical selections. Later you can go on and do the wildest and most magnificent things in a different vein. But mimicry comes first.

A&C Since you just shared that childhood story about drawing a picture of Lincoln, it's probably a good time to ask you how you became an artist.

LJA My family tells me that I drew recognizable pictures at the age of eighteen months. My aunt claimed that I drew a picture of a mother wheeling a baby carriage with a child in the carriage waving a rattle when I was a year and a half years old. What I do know is that I was always drawing, as far back as I can remember. I had the perfect environment of positive encouragement. That was the biggest thing that kept me going.

A&C How did your work at Disney Studios influence the books that you've done?

LJA That's a great question. I worked for Disney a total of three months. That's a whole three months, mind you! I didn't really understand or realize how much that experience influenced me until I did some drawing books for Simon & Schuster called *Mickey's Drawing Class*. One was devoted to the drawing of Pluto, one to Mickey and Minnie, one to Donald and Daisy, and one to Goofy. I didn't realize until then that what I had learned in that very brief period at Disney Studios was, in fact, the precise, simplified method that I'd been using in my books all along. It was the construction approach—the idea of making Mickey based on two circles of about the same size, one for the head, one for the body, but not to regard the circles as circles, to instead feel and sense them as spheres. This was all learned during a two-week course that I got there at the Disney Studio.

A&C People often say that the Lee J. Ames books teach youngsters how to draw cartoons. Is that an accurate assessment of what your books get people to draw?

LJA No, not at all. If you take any of the vehicles in *Draw 50 Cars, Trucks, and Motorcycles*, those things are anything but cartoons. If you had someone come up with a drawing of the Taj Mahal, it's certainly not a cartoon. I've done one specific book on cartoons, as we generally classify illustrations to be called cartoons. I am a member of the National Cartoonist Society, and I have been a cartoonist. "Cartoons," however, is the wrong term for the drawings in my books. More often than not, "line drawings" would be a proper description of what the results are. Sometimes the drawings that I show in the books go beyond line drawings. They have tone qualities and can properly be described as fully rounded drawings, graphites, or complete pencil drawings.

A&C In your books is there a conscious progression from one illustration to the next? Do the drawings get harder as the youngsters progress through each of the *Draw 50* books?

LJA When I give my work to the publisher, I try to have a mix of relatively simple things and some more complex things. It has been a publisher decision whether to put the simple ones first or to organize the books in another way. I know in *Draw 50 Animals* the simple drawings were up front and they became a little more complex as you went along. But then you've got the problem with a book that looks at a variety of subjects like boats, ships, trucks, and trains. Here you've got to decide within categories whether to go from simple to more complex or to mix the drawings. In any case, it has been a publisher's decision that I really haven't bothered to pay much attention to.

A&C How does an editor edit a Lee J. Ames *Draw 50* book?

LJA I certainly will consider and respect the editor's opinion as to my choice of subject matter. I may come up with something that the editor will feel is inappropriate for a lot of reasons and I may or may not agree. One thing we both look for constantly is the kind of things that will motivate the sales force. When I say that I'm not talking just about selling books, which of course, is a lovely purpose here, but I do believe that the sales force has its finger on the pulse of what the public wants. So these are considerations that I will get into with the editor.

A&C How do you decide or how does the editor decide which pictures are to be paired together? For example in *Draw 50 Famous Faces*, you've got Einstein next to Aretha Franklin, Mick Jagger next to Mao Tse-tung, and Princess Di next to Joseph Stalin. Are we to make anything out of those interesting pairings?

LJA You'd better not or we're all in trouble if you do. I left those pairings up to editors. I will tell you that I was amused when I saw the page opposite Richard Nixon—it was Frankenstein's monster!

A&C So there's not a message that you're trying to put out to the world, Lee?

LJA No, there is not, and if there were, I wouldn't let you know.

A&C How did you arrive at the *Draw 50* format originally, and did you have a difficult time selling the idea to a publisher?

LJA Back in 1962, I was working in-house for Doubleday. I was an artist-in-residence hired along with Roy Gallant. We were supposed to be a team. We did some books together and have remained close friends for all these years. In any case, there came a point when my editor, William Hall, ran out of things for me to do, so he asked me to write a book. I told him I'd never written a book, but he said, "Write," and I did a book called *Draw, Draw, Draw.* It was published. I did it while on salary

Figure 8. Frankenstein and Nixon from *Draw 50 Famous Faces*.

and I got a royalty on sales of ten pennies per book. Over the years the book sold 30,000-40,000 copies, and I was pleased. The book sold for $1.75 back in 1972. In any case, I left Doubleday as artist-in-residence, but I did want to do a sequel to *Draw, Draw, Draw*. I came up with an idea that I proposed to an editor, whose name was Seth Agnew. The book was to be something like *Draw 200 Different People, Places, Things and More*. They gave me a $1,000 advance. This book was like the *Draw 50*s. Each page was devoted to a different subject, but [it was] a much, much larger book. However, they had a tough time dealing with that title, and the book was to sell for $3.75. So they kept postponing the book because they didn't know what to do with it. Seth Agnew suggested calling it *A Drawing Dictionary*. That didn't make sense at all, and so we waited. The deadline for the book was approaching when Seth died. The book was shelved. The new editor came in and had the same problem with the book. She didn't know what to do with it. I just kept working on the book and had a good deal of it done and approved by the new editor, Blanche Van Buren, when she died. John Ernst became the editor and as and he looked over his newly acquired problems, called me and said, "Look, why don't you keep the advance, promise not to take the idea anywhere else and let's have done with it." I gathered John did not want to die! One day, years later, around 1970,

I called Tom Aylesworth at Doubleday and he suggested we have lunch and talk book ideas. Tom suggested that since we still had that viable contract, I ought to go back to the original *Draw 200* book and limit it to fifty drawings of animals. That's how the first book *Draw 50 Animals* came to be. The story doesn't stop there, however. When Tom told his wife, Ginger, who is an art teacher, about the book, she said it was ridiculous. Her comments were my first review. She said it was a step-by-step strictly rote approach to drawing—a not very desirable teaching method. But, we had the makings of the book. We had the contract, and I put together *Draw 50 Animals*. It took off and hasn't stopped since.

A&C I know you spend a good deal of time visiting schools, and you're getting ready to go to Alaska. What grades do you like to work with and what do you do in the presentations?

LJA I suffer a lot and I get butterflies, but I love the kids. I love dealing with them, but I just don't like to draw in front of them which, of course, is what I'm called upon to do. The kids are just wonderful, and fourth, fifth and sixth grades are probably the easiest for me. They ask wonderful questions, and they write to me. I've yet to see one letter from any child anywhere that isn't, in some respect, a total delight and usually filled with wonderful surprises. In addition to asking about how much money I make, they ask very personal questions about my wife and children. They ask how I learned to draw and suggest subjects for other *Draw 50* books. The letters are delightful.

A&C Do you believe your readers are doodlers or budding artists?

LJA Some, I hope, are budding artists. Others are misled into believing that my books will teach them how to be artists in one quick swoop. I can't really give you an answer. I've seen work come to me from kids that has gratified me tremendously. I have also received pictures from kids who have simply traced that final drawing. On occasion, I've received from kids tracings of the entire page, including each and every step. So, I don't know. But one thing I do know. My biggest gratification is that I've gotten some youngsters to like books who might not otherwise have gone in that direction.

A&C Tell us something about the other people behind your books. I see you share the copyright of many of them with Murray Zak but you also frequently acknowledge Holly Moylan, Warren Budd, and Ray Burns.

LJA OK. Murray Zak is my business partner. Holly Moylan helps me with research and things of that nature. She's a very special person. Warren Budd is the present art director that we've got at the studio. Warren Budd and I are working on a book that is coming out shortly. Actually, I'm having him work much more heavily on it. I think it will be titled *Draw 50 Sharks, Whales, and Other Creatures of the Deep.* What I've started to do is to get artists in with me, like Ray Burns, with whom I did *Draw 50 Holiday Decorations* recently. My thinking here is to show other artists' work using my constructive approach to drawing. The latest artist that I'm working with is Mort Drucker. The book is to be *Draw 50 Caricatures* by Mort Drucker and Lee J. Ames. Mort is the guy who just took the National Cartoonist Society's Reuben Award, which is the cartoonists' equivalent of an Oscar. He's the guy who did the *Ollie North Coloring Book*, the *Ronald Reagan Coloring Book*, and he is one of the top artists at *Mad Magazine*.

A&C What advice do you give youngsters who tell you they want to become artists?

LJA If you like to draw, don't be discouraged. Just keep drawing. If you want to draw and you've got it within you to be a artist, you will be. Nothing in the world can stop you. Don't be discouraged, and if you enjoy it, keep at it. The very worst that can happen is that you don't become an artist, but you will have developed an ability to do something that you like to do. Nobody can take that away from you.

A&C Last question. What gives you the greatest satisfaction as a creator of such popular drawing books. What's the real thrill of it, Lee?

LJA The real thrill of it is that youngsters have been pleased. That's what makes it all worthwhile.

BOOKS BY LEE J. AMES

***Draw Fifty Airplanes, Aircraft & Spacecraft.* (1977) Garden City, NY: Doubleday.

***Draw Fifty Animals.* (1974) Garden City, NY: Doubleday.

***Draw Fifty Athletes.* (1985). Garden City, NY: Doubleday.

***Draw Fifty Beasties and Yugglies & Turnover Uglies & Things That Go Bump in the Night.* (1988). Garden City, NY: Doubleday.

Draw Fifty Boats, Ships, Trucks & Trains. (1976). Garden City, NY: Doubleday.

***Draw Fifty Buildings & Other Structures.* (1980). Garden City, NY: Doubleday.

***Draw Fifty Cars, Trucks, & Motorcycles.* (1986). Garden City, NY: Doubleday.

***Draw Fifty Cats.* (1986). Garden City, NY: Doubleday.

**Draw Fifty Dinosaurs & Other Prehistoric Animals.* (1977). Garden City, NY: Doubleday.

***Draw Fifty Dogs.* (1981). Garden City, NY: Doubleday.

***Draw Fifty Famous Cartoons.* (1979). Garden City, NY: Doubleday.

***Draw Fifty Famous Faces.* (1978). Garden City, NY: Doubleday.

Draw Fifty Famous Stars: As Selected by Rona Barrett's Hollywood Magazine. (1982). Garden City, NY: Doubleday.

***Draw Fifty Horses.* (1984). Garden City, NY: Doubleday.

***Draw Fifty Monsters, Creeps, Superheroes, Demons, Dragons, Nerds, Dirts, Ghouls, Giants, Vampires, Zombies & Other Curiosa...* (1986). Garden City, NY: Doubleday.

**Draw Fifty Vehicles.* (1978). Garden City, NY: Doubleday.

How to Draw Star Wars Heroes, Creatures, Spaceships & Other Fantastic Things. (1984). New York: Random House.

*Ames, Lee J. & Ames, Lee J., Jr. (1987). *Draw Fifty Boats, Ships, Trucks & Trains.* Garden City, NY: Doubleday.

Ames, Lee J. & Burns, Ray. *Draw Fifty Holiday Decorations.* (1987). (Written with Ray Burns). Garden City, NY: Doubleday.

* Indicates edition is paperback
** Indicates a paperback edition also available

CHAPTER 3
Accuracy

Whether young adults live in remote or urban areas, patronize your library, attend your English class, or share your dinner table, they read nonfiction. During this process, they encounter innumerable observations, opinions, and facts. Some of them may have seen this material:

> Q. Can people get AIDS from mosquito bites?
> A. Not as far as is known.[1]

> Now—if time is not the same for all observers, neither is space.[2]

> Although the South had few large seaports, and the West wasn't even near the ocean, they resented British high-handedness at sea.[3]

> An intercontinental ballistic missile takes about thirty minutes to travel between the United States and the Soviet Union.[4]

Quite possibly teachers or librarians recommended the books containing these quotes to young adult readers, considering these particular explications valid, interesting, or useful enough to pass on to another person. Were they right? Is the above information accurate? How do you know?

Accuracy is the most daunting criterion for teachers and librarians judging an informational book, particularly one covering an unfamiliar subject. How can evaluators determine factual accuracy in a subject like science, mathematics, or history that they may know little about? Priscilla Moulton voiced these sentiments as early as 1966, when she reported that twenty-five librarians in reviewing books for children, "each in turn and with near desperation, cried, 'Give me anything but science books!'"[5]

This anxiety encapsulates the predicament many professionals encounter as they attempt to evaluate fairly those books they will recommend to young adults. Librarians and teachers worry that they may either endorse volumes filled with inaccurate information or that the reverse might happen: They will overlook those books that accurately reflect the cutting edge of an unknown discipline. Consequently, individuals turn to professional reviewing sources for guidance, often without realizing that reviewers frequently face the same dilemmas as does the lay population.

Roger Sutton, associate editor for *The Bulletin of the Center of Children's Books*, explains that when writing reviews of nonfiction works, *The Bulletin's* editors often rely on the expertise of their advisory committee and content area specialists in matters of accuracy, incorporating their perceptions into the resulting reviews. Sally Estes, young adult editor at *Booklist*, says that reviewers will also consult reference sources and outside authorities for special books, but that frequently time constraints prohibit lengthy collaboration. However, *Booklist* employs professional, full-time reviewers, and each has been able to develop special areas of nonfiction expertise: Sue Ellen Beauregard in sports, Hazel Rochman on the subject of South Africa, and Stephanie Zvirin in the area of self-help books.

School Library Journal, on the other hand, uses a pool of four hundred reviewers to ensure accuracy and provide expertise in subject fields.[6] While this diversity occasionally produces uneven critical analyses, the fact that books are carefully matched with reviewers strengthens the overall reliability of the resulting reviews. When Dorothy Broderick recruits reviewers for *VOYA*, she sends a checklist of forty-two major subjects (with numerous subdivisions for specificity) and asks potential contributors to indicate areas of expertise, hobbies, and special interests. While three reviewers may indicate knowledge in computers, for example, only one may have the background to review books on PASCAL rather than BASIC or MS DOS machines instead of Apple IIs. The detailed interest forms provide the specificity necessary to discover these differences, thus allowing Broderick to assign properly informed reviewers to each book.

Appraisal, a highly respected reviewing source devoted exclusively to science and mathematics books, employs yet a different strategy. Each book in this journal receives two reviews—one written by a scientist/mathematician and one written by a librarian, with the former focusing on content and the latter on style, format, and appeal.

Even though various reviewers may contact content area specialists or request the opinions of others, an individual may still unknowingly recommend a book containing subject matter inaccuracies or even reject a book covering the most up-to-date material. Such books don't slip by all reviewers, and that's one reason why teachers and librarians do not depend on a single review journal, but look to several for guidance. What one reviewer misses another will probably catch.

Consider the reviews for Switzer and Costas's *Greek Myths: Gods, Heroes and Monsters: Their Stories and Their Meanings*, a collection of Greek tales ranging from creation stories to the adventures of Odysseus. Writing for *VOYA*, Margaret Miles, the youth services librarian at New Hanover County Public Library in Wilmington, North Carolina, and an undergraduate classical archaeology major at the University of North

Carolina at Chapel Hill, pointed out several serious flaws in this particular book that had gone undetected by other professionals. Miles expands her original conclusions in a later correspondence:

> There is no such thing as an "official" version of a folktale, and had they [Switzer and Costas] chosen to tell the stories in this book purely as modern collected folktale versions, one could not fairly speak of "errors" in facts as related in the stories, though gross divergence from a widely held tradition should probably be explained. Certainly there are plenty of contradictions even in the classical texts. However, Switzer and Costas have chosen to open each chapter or section of the book with a note on "Sources." In a few cases they refer in these source notes to versions they heard in Greece: stories in the section "The Royal Family of Gods," and current local beliefs about the characters Theseus ("Theseus: The Favorite Hero of Athens") and Odysseus ("The Adventures of Odysseus"). Elsewhere the source notes discuss classical authors, and occasionally relevant modern literature. And if the source is a written classical text, the retelling of the story must reflect that original.
>
> For example, young adults read and enjoy Homer's *Odyssey* in translation; we should certainly expect that a retelling of Homer's *Odyssey* aimed at young adults will be faithful to the original. . . . Yet, in their retelling of Penelope's testing of her suitors (the story told in Book XXI of the *Odyssey*), they [Switzer and Costas] have changed the details of the test."[7]

Miles notes other inaccuracies in these retellings: Switzer and Costas use the Roman name Hercules rather than the Greek form Heracles (meaning the "glory of Hera"); they substitute Mount Aetna (in Sicily) for Mount Oeta, near the city of Trachis on the Greek mainland[8]; and they incorrectly place Odysseus in the land of the Phoenicians rather than with the Phaeacians.[9] Historical facts suffer similar reconstruction problems. Switzer and Costas write of kings during the time of Aeschylus[10] (525 to 456 B.C.) although the "hereditary monarchy in Athens existed no later than 683-682 B.C. when the first annually elected archons took office."[11] It appears that democracy operated during Aeschylus' lifetime. If not, democracy certainly replaced a dictatorship rather than the monarchy indicated in this book.

While reviewing sources can alert librarians and teachers to inaccuracies, they primarily serve as general buying and selection guides, and can never address all the idiosyncratic reading and research needs of a particular young adult audience. No matter how conscientious or how careful, reviewers can never specifically pinpoint the perfect book to tie in with Mr. Smith's fourth-period class on world problems, or that certain volume that will speak to the special reader just fascinated by batteries and bulbs. Librarians know their individual patrons, teachers know their students; and both find themselves in the positions of evaluating many informational books for which they lack the content area background to judge the factual accuracy of a particular work.

Fortunately, several reasonable solutions exist for dealing with this problem.

QUALIFICATIONS

First, examine the authors. A look at who they are, what their scholarship base is, and how they present their material will provide several important clues about their work. Although the depth of a writer's qualifications certainly doesn't guarantee a well-researched book, it does reveal clues about the probable quality of the work. Authors committed to particular subjects find that these and related topics become a real part of themselves. To feed their interests, these writers exhibit the same behaviors most professionals do when caught up in a subject: They research an area, read widely in related fields, and talk to others with similar specialties.

All authors will not exhibit the same level of subject-matter knowledge. The best books aren't necessarily written by PhD's, nor are the weakest written by amateurs in a field. Fine books that appeal to young adults come from authors with diverse backgrounds—like Carl Sagan, a respected scholar of astronomy and physics; Seymour Simon, a former science teacher; Ross R. Olney, a sports enthusiast; Lee J. Ames, a commercial artist; and Helen Roney Sattler, a former school librarian who shares her grandchildren's interest in dinosaurs. In each of the above cases the writers exhibit deep interests in and solid knowledge about their content.

Not only should authors have some subject matter qualifications, but these credentials need to be made known to readers. Teens need to begin to develop independent skills for eventually choosing books on their own. Evaluating the qualifications of authors represents the first step they will take in the process of developing autonomy in book selection.

Young adults look for particular books to read either because they want to or because they have to, and knowledge about the writers of these books will begin to give them a sense of the reliability about the authors' assertions. Sometimes teenagers know a writer by reputation. Possibly they have found pleasure in several drawing books by Jim Arnosky, and predictably search for other works by this favored author. Or maybe they respect Larry Bird's talent and want to read his tips on field goal shooting. Despite such examples, young adults generally know little about the authors they will encounter.

Even limited prior knowledge may prove inadequate for evaluating a writer's specific subject matter expertise. Michael Crichton's novels, such as *The Andromeda Strain* and *Sphere*, have proven popular with teenagers, and many identify him as a fine storyteller. Others know him in connection with the futuristic movie *Westworld*. Yet, none of these images helps in assessing his qualifications to write about technology, which, as it happens, he does very well in *Electronic Life: How to Think about Computers.*

If young readers elect to find out about an author before choosing a particular title, more than likely they will do so by checking only those credentials recorded on the book jacket or within the book. Adolescents certainly possess the talent to locate brief biographical entries about authors in various reference sources, but they shouldn't have to search outside volumes for fundamental facts.

Since these biographical sketches included within books play such an important part in developing critical reading skills, they should be written carefully. All too often, however, personal information supersedes professional credentials, and anecdotes form the bulk of biographical data in young adult literature. In Rhoda Blumberg's *Sharks* the author's total knowledge of marine life is defined through the following statements: "Last year she hooked a very large nurse shark off the Florida Keys. When it surfaced, her husband took the rod and reeled the shark near enough to the boat for her to photograph it. Then it was let go."[12] In the absence of any other pertinent biographical information, these observations fail to establish her credentials, and, in fact, negate the serious scholarship evident in much of her work.

On the other hand, many works exist that contain biographical information that accurately reflects the superficial treatment the author has given a particular subject. In *The Great White Shark* author Eve Bunting professes to have been "fascinated by the sea" and states that she has written books on other "mysterious creatures." But sharks aren't mysterious at all. They've been studied extensively, both in captivity and in their natural surroundings; they've been dissected in laboratory settings; and their habits have been chronicled and detailed. Sharks may be big, frightening, or intriguing, but they aren't mysterious. Bigfoot is mysterious; the Abominable Snowman is mysterious. But sharks are not. And for an author to show such little respect for accuracy reveals an orientation toward the nonscientific and the sensational. The dismal jacket information for this book, which includes lurid accounts of great white shark attacks illustrated by shocking stills from grade B movies, underscores the paucity of serious investigation so evident in the final product.

Inflated and nonspecific credentials offer another form of inaccuracy. Biographical sketches should indicate the fields of expertise of teachers and professors, specifically name institutional affiliations, and identify awards. If an author of a history book were described as "an administrator for over twenty years at an eastern university and the recipient of four writing awards," such a description could well refer to the head of a catering organization who has won recognition for a question/answer column in a campus newspaper. By encouraging young adults to critically examine an author's qualifications with the same reservations one would employ when looking at a résumé, teachers and librarians can dimish the impact of such glittering generalities.

Despite negative examples, many fine books offer a fair accounting of the authors' backgrounds, their personal reasons for writing a particular work, and even lively vignettes relating to their subject matter orientations. Helen Benedict's *Safe, Strong, & Streetwise*, a no-nonsense manual on sexual safety, mentions her other works, her training in rape crisis counseling, her extensive research, and this motive for writing: "The young in particular seemed sheltered and misled, so I decided to write a book that would educate them about what sexual assault is, how to avoid it, and how not to do it to anyone else."[13] This spare sketch accurately reflects Benedict's straightforward text and professional tone.

The biographical information James Jespersen and Jane Fitz-Randolph choose to share with their readers mirrors their near reverence for subject, so evident in *From Quarks to Quasars: A Tour of the Universe*. Jespersen writes that his interest in the universe began as a high school student when he first read George Gamow's *One, Two, Three Infinity*, and that he eagerly pursued this field in college, eventually under Gamow's tutelage. Similarly, Fitz-Randolph shares her "ongoing search for truth," and her fascination with the way society approaches new ideas and the people who formulate them.

And Laurence Pringle's profile on the jacket of *Throwing Things Away* not only points out his formidable background as a biologist, teacher, editor, and author of numerous books, but also recounts his reasons for writing in a light, personal way: "Research on this project brought me in touch with archaeologists, biologists, landfill managers, and other experts all over North America. My feet sank into landfill surfaces from Denver to Miami. Parts of the book evoke personal memories: As a teenager I shot dump rats at night, and through the years I've acquired lumber, my lawn mower, and other valuables at dumps. For me, taking trash to the local landfill is not a chore, but an adventure."[14]

SCHOLARSHIP

Simply knowing who the authors are is only the first step in evaluating the accuracy of an informational book. The second is an inspection of the acknowledgments. Did the author consult authorities for firsthand information or to fact-check the manuscript? Far from trivial, these credits imply serious scholarship and suggest that writers have made an honest effort to verify their facts and assumptions.

The third step involves an examination of the resources used. If, for example, a team of authors produced what appeared to be a factual psychology text, but based all their research on the *Reader's Digest* monthly column "Life in These United States," thoughtful readers would naturally suspect the validity of many of their assumptions. On the other hand, if these mythical authors included case studies, research reports, and scholarly texts instead of popular accounts, they would underscore their attempts to produce an accurate work and in turn would invite readers to seriously consider their facts and conclusions.

An examination of bibliographic references reveals whether, on the surface, authors have done their homework, whether they have used a variety of source materials, and what type of information they have relied on. In addition, the inclusion of a bibliography contributes a subtle yet important message to the young adult reader. Formal references indicate that research happened before writing began.

Our experiences with teenagers who are asked to write school reports show they assume that either adult authors are born knowing the information they share in books or that they acquire that information through exotic life experiences. The perpetual advice, "Write about something you know," is repeated in English classrooms and writing workshops across the country. But this recommendation proves futile unless young adults encounter models for acquiring that information. If these students never see examples of an author's research, then the inevitable conclusion—that they can't begin to write because they just don't possess enough information—appears perfectly logical. The mere presence of a bibliography attacks this notion: Writing doesn't just happen automatically; it involves study and scholarship as a part of the process.

Although bibliographies should include major sources, they don't have to be exhaustive. Many references used by sophisticated authors with vast resources at their disposal will prove unavailable to secondary school students, and highly technical or arcane sources can reasonably go unmentioned. On the other hand, bibliographies must not be too selective, and should include pertinent adult source material on the assumption that mature and interested readers will avail themselves of interlibrary loan networks, as well as local resources, to satisfy a personal interest.

Responsible authors deal with this problem of documentation in several ways. In *Rescue: The Story of How Gentiles Saved Jews in the Holocaust*, Milton Meltzer not only provides a traditional list of selected source material, but personalizes his bibliography by pointing out the variety of sources he employs, as well as those references he found particularly useful. In *Let There Be Light: A Book about Windows*, author James Cross Giblin explains the design of his superior bibliography, which not only serves as a list of sources, but facilitates the interested reader's own research:

> The listing is organized by chapter, and in sequence within each chapter. As a result, it can be used to pursue a topic that the reader wants to explore further. Those books that were written for young people are indicated with asterisks. In addition to books and articles

the listing includes mentions of exhibits, lectures, and tours that contributed importantly to the author's research.[15]

The recognition of atypical resources, like Giblin's inclusion of exhibits, lectures, and tours, not only alerts teenagers to the infinite research possibilities around them, but also underscores the premise that no one produces work in a vacuum. In *Draw Horses with Sam Savitt*, the author also promotes this notion by offering a unique, informal, statement of attribution. In an afterword Savitt acknowledges four artists—Will James, Paul Brown, Lionel Edwards, and Alfred Munnings—who have influenced his work:

> I admire each artist for what I believe he did best: Will James for his Western-horse action; Paul for his precise detail; Edwards for his simple, unaffected style; and Munnings for his wonderful, free handling of paint and his depiction of the classic horse. But the one thing they had in common was a marvelous ability to draw, which was evident in every picture they created. I have learned things from these artists that I might never have discovered for myself, for there were times when one word or illustration clarified the answer to a problem that had been troubling me for years.[16]

The message Savitt imparts to his readers is that he became a fine artist not simply because all of a sudden he discovered a God-given talent, but that he seriously, thoughtfully, and systematically developed his craft.

Similarly, in *Drawing Dinosaurs and Other Prehistoric Animals*, author/illustrator Don Bolognese recognizes an important community resource by acknowledging the models from the American Museum of Natural History in New York City he used for several illustrations. To further aid interested readers, his text includes a list of museums with permanent dinosaur exhibits, and he prompts young artists to visit these sites and take advantage of opportunities to sketch their three-dimensional models from different perspectives.

The tendency to share the research process characterizes many traditional bibliographies as well. As John Christopher Fine states in *The Hunger Road:* "A bibliography is really the beginning, not the end of a book."[17] And Stephen Tchudi concludes *Soda Poppery: The History of Soft Drinks in America* with the message that research constitutes an ongoing process. He encourages inquisitive readers to check in their local libraries for titles other than the ones he's mentioned, and he reminds them that new information will appear in more recent issues of the *Reader's Guide to Periodical Literature*. Tchudi even provides a head start by suggesting subject descriptors to use when looking up specific information.

Closely related to the issue of bibliographies is that of footnotes. The appearance of footnotes in informational books indicates not only that authors have consulted other sources, but also that they do not set themselves up as absolute authorities whose facts and opinions should be unquestionably accepted. This attribution involves more than professional courtesy. Footnotes suggest that the verification of facts and opinions is a valid and appropriate step in scholarship. Their presence acknowledges the reader as a critical individual, capable of evaluation and, ultimately, competent to accept or reject the ideas within a particular work.

Hazel Rochman, assistant editor of books for young adults at *Booklist,* points out that shoddy or nonexistent documentation delivers a subtle but powerful message from authors to readers: "Trust me. I've looked at the evidence and I'll tell you."[18] This attitude reflects the antithesis of critical reading skills—to never unquestionably accept what is in print, to check statistics and sources, and to think for yourself—that form the core of respected secondary reading and English curricula. Librarians and teachers cannot develop critical thinkers if the raw materials they use encourage passivity.

As late as 1985 few informational books aimed specifically at young adults included footnotes. Generally authors employed text referencing to validate their information, although specificity frequently suffered in the process. One such work includes references to "a scientist" who suspected that the solar system contained a tenth planet,[19] and another mentions "one writer" who drew conclusions about the voracious eating habits of starfish[20]—both without further identification. Similarly, in describing basking sharks, Rhoda Blumberg gives this lightweight observation: "They don't always cruise along calmly. Sometimes they leap out of the water. One of these big, heavy giants was seen jumping so high that its tail was six feet above the water."[21] This casual allusion prompts several unanswerable questions. Who saw the shark? Was this person a reliable judge of distances, particularly over water? Could this person accurately identify a basking shark?

Of course, not all of the older titles on library shelves contain imprecise quotations from experts. In *The World of the Snake,* author Hal Harrison, discussing the life expectancy of snakes, offers the following: "Dr. Herbert Hechenbleikner, Professor and Chairman of the Department of Biology, University of North Carolina at Charlotte, kept a rattlesnake named Oscar for over 28 years; another named Rudolph lived for 24 years 7 months. At the San Diego Zoo in California, Mr. Charles E. Shaw and his predecessor, Mr. C. B. Perkins, kept an African cobra, *Naja melanoleuca,* alive for a little over 29 years."[22] By including both the names and the professional associations of these herpetologists, Harrison provides important facts that aid young adults in judging the validity of the scientists' observations. Harrison respects his readers' inquisitiveness and their search for reliability of sources.

Even in more recent publications the practice of text referencing for formal sources all too frequently gives only enough information to provide surface legitimatization for statements, but too little documentation for the interested student to check a particular quotation, read the context in which it was given, or simply further explore a topic. Consider Nat Hentoff's *American Heroes: In and Out of School*. In this vigorous discussion of ten individuals—students, teachers, librarians, civil libertarians—who have stood fast for human rights, Hentoff devotes one chapter to Kathy Russell's successful fight against censorship in Washington County, Virginia. In outlining background material he mentions:

> Virginia was also, of course, the home of Thomas Jefferson, who in 1814, when he heard that a book might be banned because certain authorities objected to its religious views, wrote a bookseller.
> "I am really mortified to be told that in the United States of America . . . [a book] can become the subject of inquiry, and of criminal inquiry too. . . . Are we to have a censor whose imprimatur shall say what books may be sold, and what [books] we may buy? . . . Whose foot is to be the measure to which ours are all to be cut or stretched?"[23]

Since the source of this quotation isn't provided in the bibliography, interested readers have little choice but to accept Hentoff's brief context and selective interpretation. Furthermore, even the higher level of specificity in text referencing that Hentoff offers in other sections of this book proves inadequate. In one chapter he quotes activist Joan Baez, mentioning that this information came from an interview that he conducted and that appeared in *Playboy* magazine. Although Hentoff's inclusion of authorship, subject, and source provide enough clues for inquisitive readers to find the exact reference, his negligence in citing the specific issue and page number where the quote appears relegates this verification to only the most tenacious teenagers.

Nat Hentoff is not the only author who provides imprecise documentation, and *Heroes In and Out of School* should not be dismissed simply because of this feature. It is a fine book which energetically discusses complex issues within a framework easily accessible to many young adults. The lack of complete referencing detracts from, but does not damn, the complete work.

Similarly, Ann Weiss's *Lies, Deception and Truth* is a solid work for young adults, even though flimsy documentation diminishes the overall quality. For example, she mentions incidents in which she says former President Reagan told lies: once concerning his wartime service and once regarding a mythical welfare recipient. Especially since the very topic of Weiss's book is deception, the irony that young adults can't even check or authenticate her sources partially negates her otherwise thoughtful examination of truth.

Historically, two false assumptions have precluded the decision to eliminate footnotes. First is the presumption that young adults will automatically reject books with formal footnotes, that the inclusion of such documentation labels a book as too academic and pedantic for adolescent tastes. The second surmises that teenage readers want only easy answers, that they use nonfiction merely to satisfy school assignments, and that they approach these volumes with no more drive and curiosity than is necessary to find the solution to a stuffy research question.

As with many deep-seated practices, there is a degree of truth attached to these two assumptions. Certain methods of documentation, such as the American Psychological Association's format with information included in parentheses in the text, may well prove cumbersome for teenage readers, for such styles often interrupt the flow of text and intrude on the reading process. But there is no evidence that end-of-chapter or final notes will dissuade young adults from any particular work. If they choose to ignore the documentation, they are certainly free to skip those appended sections.

Many young adults do indeed consult informational books merely to satisfy school assignments, and have little motivation to explore a topic more fully. Still, these students must see the modeling of proper documentation for their own writing. In addition, apathetic students do not represent the sole readership of a good book. Today's young adults will become tomorrow's scientists, politicians, doctors, researchers, and teachers. By not insisting on proper documentation, librarians and teachers tacitly deny these inquisitive readers the opportunities to learn more about a subject, to consult original source material, or to question the assumptions of an author.

Aware of these concerns, many authors now adroitly incorporate evidence of research in their books. Lyall Watson's *The Dreams of Dragons* serves as a model of documentation. This collection of essays explores the soft sciences with Watson hypothesizing about the predominance of right-handedness, the homing senses of animals, and the existence of dragons. He references scientific studies and papers within the text by providing the author's name and background, but, in a separate appendix, Watson also includes specific documentation—author, title, date and place of publication, and page number—for sources mentioned in each chapter. Likewise, Carl B. Feldbaum and Ronald J. Bee provide extensive footnotes in their superb work *Looking the Tiger in the Eye*. This book delivers an unflinching examination of nuclear warfare, and Feldbaum and Bee's impeccable scholarship underscores the seriousness of their theme. Not only do these writers document data, but they also validate information that without proper referencing would be considered fictionalization. When they mention a person's thoughts, emotions, or feelings, they invariably refer the reader to the primary source material from which they drew these observations.

Authors who decide to include footnotes in their works face a perplexing dilemma. They must wonder how many footnotes are sufficient, and whether too many may prove off-putting to the teen reader. As Tchudi notes in *Soda Poppery*, "To list the reference to every statement or quotation in this book would have cluttered each page with footnotes, many of them to sources that are hard to come by."[24]

In such cases authors, editors, and publishers should consider the sophistication of their primary audience, recognizing that in many instances informational books serve as models for writing. Junior high school students are required in their own investigations to include minimal documentation for their facts and opinions, while senior high researchers face more stringent demands. These young adults will never understand or accept the need for attribution in their personal papers unless they encounter it in the very books they utilize for their own assignments. English teachers may inform their students that real writers document their texts, but unless these young adults see specific examples of that verification they will develop their own ideas: Real writers don't research or document, and footnotes and bibliographies are simply meaningless exercises invented by teachers for the purpose of making the lives of all their students miserable.

One final question remains concerning documentation: Is it necessary to fully reference and document popular reading—books about sports, or unidentified flying objects, or movie monsters? In a word, Yes! Authors, editors, librarians, and teachers cannot know which books readers will use for serious research and which ones they will use for popular reading. No outsider can define a reader's stance. One reader will peruse *Superman from the 30's to the 80's* to vicariously engage in the Man of Steel's thrilling escapades, while another will study the same volume as a reflection of popular culture and taste. Yet a third reader will look for differences in production and artistic styles over the fifty-year period. No matter how frivolous a work may appear to an adult, it may well be the beginning of a lifelong interest for a teenager.

FACT AND OPINION

Authors begin with facts. They sift through them, they choose appropriate ones, they arrange them, they ask why they occur, and what these facts indicate about the human condition or the natural world. In so doing, they develop their opinions. Both appear in any work, and writers owe it to their readers to let them know when they are shifting gears—when they are discussing facts and when they are discussing opinions.

At its simplest level, this obligation requires that authors preface their opinions with disclaimers such as "I believe," "it appears," or just simply, "perhaps," and omit such qualifications when recounting statements of fact. Many authors comply with such conventions. In *Journey to the Planets*, for example, Patricia Lauber discusses the rings of Jupiter. She mentions how surprised scientists were when they saw photographs of the rings by *Voyager 1* and then later by *Voyager 2*, for the rings had gone undetected by both astronomers and scientists studying photographs from the earlier *Pioneer* explorations. The *Voyager* photographs generated new questions and, predictably, tentative opinions about the rings. Lauber raises three of those questions, clearly responding to them with an opinion: "Where do the [ring] particles come from? Why don't they fall into Jupiter? Or, if they do fall into Jupiter, what is the source of new particles that replace old ones? The best guess is that the particles come from material thrown out by Io's volcanoes."[25]

Based on tangible fact, *Journey to the Planets* offers speculative opinions that attempt to explain observed scientific phenomena. In other works, opinions rather than facts form the content base. Marjorie Braymer's *Atlantis: The Biography of a Legend* illustrates this point. Although people have believed in the lost continent for centuries, no one has ever proved the existence of Atlantis. In order to validate the subject matter of her book, Braymer must describe the evolution of a legend. In doing so, she reverses the process many authors follow when they draw opinions from facts: Braymer must explain why humans persist in believing in a theory without a shred of physical evidence. She accomplishes this task by examining the detail and documentation in Plato's original account of Atlantis, the differences between evidence and proof, the inclination for humans to ignore facts and figures when it so pleases them, and the overwhelming fabrications of the story in literature and legend. Braymer had another option open to her; she could simply have claimed the existence of Atlantis, in much the same way the supermarket tabloids report that Elvis is alive and wandering the malls of Kalamazoo, Michigan. But such a path would lead only to passing sensationalism; instead, Braymer provides substance to her highly suspect topic by critically evaluating it.

Separating fact from opinion becomes an even trickier matter when dealing with the social sciences, for readers' own political predispositions invariably affect their responses. Just as writers form opinions during the writing process, readers also create, or validate, their own opinions during the reading process. They do not approach books in a vacuum, but instead bring their experiences, beliefs, and self-interests into play whenever they interact with text.

Jeanne Vestal, senior vice president and editorial director for Franklin Watts, acknowledges this problem. At Watts, all nonfiction manuscripts are sent to concept readers, or experts in the fields under discussion, for general impressions about accuracy and points of view. But politically oriented manuscripts can pose a problem; unless the author's point of view is that of the concept reader's, it is particularly difficult to obtain an objective consensus about the worth of the manuscript.

Aware of this potential problem, conscientious evaluators must ask themselves: Am I rejecting an idea because I disagree with it, or am I accepting an undocumented opinion because it has become part of my value system? Young adults, though, may not possess the background to make such distinctions. Therefore, authors should take particular pains to state their orientations. In *Taking on the Press: Constitutional Rights in Conflict*, Melvyn Zerman institutes such a discussion on the first page:

> About two hundred pages from here I remark on how difficult it is to maintain complete objectivity in reporting. Since I most certainly do not exempt myself from this observation, it seems only proper that I prepare the reader for my bias at the outset, before evidence of it comes creeping into the text.
>
> I am usually inclined to stand at the side of the press when it opposes efforts to punish or restrain or—worst of all—silence those who would report or comment on the news. Note that I say "usually," not "always," for I do believe that the press must operate within boundaries of decency, compassion, and responsibility. Because these boundaries sometimes are clouded over and hard to define, and because on occasion they are unquestionably breached, my sympathy for the press has been known to fade into ambivalence or even turn into outright hostility.
>
> But such lapses in allegiance are rare, and I confess my bias so that readers, aware of it, can better make up their own minds about the controversies that churn through the pages ahead. Feel free to question and doubt and disagree. Feeling free to criticize is really what this book is all about.[26]

Zerman plays fair with his readers; he lets them know the rules of the game before they begin the contest. He tells them that opinions will present themselves in the work, cautions them to look for his point of view, and encourages them to approach his conclusions with skepticism.

In the twenty-third edition of *Africa 1988*, Pierre Dostert also incorporates his opinions into his narrative; but, unlike Zerman, Dostert does not alert his audience to his bias. In an afterword, Dostert admits that "there almost always is more than one viewpoint on even the most minute of issues and the way in which they are described,"[27] but he offers no further clues concerning his own convictions. And unquestionably these viewpoints appear in his work. In what on the surface appears to be an objective overview of Africa, Dostert defends a pro-apartheid stance for South Africa. He equates the process of banning, where individuals are forbidden to even speak with more than two people concurrently, to America's sedition laws, but fails to note that only in the fictionalized *The Man Without a Country* has an American citizen been exiled from his native land; he describes Archbishop Tutu, an official of the Anglican Church and the recipient of the Nobel prize for peace, as a "publicity-seeking sensationalist"[28]; and blames the foreign press for sensationalizing, encouraging, and even instigating racial violence. He further castigates the news media for their attitude toward Tutu by writing "The press always gives him a welcome audience, always reverently referring to him as a 'Nobel Peace Prize laureate.'"[29] To adopt the South African ruling government's political stance is well within an author's prerogative, but to present that position as fact without warning readers of the orientation is unacceptable.

Books should, when appropriate, also point out problems of incorrect and unverifiable factual information. James A. Oliver's *Snakes in Fact and Fiction* meticulously attends to the differences between documented data, incorrect assertions, and facts and opinions. In the first chapter, for example, Oliver details the problems of recording the measurement of the largest snakes. He mentions several questionable newspaper accounts and justifies his skepticism by citing various official methods of measurement noted in reputable instances. He examines the problems of estimating length experienced by both professionals and nonprofessionals: the discrepancies between measurements of snake bodies and their removed skins, and the logistical problems that occur when attempting to measure a particularly large snake. What may have seemed like a simple question (What is the largest snake?) thus becomes a model of scientific inquiry.

Differentiating between facts and opinions and recognizing point of view marks a mature, sophisticated reader. Young adults will never reach that plateau by accepting all that is printed as the truth. Authors who consistently distinguish between facts and opinions and conscientiously point out their own values and points of view alert teenagers to the age-old caution: Don't believe everything you see in print.

SENSATIONALISM

The sensationalism of facts creates still another form of inaccuracy and yet another dilemma for book selectors. Historically, young adults gravitate toward the sensational. Circulation records confirm that junior high students regularly check out titles concerning world records, movie monsters, and super bowls, books considered sensational because they deal with extremes—the best, the most unusual, and the strangest. Older teens gravitate toward human and societal extremes. High school students choose topics such as incest, devil worship, and AIDS for required term papers, while rejecting tamer topics on the nuclear family structure, the growth of traditional religious denominations, and the eradication of smallpox. Given a choice, the majority of teenagers will elect to read books about sharks instead of goldfish, world records over census tabulations, the Ku Klux Klan rather than the rotary club, and anorexia nervosa over the four food groups. Without a doubt, it is the aberrations that attract young adults to such subjects in the first place. To dismiss all books dealing with sensational topics would not only suppress a very real reading interest, it would also result in a simplistic measure for solving a problem—like throwing the baby out with the bath water. Sensational subject matter is not the issue. The presentation and treatment of that content does, however, demand attention.

A case in point occurs with Anita Gustafson's *Guilty or Innocent?* In this book Gustafson presents ten crimes and asks young adult readers to second-guess the legal system by judging the guilt or innocence of the accused parties. Her initial cases concern cannibalism: The first describes a particularly gruesome historical incident in which a seventeenth-century family preyed on travelers for three generations, while the second recounts the methods of survival of the Uruguayan rugby team stranded in the Andes Mountains in 1972. While both accounts present sensational material, they do so straightforwardly and without exploiting the young adult reader.

In subsequent sections, however, Gustafson shows much less restraint. Note the following passage reporting the death of Lizzie Borden's mother: "Abby lay in a pool of blood, her head nearly separated from her body. The blood from her nineteen blows was dark and congealed."[30] In another chapter Gustafson has Dr. Sam Sheppard encountering this scene of his wife's murder: "Bits of her teeth were broken in the attack. The bedroom walls were spattered with blood. A trail of stain led down the stairs to the first floor of their suburban Cleveland home."[31]

In neither example does the physical state of the murder victim or the descriptive scene of the crimes have any bearing on the information Gustafson provides as clues for the reader to decide the guilt or innocence of the accused. It's not the sensational nature of the scandals that present a problem in this book, but rather the needlessly lurid descriptions of the physical settings. While a forthright discussion of sensational matters is acceptable, exploitation of these topics is not.

Frederick Drimmer's *Born Different* also explores an extraordinary topic. In describing the lives of seven people born with severe abnormalities—Tom Thumb, the twenty-four-inch-high dwarf; Robert Wadlow, the tallest man in the world; Julia Pastrana, known as Apewoman; Joseph Merrick, immortalized as the Elephant Man; Herrmann Unthan, the musical virtuoso born without arms; and the Siamese twins Eng and Chang Bunker—Drimmer takes particular pains to downplay the sensational nature of his book. With compassion he presents these individuals as both victors and victims, revealing their pettiness, foibles, disillusionments, and triumphs. When describing their physical anomalies, Drimmer takes special care to calmly, objectively, and scientifically recount both the biological explanations and their physical manifestations. Whereas Drimmer could have set himself up as the P. T. Barnum of young adult authors, he is instead a writer who deals with a sensitive subject with empathy and restraint.

At certain times, however, authors are compelled to include graphic, gruesome, and even terrifying details in order to honestly address a particular issue. In *Smoke and Ashes: The Story of the Holocaust*, author Barbara Rogasky meets this problem head-on. Although she warns readers, "This book was not written to give you nightmares,"[32] she unflinchingly recounts the horror that we know as the Holocaust: From 1933 to 1945 over six million humans were systematically, coldly, and ruthlessly murdered. Bigotry, persecution, torture, and genocide—the unrelenting progression of four of humankind's most heinous and repulsive crimes—can neither be explained nor understood simply by telling readers that they occurred. Such an approach doesn't allow the audience to judge the facts for themselves, but rather asks that they accept, or reject, the author's word.

Barbara Rogasky takes the reader into hell, but incredibly, she accomplishes this without exploitation, remaining true to her role as historian and recorder. She outlines the history of anti-Semitism in Germany, the rise of Hitler's dictatorial power, the effects of early Nazi violence against the Jews, the purpose of the special action groups, the terror of life in the ghettos, the design of the Final Solution, the panic of transportation to the camps, the trial of selection procedures, the horror of the gassing, and the ordeal of life within the camps. Is this roll call of human atrocities necessary? Yes, for without the sum of the crimes the horror that was the Holocaust loses its power.

A particularly annoying bid for sensationalism occurs when authors use exclamation points in an artificial attempt to generate excitement over bland subject matter. While the information in the following excerpt from *Wonders of Starfish* by Morris Jacobson and William Emerson might prove interesting, it doesn't deserve the enthusiasm the punctuation demands:

> Starfish find their food by a strong sense of smell. It was found that a starfish in a tank was able to detect a food fish at a distance of 60 centimeters, almost 2 feet! And another scientist reported that one can lead a starfish around, like a donkey with a carrot, by holding a piece of dead crab five centimeters (2 inches) away from one of its tips. Truly a remarkable feeder is the starfish and an interesting one to watch![33]

Illustrations as well as text can be sensationalized. Luring young adults into books with shocking photographs can only be likened to tabloids screaming at potential purchasers through thrilling, eye-catching headlines. Sensational books can, of course, include exploitive and manipulative photographs and illustrations, but selectors don't have to endorse these works.

The cover illustration (see Figure 9) of Guido Dingerkus's *The Shark Watchers' Guide* represents a blatant attempt to fool readers about the book's contents and, in fact, belies the author's stated purpose, which is to show that sharks are not "large, menacing monsters lurking near every beach, waiting for people to go swimming so that sharks can eat and attack them."[34]

Shark books will, and should, include photographs of man-eaters, case histories of shark attacks, and precautions to take while swimming and diving, but for an initial illustration to focus on such issues, when

Figure 9. Cover Illustration from *The Shark Watchers' Guide*.

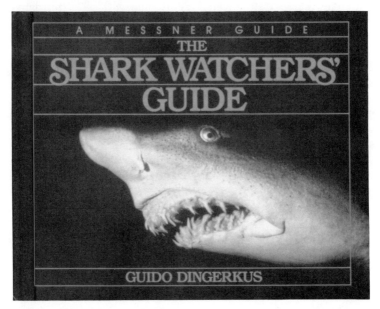

the entire book proports to disclaim this attitude, is nothing short of sensational.

Notice the contrast in the cover illustration (see Figure 10) of Helen Sattler's *Sharks, The Super Fish*. The illustrator, Jean Day Zallinger, clearly shows the primitive grace of the shark in its underwater habitat. While the shark's size is menacing, it is neither frightening nor overwhelming within the vast environmental context of the oceans, and it doesn't overpower or distort readers' perceptions toward the book.

Facts, opinions, and illustrations may cover exciting and thrilling topics, but in themselves they must not sensationalize. The exploitation of young adult readers is underhanded and reprehensible, for it subtly identifies them as an audience able to select reading material for little beyond its shock value. That condescending message conveys little respect for the reader.

STEREOTYPING

Whether referring to physical, sexual, racial, or cultural characteristics, stereotypes provide tidy perceptual packages begging to stay neatly wrapped so that the inquisitive will not actively explore their contents. Stereotypes trade the baffling complexities of what *is* for the comfortable simplicities of what might have once been or even for what never was. As such they represent a form of inaccuracy. For writers to toss off a concept through a stereotype or conventional label indicates that they have not put original thought into a problem or looked past their own prejudices when writing. If authors don't employ meaningful analyses, then readers will not feel challenged to do the same. Critical thinking thus meets an impasse and reading becomes only an act of affirmation.

Such a situation defies one of the major purposes of teaching and encouraging reading. After all, it is reading that allows young adults to travel outside their own spheres of self-interest and to confront what is different—whether it is a time period, a scientific theory, an individual, a society, or an idea. Confrontation may not challenge readers to change their opinions, but without it they will not have the opportunities to begin to think critically. In the best of all literary encounters, young adults use books as tools for widening their own knowledge bases and, as by-products of that process, to question, alter, or confirm their prior assumptions.

Figure 10. Jacket Cover Illustration from *Sharks, the Super Fish.*

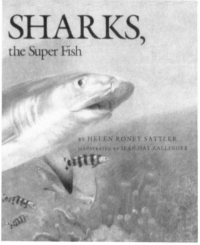

Ironically, some of the very books designed to open doors for young adults may actually close them. Books about unfamiliar regions and countries, for example, should not only be free of stereotypes, but should also hold the potential of allowing young adults to question some of their own preconceived notions. This situation does not always occur. As Hazel Rochman so cogently points out: "Travel isn't necessarily broadening, and neither is reading about foreign places. Many tourists return from the experience with the same rigid stereotypes about 'us' and 'them.' Too many children's books about other countries—written without knowledge or passion—take the tourist approach, stressing the exotic or presenting a static society with simplistic categories."[35] For example, in *Voices of South Africa*, Carolyn Meyer, writing about South Africans' obsession with etiquette, is lulled by the charm of white society, overlooking the sordid living conditions of the majority of the population[36]; Bill Harris, in *Texas*, describes Texans as those who wear "cowboy hats and Lone Star belt buckles, boots with pointed toes and high heels and drink their beer straight from the bottle"[37]; and Patricia Ross, in *Mexico*, ignores the abject poverty of that country by presenting its citizens as content because "they love their children and want big families, even if it means sacrifice and more work. They are usually happy, since they have love and religious faith."[38]

On the other hand, conscientious authors who honestly present issues realize their potential for breaking various stereotypes. In *The 60s Reader* James Haskins and Kathleen Benson make liberal use of original source material and painstakingly develop a sense of that time, so that readers will at least have the opportunity to leave their book with a more complex view of the decade than one perpetuated by overexposure to photographs of garishly decorated VW vans, love-ins, and stoned hippies. Similarly, Jean Fritz's *China's Long March* portrays the Red Army not as a thundering horde of fanatics, but as a dedicated group of desperate men and women surviving an incredible ordeal they saw as the only way to instigate much-needed change in their country. That Fritz takes the time to examine the individuality of various participants—from the man who loved wildflowers to seventeen-year-old Li Xiauxia, passionate about the opportunities for women, to the garrison thrilled by the reality of electricity—underscores the concept that this army was not a faceless group but a mixture of unique individuals. And perhaps unconsciously, in *The Riddle of the Dinosaur*, John Noble Wilford emphasizes the perception that scientists aren't necessarily detached experimenters but, rather, humans who "sometimes make mistakes, and compete or squabble among themselves,"[39] when he introduces the petty jealousies and mean-spiritedness of Othniel Charles Marsh and Edward Drinker Cope as each one tries to monopolize archaeological digs, discredit the other, and establish himself as the most respected paleontologist in the late nineteenth-century "dinosaur wars."

Stereotyping occurs in illustrations as well as text. Although Charles Coombs dutifully includes two photographs of women in *Soaring*, a book that introduces teenagers to sailplaning and gliding, in both illustrations the women are placed in passive roles. In one, a young woman receives a lesson from a male instructor, and in the other she merely occupies the cockpit of an airplane. Where's the joy, the thrill of being a part of nature, the shared enthusiasm in a popular sport? Certainly not in these two photographs.

Other illustrations may build stereotypes. Photographs of a *Jaws*-like great white shark emphasize the perception that the harm sharks cause occurs only through direct physical assault, negating the frequent and tangible damage attributed to basking sharks that tear numerous fishing nets. Dinosaurs also suffer from pictorial stereotyping. Illustration after illustration shows these animals killing, hunting, eating, or standing with looks of anticipation—as if they are about to attack or be attacked. In cases where certain characteristics are known about one species, that characteristic is depicted almost exclusively. For example, Triceratops is often fighting in order to illustrate the battering feature of its three-horned head, and Allosaurus is generally shown stalking or eating Apatosaurus, because several specimens of the latter have been found with Allosaurus teeth marks. Such illustrations make sense, but when all other behaviors, like resting or traveling or mating, are excluded, readers may begin to wonder if Triceratops did anything besides fight or whether Allosaurus spent its entire life span feasting on Apatosaurus.

Reading has the potential of allowing young adults to venture outside their immediate, provincial selves, but they will never make that journey if along the way they encounter only what they already know, or if they find panaceas rather than solutions, caricatures instead of individuals, and bias in place of inquiry.

ANTHROPOMORPHISM AND TELEOLOGY

Two final categories to examine in terms of accuracy are anthropomorphism and teleology. The former attributes human traits to nonhuman subjects, while the latter defines natural phenomena in terms of purpose. Both result in flawed observations.

In its most common metamorphosis, anthropomorphism occurs when authors ascribe human characteristics to animals in an attempt to provide readers ready identification with these creatures, in much the same way young adults would identify with characters in fictional works. But animals aren't human, and books that encourage teen readers to view them in terms of human intentions, emotions, and behaviors rather than in their own circumstances present the animals inaccurately and do young adults a disservice.

In *The Happy Dolphins*, a book recounting author Samuel Carter's experiences training two dolphins, Dal and Suwa, off the Florida coast, Carter writes of the mutual pleasures he and the animals found in each other, and how the dolphins would laughingly greet him. But dolphins neither smile nor laugh. The formation of a dolphin's jaw, with the lower portion hooked over the upper section, creates a smile-like visage, but it is not a grin. And while a dolphin's bark may bring joy to human ears, it certainly isn't a laugh, just like a dog's howl or a cat's meow or a bird's call aren't chuckles. To appropriate human characteristics to describe these mammals only camouflages their unique attributes, and denies young adults the opportunities and pleasures of studying them as creatures of the sea rather than as surrogate friends.

Don C. Reed's *The Dolphins and Me* also explores the bonding between human and beast. Reed, a former scuba diver at Marine World/Africa USA, worked primarily in the dolphin pool, and he lovingly recounts his rich experiences there. He writes of the joys of riding on the dolphins' backs, of his affectionate play with the animals, and of his special sensitivity toward Ernestine, one particularly gentle female dolphin. But Reed always distances his observations. He notes that the dolphins exhibit certain behaviors that one might construe as human, but he never labels them as such, and takes particular care to offer other speculations on their purpose. Reed doesn't assume these mammals are oceanic copies of himself. Through such restraint, he allows young adult readers to consider the animals' true nature.

Anthropomorphism does not limit itself to books about the natural world. Books about computers, for example, frequently assign human-like qualities to the machines. Statements such as "It [a computer] can memorize entire encyclopedias,"[40] or "A computer can deliver a joke with a straight face and perfect timing,"[41] cross the line between metaphor and personification. Poetic comparisons between the central processing unit and the brain, keyboards and ears, and monitors and eyes that italicize or put the human qualities inside quotes avoid the anthropomorphic.

Simple teleological explanations offer pat answers to conceivably complex situations. As children's author Millicent Selsam clearly points out, statements like "Birds suddenly leave one locality and fly hundreds of miles to another place *so that* they will have food and a warmer climate in the new location"[42] ignore valid theories concerning reproduction—that migration patterns may have developed during the Ice Age, since experiments indicate that extended hours of sunlight may affect the birds' reproductive organs. Selsam concludes that the best alternative to that teleological explanation would be to report the scientific observations known about migration and extrapolate the best theories, allowing readers to find new areas for personal observations.

In other cases teleological explanations personify nature as a benevolent earth deity who plans and oversees the natural world. Generally, these discussions begin with an observable fact and superimpose an intent on it. For example, scientists know that in the evolutionary chain human ears have developed into efficient devices for hearing. To state humankind was given ears in order to hear, however, implies causation from an unrelated effect and denotes purpose for which there is no scientific evidence.

In *The Great White Shark*, Eve Bunting mentions that these gigantic fish are often loners, and says by way of explanation, "It is as though nature understands that one great white at a time is terror enough."[43] She ignores the theory that they may travel alone partly because they cannot compete for food with other predators of their size. Such explanations hinder valid observations and have no defensible place in information books.

Yet, when authors define the word "purpose" as *function* rather than *intent*, they are perfectly within the boundaries of scientific inquiry. Such observations do not close off all areas of inquiry, but rather open avenues for new hypotheses, the very nature of scientific questioning. In dinosaur books, for example, authors frequently raise questions about the plates of the Stegosaurus: What were the plates for? The possibilities—that these plates were used for cooling devices, camouflage, or protection—invite complex suppositions based on sophisticated hypothesis rather than providing simple answers and shutting out the inquisitive.

How do librarians and teachers fairly evaluate accuracy in a subject they may know little about? For general purchase, they rely on opinions from a combination of reviewing sources and selection aids, as traditionally recommended for establishing and maintaining a book collection. But when seeking out recommendations for recreational reading and suggestions for curriculum development, librarians and teachers will best serve young adults by weighing the strengths and weaknesses of individual volumes in terms of the scholarship and qualifications of the author, the delineation between fact and opinion, sensationalism, stereotyping, anthropomorphism, and teleology.

NOTES

1. Nourse, Alan E. (1989). *AIDS*. Rev. ed. New York: Franklin Watts, p. 115.

2. Jespersen, James and Fitz-Randolph, Jane (1987). *From Quarks to Quasars: A Tour of the Universe*. New York: Atheneum, p. 74.

3. Marrin, Albert (1985). *1812: The War Nobody Won*. New York: Atheneum, p. 15.

4. Pringle, Laurence (1985). *Nuclear War: From Hiroshima to Nuclear Winter*. Hillside, NJ: Enslow Publishers, p. 55.

5. Moulton, Priscilla Landis (1966). An Experiment in Cooperative Reviewing by Scientists and Librarians. *The Horn Book, 42*, p. 345.

6. Avi (1986). Review the Reviewers? *School Library Journal, 32*, p. 114

7. Miles, Margaret (1989). Letter to Betty Carter. February 19, 1989.

8. Switzer, Ellen, and Costas (1988). *Greek Myths: Gods, Heroes and Monsters: Their Sources, Their Stories and Their Meanings*. New York: Atheneum/A Jean Karl Book, p. 100.

9. Switzer, Ellen, and Costas (1988). p. 198.

10. Switzer, Ellen, and Costas (1988). p. 67.

11. Miles, Margaret (1989). Letter to Betty Carter. February 19, 1989.

12. Blumberg, Rhoda (1976). *Sharks*. New York: Franklin Watts, p. 79.

13. Benedict, Helen (1987). *Safe, Strong, & Streetwise*. Boston: Joy Street Books, book jacket.

14. Pringle, Laurence (1986). *Throwing Things Away*. New York: Thomas Y. Crowell, book jacket.

15. Giblin, James Cross (1988). *Let There Be Light: A Book about Windows*. New York: Thomas Y. Crowell, p. 145.

16. Savitt, Sam (1981). *Draw Horses with Sam Savitt*. New York: Viking, p. 96.

17. Fine, John Christopher (1988). *The Hunger Road*. New York: Atheneum, p. 139.

18. Rochman, Hazel (1986). "The YA Connection: Footnotes and Critical Thinking." *Booklist, 82*, p. 639.

19. Anderson, Norman D. and Brown, Walter R. (1981). *Halley's Comet.* New York: Dodd, Mead and Company. p. 30.

20. Jacobson, Morris K. and Emerson, William K. (1977). *Wonders of Starfish.* New York: Dodd, Mead and Company. p. 30.

21. Blumberg, Rhoda (1976). *Sharks.* New York: Franklin Watts, p. 37.

22. Harrison, Hal H. (1971). *The World of the Snake.* New York: J. B. Lippincott, p. 39.

23. Hentoff, Nat (1988). *American Heroes: In and Out of School.* New York: Delacorte Press, p. 28.

24. Tchudi, Stephen N. (1986). *Soda Poppery: The History of Soft Drinks in America.* New York: Charles Scribner's Sons, p. 143.

25. Lauber, Patricia (1988). *Journey to the Planets.* Rev. ed. New York: Crown, p. 68.

26. Zerman, Melvyn Bernard (1986). *Taking on the Press: Constitutional Rights in Conflict.* New York: Harper & Row, p. ix.

27. Dostert, Pierre Etienne (1988). *Africa 1988.* 23rd Annual Edition. Washington, DC: Stryker-Post Publications, p. 186.

28. Dostert, Pierre Etienne (1988), p. 115.

29. Dostert, Pierre Etienne (1988), p. 116.

30. Gustafson, Anita (1985). *Guilty or Innocent?* New York: Holt, Rinehart & Winston, p. 30.

31. Gustafson, Anita (1985), p. 77.

32. Rogasky, Barbara (1988). *Smoke and Ashes: The Story of the Holocaust.* New York: Holiday House, p. 3.

33. Jacobson, Morris K. and Emerson, William K. (1977). *Wonders of Starfish.* New York: Dodd, Mead, pp. 34–35.

34. Dingerkus, Guido (1985). *The Shark Watcher's Guide.* New York: Julian Messner, p. 10.

35. Rochman, Hazel (1989). "Booktalking: Going Global." *Horn Book, 65,* p. 33.

36. Meyer, Carolyn (1986). *Voices of South Africa: Growing Up in a Troubled Land.* San Diego, CA: Harcourt Brace Jovanovich.

37. Harris, Bill (1979). *Texas.* New York: Mayflower Books, p. 35.

38. Ross, Patricia (1971). *Mexico.* Grand Rapids, MI: Fideler, p. 113.

39. Pringle, Laurence (1981). "Science Done Here." In Betsy Hearne and Marilyn Kaye, *Celebrating Children's Books.* New York: Lothrop, Lee & Shepard, p. 113.

40. Lampton, Christopher (1983). *Programming in BASIC.* New York: Franklin Watts, p. 1.

41. D'Ignazio, Fred (1983). *Invent Your Own Computer Games.* New York: Franklin Watts, p. 18.

42. Selsam, Millicent E. (1967). "Writing about Science for Children." In Sara Innis Fenwick, *A Critical Approach to Children's Literature.* Chicago: University of Chicago Press, p. 97.

43. Bunting, Eve (1982). *The Great White Shark.* New York: Julian Messner, p. 13.

CHAPTER 4
A Conversation with
Milton Meltzer

For years Milton Meltzer has been a voice speaking about the importance of nonfiction in the juvenile book field. His articles and speeches have helped to refocus professional attention on nonfiction. Meltzer has written more than seventy books. He has been nominated five times for the National Book Award. In addition, he has received Jane Addams, Christopher, Jefferson Cup, Carter G. Woodson, Washington Book Guild, Golden Kite, and Olive Branch awards.

Milton Meltzer

A&C In an old biographical sketch about you, it says that as a young man you wanted to teach, but since it was during the Great Depression, you "turned instead to social and political journalism in an attempt to change what was wrong with society." Looking back over the more than seventy books you've written, are you still trying to change what is wrong with society?

MM Yes, I feel the same way. You'll never find perfection in any society, but it's the responsibility of us all to try to make life for everyone as good as it can be.

A&C We just finished reading a new book of yours, *Voices from the Civil War*. In the book you weave letters, speeches, interviews, diaries, and newspapers into a vivid picture of that war and the personal experiences of people who fought in it. How do you create a book like that?

MM Voices from the Civil War is characteristic of one strong vein in my writing—the direct use of documentary material. I believe the approach used in that book helps to make history come alive for young readers. Sometimes I take a narrative approach to history into which I weave the kind of documentary material that makes up *Voices.*

The first book I did in the *Voices* form was published by Knopf in 1967: *Bread and Roses: The Struggle of American Labor.* The idea came from John Anthony Scott, who conceived the series and edited it for Knopf. He felt the kind of documentary material given to university students ought to be available to younger people as well. He asked me to do the first book. I liked working with that form and felt it was a very exciting way to present history to youngsters. I then wrote another book in the series, *Brother, Can You Spare a Dime?*, about the Hoover years of the Great Depression. Since then many of my books have been done in this manner.

Figure 12. Jacket Illustration from *Voices from the Civil War.*

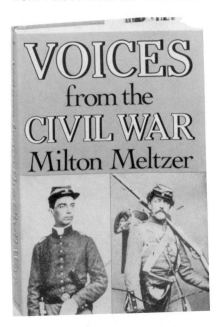

A&C We're interested in where you go to get the first-person accounts that fill books like *The American Revolutionaries.*

MM In researching the distant past, such as the American Revolution or the Civil War, you find that there's little new to dig up. Almost everything you can think of—diaries, notebooks, memoirs, journals—has been collected in one form or another. These documents are often published in obscure historical journals. Some of the documents I've used come from the files of state or local historical societies. Someone digging in the attic finds an ancestor's letters written when he was a soldier in the Union or the Confederate

---

Cover photograph of *Voices from the Civil War* by Milton Meltzer. Published by Harper & Row, 1989. Used by permission of William C. Morris, Harper Junior Books Group.

forces. The letters are often handed over to the local library where some scholar finds them and publishes the documents in a local or state historical journal. Some scholars edit anthologies of such documents. So I certainly look for existing collections of letters and documents. I'm grateful to the original researchers when I draw upon them to reach my audience of young readers.

A&C How do you take all those various documents from a particular historical period and put them into some kind of form?

MM In doing research I use three-by-five-[inch] pads of paper. I note what interests me in the reading I'm doing. I might focus on a quote or a fact or maybe a situation. I have my own self-developed shorthand for codifying the sources so that I can get back to them if necessary. I usually have a rough chapter outline for a proposed book. I file the three-by five-[inch] slips in a box; each slip has the number of each chapter that I'm covering. When I get to the closing stage, I simply take out the notes on Chapter 1 and shuffle them around on my desk until I find a coherent pattern for it. I put a slash mark through the notes I use but save the others in case I need to go back later and fill in a hole. When my work goes through an editor's hand, he or she may raise questions about things I haven't covered in the book. Or I might be asked to elaborate on a particular point. The material I need may well be on one of the three-by-five-[inch] slips that I hadn't intended to use, so I save everything.

When doing a book of this kind for young readers I try to select documents that convey the experience of young people, so the link between reader and subject is that much closer. In *Never to Forget* there is a good deal of testimony on the Holocaust from its younger victims. In *Bread and Roses* I hunted for evidence of what young people went through in the time before child labor was banned and kids worked in coal mines, in textile mills, in sweatshops. Of course the experience of adults is included, but I keep an eye out for youth. The same is true of my book *Poverty in America*, and so on. In my recent documentaries on the American Revolution and the Civil War I was able to convey the experience of the many teenage soldiers who fought in both conflicts.

A&C What kind of time do you give yourself for completing a book?

MM The time often depends on the availability of materials. Ten years ago my adult biography of Dorothea Lange was published. That book took two-and-a-half years to do because a good part of it was based on interviews. Lange died ten years before I began work on her life, so much material came from talking with or writing to about one hundred people all around the United States. I did a good deal of traveling to interview people, sometimes even going back for a second interview when I found contradictions or holes in eyewitness accounts. So you see why that kind of book takes up a great amount of time.

But, if it's a book on a subject that I've already done a lot of work on, each successive book in that field may take somewhat less time. The research I did for *The American Revolutionaries* was helpful in doing my biographies of Benjamin Franklin and George Washington. Right now, I'm in the middle of a book about the Bill of Rights, which comes out of the same revolutionary period. In this case, half of the book will deal with what's happened to the Bill of Rights in the two hundred years since it was adopted, so that's a different kind of research. But with each book, I'm able to build on what I learned about the Revolution in the earlier books.

A&C With seventy or more books to your credit, you must be a disciplined writer.

MM The word "disciplined" has a pejorative ring to it. It's as though you feared writing or would rather be doing something else. That's not true for me. Writing history and biography is very much a labor of love. I go to my desk every morning very happily. I'm glad that I'm privileged to be able to do what I like and make a living at it. I do, however, tell people who want to write that a regular work schedule is necessary. A writer must sit down daily at the desk whether or not he thinks he has something to say.

A&C Most of the textbooks on children's or adolescent literature have a list of criteria for what makes a good nonfiction book. We're wondering if you have your own set of standards for how you judge a nonfiction book. What makes a good one?

MM The writer's voice must be heard on the pages of the book. Teachers and librarians refer to nonfiction as *informational books*. I don't like the term because it is a kind of put-down. It implies that to do a nonfiction book is something like compiling a telephone directory—just mechanically assembling facts with no feeling behind it. In reading a nonfiction book, I look for the passion that shows the writer's concern for what he or she is writing about.

People often raise the question of objectivity. I think it's false for authors of nonfiction books to say they are totally objective. I don't think there is any such thing as being totally objective. You'd have no personality, no point of view, no evidence of experiencing life. Whatever you write comes out of your own origins, your upbringing, your education, the work you've done, the people you've known, the ideas you've had, the politics you've been involved in, and the approach you take to any subject reflects all those life experiences. If you try to conceal your point of view, you are simply denaturing your own work.

A&C We know that you have written about the problems with history textbooks used in the junior and senior high schools. Would you talk about the problems with those textbooks and how they differ from your approach to history?

MM One of the major difficulties with history textbooks is that they're often the product of a committee. They are not animated by what I've just been talking about—a direct, personal, point of view on a particular facet of history or even the sweep of decades. The names of distinguished historians may appear on the textbooks, but how often were they written by them? Sometimes they simply lend their names, and a committee within the publishing house actually does all the work. In one case, a man I knew, a first-class historian, was commissioned by a publishing house to do an American history book by virtue of the very fact that he was so good. He thought they wanted his point of view. He wrote some chapters, sent them in, and got them back much rewritten. They didn't play around with his facts, but the whole tone of what he had written was grossly distorted, so he broke the contract. He wouldn't allow his name to appear over a book that wasn't his own.

A&C Is part of the problem also that the textbooks don't have the first-person accounts that you include in your books?

MM I think that is starting to change, if in a limited way. Perhaps they'll have a boxed insert with a brief first-person account. But, even that is rare. The other problem with history textbooks is they're too monumental. They are like the New York telephone directory in size and weight. I feel dropping that kind of thing on any youngster's desk is terribly depressing and discouraging, no matter how bright the student is. The many maps, pictures, and timelines distract the reader from the text, ruining narrative flow. The young reader would profit much more if trade books were used in place of the textbooks. Plenty of trade books are available on all aspects of history and are usually far livelier and more personal. California has begun to do this.

A&C Is nonfiction still a second-class citizen in the juvenile book field?

MM To a much lesser degree than it was, say, ten or twelve years ago, when I began to utter my laments in public on this subject. At the annual Boston Globe/Horn Book Award ceremonies I gave a talk called "Where Have All the Prizes Gone?" [about the paucity of juvenile literary awards that have been given to nonfiction books.] The very next year, the sponsors divided the prize—one for fiction and one for nonfiction. Now that has happened in many places, and some groups give prizes just for nonfiction—for a particular book or for the whole body of one's work in nonfiction. Even the Newbery committee broke the ice by honoring Russell Freedman's *Lincoln*. It was a terrific thing to do, but it took fifty years to do it. The few books they gave prizes to before that were called nonfiction really were not. Instead, they were books written in the outmoded vein of biography that was highly fictionalized, had invented dialogue, and sometimes concocted scenes. That's all changed today, but it took a long time.

A&C There's a trend in nonfiction today toward including more photos and graphics. Will we see more of that in your books?

MM Some of my books have had a great many pictures right from the beginning. The very first book I did for adults—*The Pictorial History of the Negro in America*, as it was then called—was written with Langston Hughes. The book is still in print thirty-five years later and has sold very widely. The basic idea was to do a pictorial history. The book used twelve hundred pieces of art that I researched, but has a very solid narrative, too. In biographies I've written recently about Ben Franklin, George Washington, and Mark Twain you'll find quite a few illustrations. One wouldn't call these picture books, for the text is very much dominant.

A&C Do you do your own research for the pictures?

MM Yes. Because I've done so much of it over the years, I have a very good notion of sources to go to in order to find the pictures I need, and New York, where I live, is very rich in picture sources. I usually confer with the editor and the art director after the text for a book has been approved. I get some general idea of how much illustration they want to do. If I know there is going to be art in the book, I'll make notes about pictures as I do the text research. That speeds up the process.

A&C How do you feel about the importance of footnotes, bibliographies, and reading lists in nonfiction for adolescents?

MM I think bibliographies are very important. Recently I have been including annotated bibliographies, organized by subjects covered in the text. This helps give the young reader an indication of the nature of the book, what it's about, and ought to be more valuable than just the listing of titles. I also indicate which reference books may be the most useful to them. Now, on the issue of footnotes, there is a difference of opinion. Hazel Rochman, at *Booklist*, thinks that the text itself should have footnotes, either at the back of the book or at the bottom of each page. I suspect a great many young readers would be put off by all these notes. I try to refer, within the text, to the source of important statements or facts and to indicate whether something is disputed. But I don't provide scholarly footnotes for young readers. All sources—books, magazines, newspapers, journals—will be in the bibliography. If I were to put footnotes into my books there might be as many as ten or fifteen on every single page. How many young readers would see that thicket of small-type notes and not be put off by it? My biography of Dorothea Lange has twenty pages of closely packed footnotes in the back of the book, but that's intended for adults.

A&C Your memoir, *Starting from Home: A Writer's Beginnings*, is a wonderful work. How did the process of writing that differ from the other books that you've done?

MM I must say I didn't spin the book only out of my faulty memory. Perhaps because of the other books I've written, I wanted *Starting from Home* to be a kind of social history of my hometown, Worcester, Massachusetts, at least as I knew it. The good schooling I had while growing up there mattered to me. The book is dedicated to a marvelous English teacher, Anna Shaughnessy. She and my history teacher, Mr. Brennan, planted seeds in me that matured many years later in the form of books I never anticipated I would write.

I made several trips back to Worcester to look again at the places where I lived and had gone to school. I went to the library and used the files of the local press for many of the years I had been in junior and senior high school. I talked to people my own age who still live in the city. I also spent time interviewing my two brothers. My older brother had a fantastic memory for early childhood, and I interviewed him at great length about experiences we shared. I needed his perspective on various incidents to see how they matched mine. As often happens with personal testimony, we sometimes differed radically not only in our interpretation of what happened within the family but even on whether it happened to me or to him. I'd tell him a particular incident I was writing about from my childhood, and he'd tell me that I didn't do that, but he did, and I was stealing his life. In 1987 I wrote a book called *The Landscape of Memory*. Some of it goes into the phenomenon of memory and how faulty and unreliable it can be.

A&C It seems to us that one of the finest portraits of a teacher is the picture that you paint of Anna Shaughnessy. What effect did she have on your life?

MM If it weren't for Anna Shaughnessy, I don't think I would have gone to college. I came from a working-class family, and she made me believe college was possible. She helped by steering me to an experimental college that was opening at Columbia, and helped me to get a scholarship to attend New College. Anna was a lively intellectual who was always eager to talk about books and ideas. She introduced me to Thoreau and other great writers. Several years later, I went back to Thoreau and began to think about the problems and issues he'd raised in connection with social reform. I'm grateful to her for making that connection. It led me to write two adult books on Thoreau.

A&C What title of yours seems to be the most popular with students?

MM Sales of books would not be a very sure guide. In nonfiction, the great majority of books are sold to the schools and the libraries, and it's the adults who make those choices. So I can only judge what youngsters like from the letters I get and the many visits I make each year to talk to kids in schools. There I often find genuine enthusiasm for what I write about and the way I do it.

A&C Do awards given to nonfiction books lead to increased sales?

MM The only award that seems to make a real difference is the Newbery. No other award does. If teachers and librarians like your work you usually do well in sales. I'm sure any awards you win have a positive effect.

A&C What do you think is the job of a good nonfiction reviewer?

MM Most reviewing media in our field give too little space to book reviews for the writer to say much of anything. They are merely snippets, with no space to develop ideas or to prove a point, be it positive or negative. It's nice to get approving reviews, and I appreciate them very much. And a negative review can be helpful. But I wish there were more journals in our field that would devote significant space to individual titles. The *New York Times* Book Review, long ago, would give a full-page to a single title. That happened to me more than once years back. And the review editor might call upon an expert in the given field to handle your book. The *Times* labor editor, for instance, reviewed my *Bread and Roses*, a labor history, and a well-known literary critic reviewed my *Never to Forget*, both at considerable length. Not only does the *Times* never do this now, but most other newspapers have dropped reviewing children's books altogether. They say it is because the publishers don't find advertising in such media worthwhile, and without ads—no space for reviews.

As for children's literature journals, some do manage to cover most or even all the books in our field. But to do that requires the briefest

Figure 13. Jacket Cover Illustration from *Rescue*.

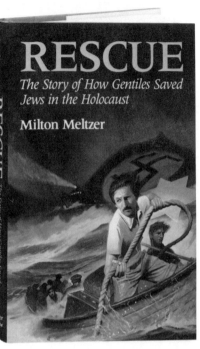

From *Rescue* by Milton Meltzer. Published by Harper & Row. Used by permission of Harper-Collins Publishers.

coverage of a vast number of books. *Horn Book* handles only books its reviewers like. I wish the journals could combine broad coverage with at least some detailed analysis of selected titles, significant for one reason or another. Sometimes such journals as *Children's Literature in Education* and *The Lion and the Unicorn* do run sizeable articles on some books or on one author's body of work, or on a theme as it is treated by a few or more writers. I remember one excellent piece comparing the different ways three or four biographers handled the life of Madame Curie, the physicist. I learned a lot from it.

A&C What book of yours are you proudest of?

MM Hard to say! But perhaps my very first book, *A Pictorial History of the Negro in America*, later retitled *A Pictorial History of Black Americans*. I was terribly lucky to be able to work with [Langston Hughes] for I was a rank novice and had much to learn from a master. (Later we collaborated on another adult book, *Black Magic*, and I wrote a biography of him.) The book was a first in its field, appearing just on the eve of the civil rights upheaval, and it immediately became a great seller, among both black and white readers. I'll never forget the moment when Langston phoned me to say he had just read in the newspaper an AP dispatch that quoted one of the college students who led the first sit-in against segregated eating places in North Carolina. Asked why he did it, he replied that he had been reading our *Pictorial History* and was seized with the desire to do something important for his people, the way many men and women before him had been portrayed resisting racism in our book. It's time for me to do *my* part, he said. By the way, Scholastic Books has revised and updated our book and is issuing it as a history text under the new title of *The African Americans*.

A&C We know that you have a grandson named Benjamin McArthur. Which Meltzer book do you want him to read?

MM My memoir, *Starting from Home*. It was written with the next generation in mind—my two daughters and the children to follow. So much of the past is quickly lost to us. I did my best to recover not only my own childhood but my parents' earlier years and their parents too. I've had many letters from other members of our family thanking me for opening up that history to them. And other readers, not related to me, have written to say how much they find in it that helps them to understand their own lives and family history. In one case, I think fifth and sixth graders read the memoir aloud in class, and then were so excited by it they embarked on researching their own family histories. That delighted me.

A&C As a writer of nonfiction, what gives you the greatest satisfaction?

MM The work itself, for one thing. I think I said before that I find great pleasure in trying to reconstruct the past, whether of a society, a period, or a person. You're always learning something new, discovering fresh ways to look at life, seeing people and character in different perspective. And of course the other part of it is the pleasure of finding that readers enjoy what you create and perhaps themselves go through the process of growth you experienced in doing your job.

BOOKS BY MILTON MELTZER

Ain't Gonna Study War No More: The Story of America's Peaceseekers. (1985). New York: Harper & Row.

All Times, All Peoples: A World History of Slavery. (1980). New York: Harper & Row.

The American Revolutionaries: A History in Their Own Words. (1987). New York: Thomas Y. Crowell.

Benjamin Franklin: The New American. (1988). New York: Franklin Watts.

**Betty Friedan: A Voice for Woman's Rights.* (1985). New York: Viking/Women of Our Time.

**The Black Americans: A History in Their Own Words.* (1984). New York: Thomas Y. Crowell.

A Book about Names. (1984). New York: Thomas Y. Crowell.

Bread and Roses: The Struggle of American Labor. (1977). New York: New American Library.

Brother Can You Spare a Dime? (1977). New York: New American Library.

The Chinese Americans. (1980). New York: Thomas Y. Crowell.

**Dorothea Lange: A Photographer's Life.* (1978). New York: Farrar Straus & Giroux.

George Washington and the Birth of Our Nation. (1986). New York: Franklin Watts.

The Hispanic Americans. (1982). New York: Thomas Y. Crowell.

The Human Rights Books. (1979). New York: Farrar Straus & Giroux.

The Jewish Americans: A History in Their Own Words. (1982). New York: Thomas Y. Crowell.

The Jews in America: A Picture Album. (1985). Philadelphia, PA: JPS.

Landscape of Memory. (1987). New York: Viking.

Langston Hughes: A Biography. (1968). New York: Thomas Y. Crowell.

Mark Twain. (1985). New York: Franklin Watts.

**Mary McLeod Bethune: Voice of Black Hope.* (1982). New York: Viking/Women of Our Time.

**Never to Forget: The Jews of the Holocaust.* (1976). New York: Harper & Row.

Poverty in America. (1986). New York: William Morrow.

Rescue: The Story of How Gentiles Saved Jews in the Holocaust. (1988). New York: Harper & Row.

The Right to Remain Silent. (1972). San Diego, CA: Harcourt Brace Jovanovich.

Starting from Home: A Writer's Beginnings. (1989). New York: Viking.

The Terrorists. (1983). New York: Harper & Row.

**Winnie Mandela: The Soul of South Africa.* (1986). New York: Viking/Women of Our Time.

World of Our Fathers: The Jews of Eastern Europe. (1974). New York: Farrar Straus & Giroux.

*Meltzer, Milton and Harding, Walter. (Written with Walter Harding). *Thoreau Profile*. (1969). Concord, MA: Thoreau Foundation.

* Indicates edition is paperback
** Indicates a paperback edition also available

CHAPTER 5
Content

Content, or what a book is *about*, involves more than a mere definition of topic. While it includes subject, content also refers to how an author treats that topic. For this reason, individual volumes cataloged in the same subject division are not interchangeable among young adult readers. Subtle content variations among apparently similar books will influence book selection as frequently as do gross differences.

Quality nonfiction provides both avenues and levels of meaning, refusing to be pigeonholed into a single, fixed category. Chris Crutcher's *Stotan!* is no more just a swimming book than is Richard Peck's *Are You in the House Alone?* merely a study of rape. Likewise, David E. Fisher's *The Origin and Evolution of Our Own Particular Universe* offers more than an examination of stars and planets, and Peter Parnell's *The Daywatchers* is more than a book about birds. These simplistic labels mask the power of the individual works. Fine novels are *about* the substance of story: plot, theme, characters, and setting. Similarly, first-rate nonfiction is *about* the elements of exposition: subject, scope, depth of presentation, and author's focus.

SCOPE

Scope influences readers as much as does subject. Each informational book must encompass a definable scope, although authors may elect to write about any point on a subject matter continuum that moves from limited to global. Nonfiction allows the latitude for Carl Sagan to tackle the entire cosmos, Patricia Lauber to travel to each of the nine planets in our solar system, Louise B. Young to explore our own earth, Lorus and Margery Milne to examine just the soil that covers this planet, and Don C. Reed to share his experiences with a single animal. Each book appeals to the varied interests of adolescents.

No matter which approach is used, scope must remain defined and logical. A book on the history of basketball may include chapters on both James Naismith and Larry Bird, but an in-depth section on Vince Lombardi falls way outside the boundaries of the work. On the other hand, a book covering the history of spectator sports in America can logically include chapters on all three individuals. The relationship between specific parts of a particular work and the overall vision must present a comprehensible association. When the relationship is clear, authors remain within their chosen scopes; when that connection blurs, they do not.

In *Spreadsheets for Beginners*, for example, Elayne Engelman Schulman and Richard R. Page introduce novice computer users to these practical and useful programs. They define a computer spreadsheet, the evolution of the software, the use of spreadsheets as tools, the purpose of special features in various commercial products, and the principles of operation. They don't stray from their topic by including peripheral chapters on Charles Babbage's analytical machine, the advantages of word processing, or the debate over artificial intelligence, and thus allow scope to remain both definable and apparent.

Occasionally informational books without a definable scope appear on our library shelves, in the same manner that fictional books that lack coherence sometimes do. One such nonfiction work is *The Guinness Book of Amazing Achievements*, an abbreviated and easy-to-read version of the more popular *The Guinness Book of World Records*. The former title, which includes ninety-one feats ranging from the oldest person who drives himself to work every day to the name of the pope chosen in the quickest papal election in history, fails to differentiate between a remarkable achievement and an amazing one. Therefore, entries such as the two mentioned above, or the one describing the oldest judge to serve on the bench, appear as capricious choices. The lack of overall unity and unspecified scope defines this book as a work missing both theme and purpose.

Occasionally an author's scope may be acceptable, but fails to include information sorely needed in a particular library or classroom. At that point, it's possible to fall into an unfortunate trap—that of evaluating the book one wishes the authors had written rather than the one they did.

In reviewing Walter Boyne's *The Smithsonian Book of Flight for Young People*, Dennis Ford deftly sidesteps this tendency:

> Flight in different periods is related partially through the stories of those involved—inventors, developers, designers, and pilots. The illustrations accentuate artistic and historic aspects rather than serve as a compendium of models. For example, the invention of adjustable propellers is mentioned but their technical advantage not explained, and some design improvements are noted but not pictured. These are not shortcomings, however, as such information is simply outside the scope of coverage. Students needing technical detail will find no shortage of other materials. This [*The Smithsonian Book of Flight for Young People*] is for general readers who need a broader view of the history of flight.[1]

Since Ford recommends the book for junior and senior high students, he not only acknowledges Boyne's scope as one appropriate for young adults, but also recognizes that other works will cover related issues not germane to this historical overview.

As knowledge has increased, methods of presentation have changed; and as the developmental stages of young adults have become more apparent, the scope of informational books has tended to narrow. The first picture book written for children was *Orbis Pictus: the World of Sensible Things Drawn; that is the Nomenclature of all Fundamental Things in the World and Actions in Life Reduced to Ocular Demonstration.* This book, published in 1657 by Moravian Bishop John Amos Comenius, fused illustrations and text with the intention of showing children "a graphic view of every one of the things in Heaven and Earth."[2] Three hundred years later, the first Newbery Medal for the most distinguished contribution to children's literature went to Hendrik Willem van Loon's *The History of Mankind,* which, in terms of scope, was a comparably ambitious narrative history.

But contrast these two works with today's hallmarks in nonfiction. The 1987 Newbery winner, Russell Freedman's *Lincoln: A Photobiography,* depicts not the whole of humankind, but instead a lone man. Designated as a Best Book for Young Adults one year later, Barbara Rogasky's *Smoke and Ashes: The Story of the Holocaust,* focuses on one aspect of one war, out of the thousands of conflicts that mark our history. And just the year before, that same committee chose to highlight a journalistic investigation into the death of one teenager in *Best Intentions: The Education and Killing of Edmund Perry,* by placing Robert Sam Anson's work on its list. Indeed, in this sequence, scope has narrowed since *Orbis Pictus.*

Considering the audience, that more precise focus makes sense. Typically as young adults mature they begin to identify more specific interests, and the books they read will reflect that concentration. Our 1987 analysis of those informational books most frequently circulated by junior high students supports this perception; only 10% of these titles were designated as global in scope.[3]

Scope does not define depth of presentation. Frequently books with a limited scope will offer abbreviated, superficial information rather than detailed and sophisticated analysis. On the other hand, a tendency to narrow doesn't necessarily produce books with limited, specialized themes. The reverse often occurs, as authors use a specific topic as a point of reference for readers to contemplate larger issues. In reviewing James Giblin's *Let There Be Light: A Book about Windows,* Roger Sutton points out this feature, "As was true of the author's *From Hand to Mouth,* social commentary runs fluently throughout: why Moslems constructed windows that allowed one to see out but not in; the differences between cultures that build windows facing a courtyard and those that built them facing the outside. This is as much a history of how people live as it is a history of windows."[4]

A proclivity toward descriptive field research and away from the use of secondary sources has also led to a more limited scope in books for young adults. For an increasing number of authors, research involves direct, first-person participation, observation, and interview rather than reliance on the discourse of others. Investigation has long been the tool of the natural sciences, and older works like George and Kay Schaller's *Wonders of Lions*, based on their direct studies of a Masai pride, reflects this process in natural science. In a more recent work in the social sciences, *Best Intentions: The Education and Killing of Edmund Perry*, author Robert Sam Anson likewise shares his descriptive investigative research. In both cases, the well-researched product offers a narrow scope.

Although many authors are writing books with more limited scope, still others consistently deliver fine works with a global focus: *The Guinness Book of World Records* and *National Geographic*'s double volume *Book of Mammals* are two such works. Similarly, reports from YA librarians across the United States indicate that *The Facts on File Visual Dictionary* and David Macaulay's *The Way Things Work* are both circulated frequently. While a tendency exists for informational books to exhibit increasingly limited scopes, there is nonetheless undisputable value and appeal in more generalized works.

DEPTH OF PRESENTATION

The depth of an author's inquiry refers to the amount of detail and level of concepts covered in any one book. Depth of presentation ranges from sparse to extensive. Books with limited depth of presentation include only surface facts and basic theories. A spare description of the Andromeda galaxy, for example, stresses physical attributes: the size, appearance through a telescope, and the numbers of light-years it lies from this galaxy. A more extensive discussion of Andromeda could reasonably cover topics such as Immanuel Kant's historical perceptions that the universe contains many galaxies, some comparison of the spiral Andromeda to our own, theories on how individual stars were created or will die, and a description of the two satellite galaxies which surround it. Depending on their background knowledge, motivations for reading, and levels of interest, individual young adult readers need, and demand, books with both extensive and sparse coverage on any given subject.

Although young adults have begun the process of limiting their reading topics, they certainly haven't developed all of the interests they will experience over a lifetime. Every day teenagers uncover new areas of fascination, and at that point of discovery they become novices to a discipline. Consequently, the initial books they read on these previously unknown subjects need to cover the basics: the specialized jargon, the physical descriptions, the general historical perspectives—in other words, they should provide a broad, overall view. Even though adolescents are unfamiliar with a field, they do need titles addressed to their particular maturity levels. Basic does not mean juvenile but, rather, implies conventional coverage of a topic.

Luckily, many fine books exist that introduce young readers to a subject. Elaine Scott's *Stocks and Bonds, Profits and Losses: A Quick Look at Financial Markets*, for example, opens with a discussion of a familiar Monopoly game, and has readers extrapolate principles from this common experience that relate to the rules of investment. Scott defines basic terms, such as *corporation, preferred stock,* and *stop orders*; mentions the varied methods of investment; looks at the history and function of the New York Stock Exchange; develops the role of a broker; explains how to read stock listings in the newspaper; and takes the reader through a simulated purchase. None of these topics is explored in-depth, but her suggested list of further readings provides sources for more detailed information.

Overview books like the one above must expect that readers will bring little or no content background to their discussion. In his introduction to *A New Look at the Dinosaurs*, Alan Charig observes this when he explains, "I have taken nothing for granted. I have assumed that my typical reader knows nothing of dinosaurs or of related matters.[5] It's an appropriate place to begin.

Hazards come when authors either talk down to their readers or offer misleading overgeneralizations in an attempt to simplify. Illa Podendorf suggests that adults evaluate generalizations in terms of the conclusions unsophisticated readers may draw from them. She uses the sentence "Plants use carbon dioxide and give off oxygen whereas animals use oxygen and give off carbon dioxide," as an example of a statement that while true, contains the potential of indicating that plants don't need oxygen and animals don't need carbon dioxide.[6] But this advice often goes unheeded; overgeneralizations continue to exist. For example, in his basic overview book, *Computers*, Neil Ardley offers this observation: "Most microcomputer owners have a dual set of disk drives so that the contents of one disk can be copied on to another."[7] The fact that information can be transferred from diskette to diskette on single-drive systems may well elude the computer novice.

After reading introductory works, many young adults will demand books that discuss the process of researching that interest. The first level of reading about a topic discusses what is; the second, how that information has evolved. In *The Riddle of the Dinosaur*, John Noble Wilford thoroughly explains the methodology of paleontology. He takes readers through the scientific sequence of exploration, collection, and observation; the generation of hypotheses; the revision of early assumptions; the reconstruction of data; and the evolution of new theories.

Similarly, author/anthropologist Ted Conover invites readers to follow him as he immerses himself in the culture of illegal Mexican immigrants in *Coyotes*. By traveling, working, and socializing with various individuals and groups, Conover writes more than a thrilling adventure; he demonstrates a model of participatory observation.

Books that reflect a third level of inquiry, that of immersion in a field, also enjoy young adult readerships, and likewise require professional attention. Collecting data is only part of the process of scholarship. Analyzing information and drawing conclusions complete the process. Seeing the process allows teenagers to vicariously experience the behaviors of journalists, scientists, computer programmers, historians, or engineers.

In writing *The Origin and Evolution of Our Own Particular Universe*, David E. Fisher clearly had this sophisticated audience in mind. As Fisher states at the onset, "One question that we want to answer is how our universe was created, but the other question, perhaps even more important, is how we learned the answer."[8] Fisher uses the German word *gedankenexperiments*, or thought experiments, to refer to "a procedure in which it is sometimes possible to 'perform' an experiment simply by thinking about it, and imagining what the results must be."[9] Through a series of these thought experiments he forces the reader not to vicariously observe the processes of others, but to actually participate in the formation and validation, or rejection, of the hypotheses which explain what we know about the structure, birth, and eventual death of our universe.

Even though some young adults may understand sophisticated quantum physics, this knowledge level doesn't indicate similar breadth in other subjects. Authors of all informational books for young adults need to keep in mind that these readers may not be able to distinguish between Italy and Florida on a map, or that they may assume the Inquisition refers to the process they endure when they ask to borrow the family car. No matter how deeply a book explores a given topic, information outside that particular subject must either be familiar to the audience or be detailed for them.

Thus, the depths of inquiry fall into three gross hierarchical levels: readers gather information, search for the processes of organizations, and immerse themselves in a discipline. Yet, transition from one stage to the next does not occur automatically. For various reasons, young adults will often choose to explore one particular level in increasing depth and detail and refuse to move to the next level. We find those teenagers who can recite seemingly every known fact about dinosaurs, computers, or astronomy, but show little interest in finding out about the evolution of that material.

Conversely, these divisions do not exist as exclusionary ones. To start with, few books subdivide into neat categories but, instead, overlap levels. And equally as important, the mind doesn't work within such constraints either. Humans are perfectly capable of understanding concepts before they can label the particulars. In *From One to Zero: A Universal History of Numbers*, Georges Ifrah offers the following example: A shepherd in a primitive society possesses no number names and no training in counting. But this shepherd needs to know whether or not he gathers his entire flock every night. In order to find out, he leads his flock into a tunnel, and notches a stick as each sheep passes. The next day when collecting his throng, this shepherd again leads them through a passage—a gate, a tunnel, a pass—and covers one notch with his finger each time a single animal goes by him. In effect, this shepherd has counted. He can't produce an exact figure on the size of his herd, for he doesn't have the language for a dozen or one hundred, but he can tell whether they are all present or not.

Librarians and teachers can certainly allow themselves to gently intrude on a young adult's interests and suggest works of increasingly sophisticated content. The concept of reading ladders, firmly embedded in the strategies for recommending fiction, also extends into the area of nonfiction, and is discussed in Chapter 13. Although it is appropriate for librarians and teachers to suggest particular books, teenagers need the options of either accepting or rejecting these recommendations.

FOCUS

Authors must have a clear purpose in mind when writing for a young adult audience. Purpose, in turn, defines focus. Individual foci not only mark particular works, but also characterize particular authors. Robert Hofsinde's purpose in writing was to share his passion for American Indian life with youngsters[10]; Eda LeShan feels an obligation to "write books I wish I had had as a child"[11]; Milton Meltzer is "trying to find some pattern or meaning in the struggle to realize his own humanity"[12]; Kathryn Lasky searches for "the story among the truths, the facts, the lies, and the realities"[13]; and Laurence Pringle wishes "to acknowledge that the world is a complex place but that the complexity can be explored and understood."[14] Brent Ashabranner reveals that "the things I felt I was learning about understanding other cultures and about people of different cultures trying to understand each other seemed worth sharing with young readers."[15] Although each of these authors reveals an individual purpose for writing, three general categories emerge from young adult nonfiction: to impose a belief on the reader (didactic), to present facts (utilitarian), or to share information (personal).

A didactic focus does not respect the reader. While individuals may sincerely not want young adults to use drugs, drink and drive, misunderstand other cultures, have sexual experiences, or engage in violence, books on these topics owe teenagers the consideration of allowing them to make their own decisions, rather than forcing them to accept the authors'. By no means does this statement indicate that books should not possess these themes, but specific works ought not to be written with the purposes of imposing certain precepts on an unsuspecting reader. Writers may share with teenagers why they as individuals support a position and they can offer persuasive arguments that may well influence a reader's decision to accept a particular stance, but they cannot expect or demand that young adults adopt similar attitudes just because they say so.

In *What to Say When You Don't Know What to Say: A Guide to Easier Conversation on Dates, in Job and College Interviews, on Life's Formal Occasions*, author Alice Fleming suggests the following conversational "don'ts": Don't talk about operations or illnesses, especially at the dinner table; don't tell racial, off-color, or ethnic jokes; don't give detailed synopses of books, television shows, or movies; don't repeat rumors or gossip; don't be overly critical of others; don't keep the conversation focused on yourself; and don't reveal intimacies with casual accquaintances. Although her advice is solid and reasonable—we've all endured seemingly endless conversations during which someone ignored one or more of these maxims—her manner of presentation is unwise. Young adults need to know why the author believes they shouldn't engage in specific behaviors, not simply that they should shun them. Fleming's didacticism defines reading as a passive act of absorption, negating not only the purposes of reading, but also the value of critical thinking.

The second common focus found in informational books is a utilitarian one. In these books authors present facts with little or no suggestion of personal or professional purpose. Many such works are both popular and successful. In *The Guinness Book of World Records*, for example, young adults may discover who has the longest fingernails in the world, the fastest time for running the mile, or the name of the oldest woman to give birth to a child. This information is presented clearly and lucidly, but without any indication of the authors' interests, feelings, or opinions about these accomplishments. Yet, year after year, this one book triggers a passionate need to know in younger adolescents that belies its functional focus.

The Guinness Book of World Records is not the only such book that appeals to teenagers. During the American Library Association's Best Books for Young Adults 1987 committee meetings, Mike Printz, head librarian at Topeka West High School in Topeka, Kansas, revealed his problems in evaluating *The Penguin Encyclopedia of Horror and the Supernatural*, another book with a utilitarian focus. Printz admitted that demand for that particular volume was so great among Topeka West's students that for several months he was unable to even find a copy, much less read it for himself.

Authors who employ a utilitarian focus will distance themselves from a work for several reasons. Occasionally they may not care much about the subject. Such an impersonal attitude quickly reveals itself in all other aspects of writing and will lead to rejection of the particular title by the reader. Another reason appears to come from the pool of stereotypes concerning nonfiction, that facts are unemotional collections of data and should be presented that way. But most often a utilitarian approach surfaces in collected works, like the above *Encyclopedia of Horror and the Supernatural,* which include multiple entries by informed and committed professionals, but, when combined into a whole collection, must of necessity adopt a uniform tone.

Books in the third category, or those with a personal focus, may be how-to titles, expository works, and historical accounts. Both real and imagined problems appear in books with personal foci. The first problem concerns objectivity. As long as people continue to write books, no work will ever result in a purely objective presentation. As Milton Meltzer states, "The writer cannot be neutral even if he wants to be."[16] The very facts writers select, the topics they highlight, and the connotations of the words they use all support distinct points of view, although the combination of a utilitarian focus and a neutral tone frequently masks this truth. Fine nonfiction with a personal focus, however, puts those positions out in the open for readers to examine them. And therein lies the problem.

One of the prevailing myths about informational books, similar to the one that defines nonfiction as true and fiction as not true, is that their authors must present both positive and negative views of an issue. Carrying this train of thought one step further, many adults immediately suspect the objectivity of those informational books with a personal focus and a stated point of view.

But books about child abuse or incest, for instance, aren't expected to provide readers with approving examples of offenders. What authors are expected to do is to equitably present their information about abuse, information that may include why such behavior takes place, what happens in such cases, how to deter abusers, and where to go for help. The author of an informational book can endorse the theme that incest is an aberration as surely as Patricia Hermes does in her novel *A Solitary Secret.*

The test for objectivity occurs most often in the political arena. Whether readers agree or disagree with an author's point of view, the job of defining objectivity is complicated. The only reliable procedure available is the evaluation of sources and documentation. Using that process, a careful reviewer can find serious problems in Pierre Etienne Dostert's *Latin America 1988.* Dostert substantiates his stance through quotations without references and assertions without documentation. Although he covers all Latin American countries with varying degrees of objectivity, in the chapter on Nicaragua, Dostert clearly supports the pro-*contra* position. On the other hand, Rita Golden Gelman in *Inside Nicaragua* clearly opposes the *contra's* stand. Her purpose for writing comes from her desire to share with American teenagers the experiences of Nicaraguan youth, their opinions on the conflict within their own country, and their feelings toward their North American peers. Gelman draws her opinions from her experiences of living in Nicaragua for seven months, through interviews, and from well-documented sources. Our evaluation of that particular work agrees with the 1988 Best Books for Young Adults Committee; they included the book on their annual list. Does that mean that we do not support the *contras* and favor the Sandinistas? No, it doesn't. Our political positions do not matter in book evaluation. An endorsement of *Inside Nicaragua* indicates that the author objectively presented her point of view; a rejection of *Latin America 1988* indicates that the author did not. It's not the focus that matters in these discussions, but rather the treatment of that focus in each individual book.

The personal focus of the Gelman book comes as an understandable by-product of her field research. The built-in problems with such inquiries—the unknown cultural prejudices of the investigator, the inability to completely submerge oneself into another culture, the inevitable bias in the individuals selected for observation, and the often unconscious willingness for people to tell and show what they think someone wants to know—never allow completely objective observations, but they nonetheless, with varying degrees of success, provide personal access to a culture. In such studies, however, authors need to alert their readers to these very real problems in addition to outlining their purposes for writing and their points of view.

Informational books are *about* more than mere subject matter. Content, including topic, scope, depth of presentation, and author's focus, defines the substance of a work. A book's *about* the sum of its parts.

NOTES

1. Ford, Dennis (1989). Review of Walter Boyne's *The Smithsonian Book of Flight for Young People* in *School Library Journal, 35*, p. 96.

2. Meigs, Cornelia, Nesbitt, Elizabeth, Eaton, Anne Thaxter, and Viguers, Ruth Hill (1969). *A Critical History of Children's Literature.* Rev. ed. New York: Macmillan, p. 101.

3. Carter, Betty (1987). A Content Analysis of the Most Frequently Circulated Information Books in Three Junior High Libraries. Unpublished Doctoral Dissertation, University of Houston, p. 439.

4. Sutton, Roger (1988). Review of *Let There Be Light: A Book about Windows* in *The Bulletin of the Center for Children's Books, 42*, p. 71.

5. Charig, Alan (1985). *A New Look at the Dinosaurs.* New York: Facts on File, p. [7].

6. Podendorf, Illa (1984). "Characteristics of Good Science Materials for Young Readers." In Pamela Petrick Barron and Jennifer Q. Burley, *Jump Over the Moon: Selected Professional Readings.* New York: Holt, Rinehart & Winston, p. 214.

7. Ardley, Neil (1983). *Computers.* New York: Warwick Press, p. 19.

8. Fisher, David E. (1988). *The Origin and Evolution of Our Own Particular Universe*. New York: Atheneum, p. 16.

9. Fisher (1988), p. 19.

10. Hofsinde, Robert (1960). Brother of the Indian. *Horn Book, 36*, pp. 16–21.

11. LeShan, Eda (1985). "The Pleasure Principle: A Lively Look at the New Nonfiction." Program presented by the Children's Book Council/ALA Joint Committee at the American Library Association's 104th Annual Conference, Chicago, Illinois.

12. Meltzer, Milton (1982). "Who's Neutral?" In Jo Carr, *Beyond Fact*. Chicago: American Library Association, p. 104.

13. Lasky, Kathryn (1985). "Reflections on Nonfiction." *The Horn Book, 61*, p. 530.

14. Pringle, Laurence (1981). "Science Done Here." In Betsy Hearne and Marilyn Kaye, *Celebrating Children's Books*. New York: Lothrop, Lee & Shepard, p. 110.

15. Ashabranner, Brent (1988). Did You Really Write That for Children? *The Horn Book, 64*, p. 749.

16. Meltzer, Milton (1982). "Who's Neutral?" In Jo Carr, *Beyond Fact*. Chicago: American Library Association, p. 104.

CHAPTER 6
A Conversation with
Laurence Pringle

Laurence Pringle has written more than sixty nonfiction books for young people. Trained as a scientist, with a graduate degree in wildlife biology, he's been a high school science teacher and editor of a science magazine for children. Pringle has won the National Wildlife Federation's Special Conservation Award as well as the Eva L. Gordon Award of the American Nature Study Society. Whether he's writing about the sober topics of acid rain, global warming trends, or nuclear power, a sense of optimism is always present. Pringle says, "If there is a single thread that runs through all of my books—including the controversial and gloomy ones like the one on nuclear war—I think it is a thread of hopefulness."

Laurence Pringle

A&C All the books in your *Science for Survival* series have been widely praised. You've written about complex environmental problems that we all face. In your opinion, what's our greatest environmental problem? Is it acid rain, the quality of the air we breathe, what we do with our garbage, or our polluted, diminishing water supply?

LP I'd have to say it's the probability of global warming. In 1985 I wrote a book called *Nuclear War: From Hiroshima to Nuclear Winter.* It's about nuclear war and the possible aftereffects. Upon finishing the research and writing that book, I actually found my fear of nuclear war diminished. Now that I've done the research on global warming, I feel more concerned about that—not in terms of human survival or the kind of devastation that results from a nuclear war—but because of the huge potential change that could occur. It wouldn't be immediate change, but rather a slow process. Our food supplies and water supplies could be affected, as could our entire quality of life. All the changes that everyone would be asked to make are potentially so great. This certainly ranks as the biggest contemporary problem.

A&C A pessimist could read your books like *Rain of Troubles* or *Throwing Things Away* or even *Here Come the Killer Bees* and come away depressed because it appears we've ruined the world. Yet your books always end with a section on possible solutions to the major problems. How important is that sense of optimism in your books?

LP It's vital. That optimism is there because I'm basically a hopeful person. I don't think people lacking in hope should be writing for children and young adults. Young people are idealists, at least most of them are, and they deserve to hear words of hope. Not false hopes, but realistic hopes—however faint—that humanity can work on things and solve problems.

A&C Do you feel that same optimism about the warming trend?

LP I do, except there's a tendency for humans to wait until a crisis is quite evident before they act. In the case of the global warming situation, that waiting for solid evidence may be costly in terms of how much temperature rise may already be unavoidable. Solving the global warming problem calls for international cooperation on a scale never before attempted, but I think it can happen.

A&C You've written that good teaching and good nonfiction writing are the same. Would you expand on that idea?

LP My teaching experience is relatively limited, but I was a science teacher for a while. What I was trying to do as a science teacher was not stuff facts and statistics into kids' heads, but leave them with some ideas about how the world works. I also tried to convey some values that I think everyone should share, like respecting nature, appreciating wild animals, things like that. In that sense, teaching and writing nonfiction are alike. When people read my books, I'm not concerned that they come away knowing a certain statistic about acid rain or some tiny fact about a wasp. If they come away with a better understanding of the causes of and possible cures for acid rain, or if they come away with a greater appreciation of the complex life of a wasp, then I think I've been teaching well.

A&C How did you become a full-time writer of nonfiction for children and young adults?

LP My interest in writing began in college, though I did have one little article published while I was in high school. I had no hunger for writing, as some do. It was more of a hunger for some acceptance from the world: A byline with an article or my name on a book jacket would suffice. So there was a thread of interest in getting a magazine article published when I was a college student, and I took courses aimed in that direction. I took a two-week course one summer at Syracuse University from an editor who works at *Better Homes & Gardens,* George S. Bush. Bush realized early on that most of the people in the class didn't need help learning how to analyze magazine markets or how to package a manuscript or write a query letter. We needed help writing simple English sentences, and I was among the people who needed that kind of instruction. He helped me enough so that several of the articles I started in his class were published. A few months later, I was looking for a job in magazines and applied to places like *Field & Stream* and *Outdoor Life.* No jobs were available in any of those adult periodicals. The only job I found, which I was lucky enough to get, was with *Nature and Science,* a magazine that was just beginning at the American Museum of Natural History in New York City. That's how I became a writer for children. If I hadn't landed a job with a children's science magazine, I might never have written for children.

A&C You have a bachelor's of science degree from Cornell and a master's degree in wildlife biology from the University of Massachusetts. How has your science background helped in preparing you as a non-fiction writer?

LP The primary help has been in the research area. One of the reasons I write nonfiction, or write at all, is that I enjoy the research so much. My academic training has been a source of ideas, first of all. Second, it has made it easier for me to get in touch with the right expert or find the right journal to get the most up-to-date, accurate information I need.

A&C You just talked about enjoying the research. Could you talk us through the creation of one of your books, going from the original idea through that research phase to finished product?

LP Some of my ideas are spin-offs from childhood interests of mine, while others, like acid rain or global warming, come from the morning newspapers. I often begin research on a project before I'm absolutely sure I'll be writing about it. I start collecting information in a file based on a feeling that I may someday write a book on a particular subject. Once an editor and I agree on an idea, a contract is signed and the research process accelerates. I enter what I call the "alert antennae" phase of research. I'm very conscious of the subject and pay more attention to what has been published and what might be out there that could be of value. I might not write about the subject for a year and a half or longer.

The actual writing is by far the most difficult part. First I try to get an overview of the subject, a broad understanding of the most important ideas. This stage involves weeks of reading, interlibrary loans, sometimes phone calls to experts, trying to pull together the most up-to-date information. I then try to work out an outline for the book. The research is fun, but then comes the most difficult part of all—starting to write the book. For me, sometimes it's like torture. The torture continues until I get several pages done. Then it gets easier. Near the end of the book I have a feeling that it may not be terrific, but that the basic ideas are in place. I can then go back and fix things up, revise and make it better.

When I finally finish the manuscript and send it in, there's a great sense of relief and accomplishment. The hardest work is over, but I know from experience that a lot of work remains after a manuscript is sent in and accepted. I still have the steps of responding to the editor's comments and changes, responding to an expert reader's comments and changes, finding illustrations, photographs, reading galleys, writing captions, doing the index, and so on. But, all these aspects of a book are fun when compared with the major task of writing it.

A&C What is the time line if you're doing a book like *Rain of Troubles* or *Water: The Next Great Resource Battle*? How long might that process take from idea to finished product?

LP The intense research and writing depends largely on the length of the book and the difficulty of the research. Young adult books on contemporary problems like acid rain or our water supply can take anywhere from as little as three months to as long a stretch as six months. For economic reasons, I can't really afford to have it stretch out as long as six months. A typical book of mine, from intense research time to submitting the first draft of the manuscript, is a three- to four-month process.

A&C In many of your books you thank various scientific experts for reading the manuscripts to improve the accuracy. As a general rule, do you use expert readers for all your books? How do you decide which expert gets the manuscript?

LP Nearly all of my manuscripts are checked by an expert. Most editors welcome this, and publishing houses pay the fee to accomplish it. Usually as I'm researching and writing a book, I come up with a candidate or two I think would be good as an expert reader. Sometimes, it's difficult to choose an expert because the book is so general, and scientists are specialists. On a few occasions, I've sent different chapters to different experts. In the case of *Rain of Troubles*, the scientist was an expert on the effects of acid rain on forests. He did critique the whole manuscript, but definitely found more things to comment on or suggest changes about in the forest chapter than the aquatic chapter. The trickiest part comes in choosing experts on controversial issues like nuclear energy. No one who is well informed on this issue is neutral. Someone in the nuclear power industry will respond quite differently from a person on the other side.

A&C In many of your early books you did the photography. Are you still doing your photos? How important do you think pictures and diagrams are in nonfiction books for young adults?

LP I still take photographs, and enjoy it more than the writing. I'll be doing more photography in some projects that lie ahead. I think illustrations are vital to communicate the ideas and to make a book more appealing. I try, especially in my young adult books, to have a diversity of illustrations. I like to work cartoons in whenever I can, although the fees for using them in a book are usually high. In my book on the animal rights controversy, I have a Gary Larson cartoon and some "Bloom County" strips to give the book's teenage readers some pleasant surprises.

Figure 15. Jacket Cover Illustration from *Global Warming*.

A&C In your book about garbage, *Throwing Things Away*, you write, "My feet sank into landfill surfaces from Denver to Miami." How much traveling do you do to research your books, or is it, more often than not, library research?

LP That line may give a false impression about how much traveling I actually do. I was in Florida on a family vacation, and later was speaking in a school near Denver. The landfills were right there. I also visited others closer to home. But I don't do nearly as much traveling as I'd like in researching some subjects. While my books are primarily based on library research, in recent years I've also been contacting experts by letter and telephone. Scientists and other experts are quite helpful, give generously of their expertise and time, and are eager to talk with someone who is trying to write a good book for kids on their subject.

A&C What makes a good piece of nonfiction for young adults?

LP The writing has to be appealing or teenagers won't read it. My prejudice is that many nonfiction subjects are inherently interesting. If the book is done well, it can spark a curiosity and enthusiasm in the reader about a subject he or she might not have considered very interesting before starting to read the book. I'm talking about an author's ability to convey his enthusiasm for a subject. That's similar to teaching. The best teachers convey to students their enthusiasm and passion for the subject they teach. Accuracy, of course, is important, and by that I don't mean so much the accuracy of every tiny little fact and statistic but the accuracy of key ideas and the clarity of the writing in explaining these ideas. That's what I look for.

Figure 16. Jacket Illustration from *Throwing Things Away*.

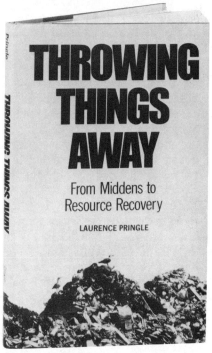

A&C How important is it that the nonfiction author display an evenhanded objectivity concerning the subject he or she is writing about?

LP I don't think objectivity is sacred. It can, in fact, be pretty boring and, in some ways, unfair to the reader. I think anyone who is well informed about a subject has a bias. It is an ethical dilemma for me and other writers. The problem is how to expose readers to all sides of an issue while keeping your own leanings but not imposing them on the reader.

A&C A good deal has been written about the importance of documentation in nonfiction books for teenagers. How important do you think things like a bibliography, an index, and list of further readings are?

LP I think an index and a bibliography are very important. Many nonfiction trade books are used for research, not grabbed off the shelf to be read for pleasure, so having an index is basic. I don't put full bibliographies in my books, but I do put in lists for further reading.

Cover of *Throwing Things Away* by Laurence Pringle. Published by Thomas Y. Crowell, 1986. Used by permission of William C. Morris, Harper Junior Books Group.

Those lists include the most important sources of information on a particular subject, and they emphasize materials that might be available in public or school libraries. Some editors have asked me to give my readers the source of every quote, including the date and issue of periodicals. I think it's bad writing to include every little detail like that because I'm not writing a research paper. I am trying to convey my feelings and ideas about a subject, and all that documentation within the prose slows things down for the reader.

A&C Would you talk about the role politics plays in your books?

LP All the contemporary problems I deal with, including nuclear energy, animal rights, and acid rain, are social and political issues as well as scientific issues. It would be unfair to readers not to include the role that politics plays in dealing with these issues. To some extent I think that most nonfiction literature that is available to youngsters on these issues may be said to have a liberal political bias. That's my bias. I believe that it is okay and appropriate for idealistic young people to be exposed to the idea that duly elected governments should take action for the public good. It can be argued that the other political side is not being well represented in nonfiction books for young adults. Let's take an extreme example. I don't know anyone who has published a book advocating cigarette smoking for young people. It's a health issue, a science issue, but also a political issue. Take a less extreme example. There are very few books for young adults that advocate, or are very accepting of, the nuclear energy business as it is currently being run in this country. So it could be argued that there is a bias against nuclear energy in most books written for young adults. But my book, *Nuclear Energy*, offers many statements and arguments of nuclear advocates.

A&C Are there three or four pieces of quality nonfiction for teenagers that you consider real touchstone books?

LP Patricia Lauber's recent books, such as *Volcano* and *The News about Dinosaurs*, are excellent, partly because they are so well designed and illustrated with full color, but also because of how beautifully they are written. In some places her text is both a model for clear communication of ideas to young people and a kind of poetry. Frankly, I have little time for reading young adult nonfiction. Books that influenced me in the past include Edward Abbey's *Desert Solitaire*, Aldo Leopold's *A Sand County Almanac*, and the writings of John McPhee. More recently I've enjoyed Tracy Kidder's books and John Hersey's *Blues*.

A&C What can be done to boost the sales and the prestige of nonfiction books for children and young adults?

LP I think the whole language movement in the schools that seems to be encouraging the use of trade books and down-playing the use of textbooks is a good step. The growth of bookstores devoted exclusively to juvenile literature appears strong, and many of those stores are giving more space to nonfiction books than you'll find in the average bookstore for adults that might have a small children's section. I think publishers have done a lot more full-color illustration of nonfiction books and the response of reviewers and buyers has been encouraging. We're competing with television, so the more nonfiction books that appear in color, as opposed to black-and-white, the more likely it is that young people will read the books.

A&C What do you look for in a good review of a nonfiction book for young adults?

LP In one sense, I think it's easier to get a favorable review if you write nonfiction. Reviewers, with a few exceptions, are not experts and may not grasp that a book is seriously wrong in some ways. Alarm bells go off when I see a reviewer has injected his or her own ideas on what a book should have been instead of just reviewing what the author actually intended to do. Also, I've seen reviews written by people who should have been copy editors instead of book reviewers, because they're nitpickers. They find something to pick at and devote half the review to minor things, neglecting to give a good idea of what the book is all about. My ideal review of a book that I've written is one in which the reviewer clearly has read the whole book and agreed with me as to what the important points and ideas of the book are.

A&C What title of yours seems to the most popular with students?

LP My best seller is my very first book on dinosaurs, *Dinosaurs & Their World*. Another popular title is *The Earth Is Flat and Other Great Mistakes*.

A&C What about the young adult books, *Water, Rain of Troubles*, or *Throwing Things Away*? Any sense of which one of those seems to be the most popular?

LP *Rain of Troubles*, about acid precipitation, seems quite popular. I expect *The Animal Rights Controversy* to attract many readers, because there is, to my knowledge, no book like it, and this subject concerns many people.

A&C What can we expect next from the word processor of Laurence Pringle?

LP I have quite a burst of books coming out. I'm excited about a book called *Bearman* that explores the world of black bears. The book is a follow-up to one I wrote called *Wolf Man*. The new one is similar in that I write about one person who has devoted his adult life to studying a wild animal. The book is illustrated with beautiful color photographs, and I think it will be very appealing to kids. I have a book coming out on the animal rights controversy. It's an intriguing, contemporary issue and a particularly difficult one to write what I consider a balanced book about. Nineteen eighty-nine marked the publication of my first fiction picture book. It is called *Jesse Builds a Road*, and was inspired by my five-year-old son, Jesse. It's a whole new field for me. Unlike nonfiction, where I can expect that just about everything I write will get published, in the fiction world I am a rookie writer with publishers rejecting manuscripts. I hope that this book is not going to be my last.

A&C Which book are you proudest of?

LP I have certain favorites, but one of the reasons I am in this field is that each book is different. The challenge of the research and writing is different for each book. The wonderful thing about the work is that it's not like making sausages or working on the assembly line. There are different satisfactions in writing a book about a wildlife biologist studying black bears and writing a book about acid rain for older readers.

A&C You may have just answered this last question. As a writer of nonfiction for juveniles, what gives you the greatest satisfaction?

LP It might be something like what a teacher feels at the end of a good day looking back at the day's lessons and seeing a hint of success at communicating some idea or value to his or her students. Actually a teacher probably has more hints of success than I do. I know very little about the impact that my books have on young readers. But that's the kind of satisfaction I strive for.

BOOKS BY LAURENCE PRINGLE

Animals at Play. (1985). San Diego, CA: Harcourt Brace Jovanovich.

Arms Race or Human Race. (1989). New York: William Morrow.

Bearman. (1989). New York: Macmillan.

Being a Plant. (1983). New York: Thomas Y. Crowell.

The Controversial Coyote. (1977). San Diego, CA: Harcourt Brace Jovanovich.

Death Is Natural. (1977). New York: Four Winds Press.

Dinosaurs & People: Fossils, Facts & Fantasies. (1978). San Diego, CA: Harcourt Brace Jovanovich.

**Dinosaurs & Their World*. (1968). San Diego, CA: Harcourt Brace Jovanovich.

The Earth Is Flat & Other Great Mistakes. (1983). New York: William Morrow.

Feral: Tame Animals Gone Wild. (1982). New York: Macmillan.

Global Warming: Assessing the Greenhouse Threat. (1990). New York: Arcade.

Here Come the Killer Bees. (1986). New York: William Morrow.

The Hidden World: Life under a Rock. (1977). New York: Macmillan/Exploring an Ecosystem.

Home: How Animals Find Comfort & Safety. (1987). New York: Charles Scribner's Sons.

***Jesse Builds a Road*. (1989). New York: Macmillan.

Listen to the Crows. (1976). New York: Thomas Y. Crowell.

Lives at Stake: The Science & Politics of Environmental Health. (1980). New York: Macmillan/Science for Survival.

Nuclear Energy: Troubled Past Uncertain Future. (1980). New York: Macmillan.

Nuclear War: From Hiroshima to Nuclear Winter. (1985). Hillside, NJ: Enslow Publishers.

Only Earth We Have. (1969). New York: Macmillan/Science for Survival.

Radiation: Waves & Particles: Benefits & Risks. (1983). Hillside, NJ: Enslow.

Rain of Troubles: The Science and Politics of Acid Rain. (1988). New York: Macmillan/Science for Survival.

Restoring Our Earth. (1987). Hillside, NJ: Enslow Publishers.

Throwing Things Away: From Middens to Resource Recovery. (1986). New York: Thomas Y. Crowell.

Vampire Bats. (1982). Hillside, NJ: Enslow Publishers.

Water: The Next Great Resource Battle. (1982). New York: Macmillan/Science for Survival.

Wild Foods: A Beginner's Guide to Identifying, Harvesting & Preparing Safe & Tasty Plants from the Outdoors. (1978). New York: Four Winds Press.

** *Indicates a paperback edition also available*
*** *Indicates a work of fiction*

CHAPTER 7
Style

In *Beyond Fact: Nonfiction for Children and Young People*, compiler Jo Carr compares fine nonfiction books to gifted teachers. The analogy fits. Just as exemplary teaching involves both an art and a science, so does the writing of quality literature. Only when both aspects of the process meld does true learning take place.

Teachers who concentrate on the science of instruction competently fulfill their job descriptions. Consistently well prepared, they follow the curriculum, they know their subject matter, and they impart knowledge to a great number of children. But those teachers who demonstrate the art of their profession go beyond these basics. They turn simple classrooms into learning laboratories. These teachers know when to push students and when to allow ideas to sit and mature; they cultivate passion and excitement in a discipline rather than encourage modest competency in subject matter; and they nurture a sense of wonder and inquisitiveness in their students rather than satisfy themselves with mere recitation of facts. What they have developed is style.

Similarly, many authors of nonfiction produce acceptable products that adhere to the principles of good writing. Their works capably present the parts of the orchestra; the ingredients for baking chocolate-chip cookies; the names, diameters, and distance from the sun of the planets in our solar system; or the land formations, the parts of government, and the imports and exports of various countries. But seldom do such publications challenge young adults to immerse themselves in a discipline or to go beyond the printed page—to question, experiment, and delight in a content area. What they lack is style. Without style, books exist only as serviceable collections of facts: Illustrations become mere decorations, physical format turns static, organization drifts into the routine, content exhibits little harmony, and prose lacks passion.

Like stellar teachers, fine nonfiction writers employ subtle, elegant skills. Beyond using the conventions of grammar, getting their facts straight, and establishing a definable scope, they allow the art of communication to guide their work. These writers know when to tell and when to show; they display the polish of using the precise word or image to clarify a point; they reveal finesse in choosing language that sounds, smells, and feels; and they demonstrate the power in developing ideas and themes that elicit understanding, surprise, and wonder. Individual expression drives each book, allowing all other literary elements to come into play. What distinguishes these writers is style.

What then, is style? We define style as a vision, far greater than the sum of its discussed parts of clarity, language levels, and tone. Style guides a work rather than making a brief appearance with a well-turned phrase or a striking metaphor. Style allows us to examine not only how authors see their content, but also how they envision their readers. And it is style that elevates a work from that of mechanical treatise to quality nonfiction. In so doing, style allows reading to become an aesthetic experience rather than a fact-finding mission.

To discuss style as distinct, quantitative components resembles those attempts to describe the human body in terms of vitamin and mineral content, muscles, cells, bones, blood, and tendons. A human's persona, that unifying and distinct psyche, remains outside and apart from the dissection, although it shapes and defines every individual. Likewise, style represents the soul of literature, an ephemeral substance that we glimpse for a moment, but ultimately remains intangible.

CLARITY

Clarity in writing emerges as the most frequently mentioned component of style. As Purves and Monson say, the writing should be "so clear that the reader is able to grasp the phenomenon that is being discussed."[1] This quality must be present in both overall design and individual explanations. What leads to clarity? Fine writers with a solid vision of their works, their audience, their craft, and their subject matters. Authors who are interested in their topics simply write better books than those who aren't. As Milton Meltzer once wrote "If the writer is indifferent, bored, stupid or mechanical, it will show in the work."[2] The reverse is also true: If the writer is enthusiastic, excited, intelligent, and insightful, it will also show in the work.

We've all met subject matter specialists thoroughly grounded in a content area, yet unable to explain the concepts to a nontechnical audience. Writers for young adults can't allow themselves such lapses. If they do, the potential exists for one of two messages to transfer from author to reader—either books aren't appropriate means of communication or the reader isn't capable of understanding that particular subject. Both assumptions spell disaster for the future of a literate society.

Writers for young adults must know their audience. They may gain this knowledge by recreating their own perceptions during adolescence, from familiarity with psychology, or from direct contact with teenagers. Young adults' interests, their methods of expression, their background knowledge, and their concerns all come into play when attempting to teach or explain a concept to them.

The following paragraph taken from *Computers* by Neil Ardley shows how muddled explanations can become when an author fails to take into account the limitations of his readers. In this introductory overview book on the function and functioning of computers, Ardley attempts to explain the concept behind Napier's Bones, a precursor to the modern-day slide rule:

> The next event did not take place until the early seventeenth century, when John Napier, a Scottish mathematician, invented logarithms to help scientists and merchants multiply and divide. He produced a system called Napier's Rods or Bones with [*sic*] consisted of long strips of wood or bone with figures marked down the sides. When the rods were moved alongside each other, multiples were shown.[3]

Now, ignore the comparison with a slide rule we've provided you with and see if you can explain the concept just from these printed words, Ardley's entire description of Napier's invention. Can you rephrase them or conjure up a mental image of precisely what Napier's Bones must have looked like or how they worked? It's a difficult task, even for adults who've had some introduction to logarithms and a math course or two beyond the junior high level. Imagine the effort a young adult must make to get even a cursory understanding of this important idea. Ardley simply forgets his audience here. His explanation serves as a reminder for mathematicians, but fails as an introduction to the untutored teenager.

Writers of young adult nonfiction must know their subject as well as their audience. In a 1988 *Horn Book* article, author Brent Ashabranner explains that "a writer who hopes to make a complex subject clear to young readers must understand it so well that he knows what he can leave out without distorting, oversimplifying, or reducing the subject to an insipid pap."[4] In our above example, Neil Ardley left out too much: a concrete, physical description of Napier's Bones, an indication of why this invention antedates modern computers, and an explanation or an example of how it worked. The oversimplification leads to inaccuracy.

As Ashabranner points out, writers must know what they can leave out, but they must also know what to put in. Too much information can prove as damaging as too little. In the following excerpt there is the potential of drowning the reader in too much detail. The quotation comes from a chapter in William Katz and Mark Crawford's *The Lincoln Brigade*, in which the authors provide brief biographical sketches of some of the members who volunteered to fight the Fascist threat during the Spanish Civil War. Although these idealists came from all over America, from farms, unions, universities, churches, and synagogues, most, like Oliver Law, claimed at least a modest history of protest and activism.

> On August 31, 1945, Oliver Law, a Texas-born black Communist, helped organize a Chicago rally for Ethiopia. Despite a ban by Mayor Kelly, it drew ten thousand people and two thousand police. Law was the first speaker, and he suddenly appeared on a rooftop to address the crowd, By the time police arrested him, there was another speaker on another roof, and another . . . until six speakers were heard and arrested.[5]

That's all the information about Law that Katz and Crawford provide in this chapter. The task that falls to the reader becomes one of filtering out the unimportant information and storing the important facts. Unfortunately, the section lacks clues to aid in that process. What is important here? That Law comes from Texas, that he is black, a Communist, or an organizer of some obscure forum concerning Ethiopia? That he spoke first—which may imply his leadership role—or that others felt a need to participate in the face of Law's arrest? That 10,000 attended the rally or that the mayor of Chicago was named Kelly? Each detail receives equal weight in the above discussion, and readers will either feel forced to try and remember all of them or gloss over the entire section without developing a perceptual framework within which to place Law when he appears in subsequent chapters.

Too many facts can also overpower main ideas and themes. In a conversation at the 1989 American Library Association's midwinter convention Elizabeth Gordon, former publisher and vice president at Harper & Row, mentioned this problem in reference to Carl B. Feldbaum and Ronald J. Bee's original manuscript for *Looking the Tiger in the Eye: Confronting the Nuclear Threat.*

Gordon commented that every chapter from the first draft of *Looking the Tiger in the Eye* could easily have been developed into a single title, each aimed at an adult audience. Feldbaum and Bee's original research exhausted all facets of their topic, and their inclusion of minute detail would have been daunting to most teenage readers. The endless roll call of fact after fact after fact was so overwhelming that the book ran the risk of presenting total nuclear warfare as inevitable, the very perception Feldbaum and Bee wanted to challenge by asking young adults to become informed citizens and make deliberate decisions concerning their responsibilities in the nuclear age. Through careful editing, the authors eliminated much of their excessive detail, thus allowing theme to emerge as the powerful focal point in their clearly developed and accessible argument.

Overall clarity improves when particular explanations and examples include meaningful analogy. Jean Fritz's description of China "with its two parent rivers, the Yangtse River and the Yellow River, and all their tributaries spilling across the country like children running away from home,"[6] creates a visual image of the physical map by using concepts well within the grasp of the audience.

Similarly, in *The Origin and Evolution of Our Own Particular Universe*, David E. Fisher employs a series of accessible metaphors to illustrate his points. The uncertainty theory of quantum mechanics, which appears to contradict natural laws, appears less exotic when Fisher compares the status of this theory to that of a foreign diplomat living in Washington but allowed to operate outside the laws of our government. Likewise, Fisher's references to the Cinderella Universe, the wheels within rims on a bicycle, and an old, warped billiard table allow readers to bring not only sharp mental images but their own experiential background to their comprehension of, respectively, the inevitable end of the universe, the elliptical patterns of the planets, and Einstein's view of space.

When carefully executed, the working combination of illustrations and text can also produce exceptional clarity. In *Pyramid*, author/illustrator David Macaulay includes a series of drawings that not only serve to explain how the ancients determined true north, but also underscore their abilities to reason and employ sophisticated concepts.

Figure 17. Creating a Horizon Line

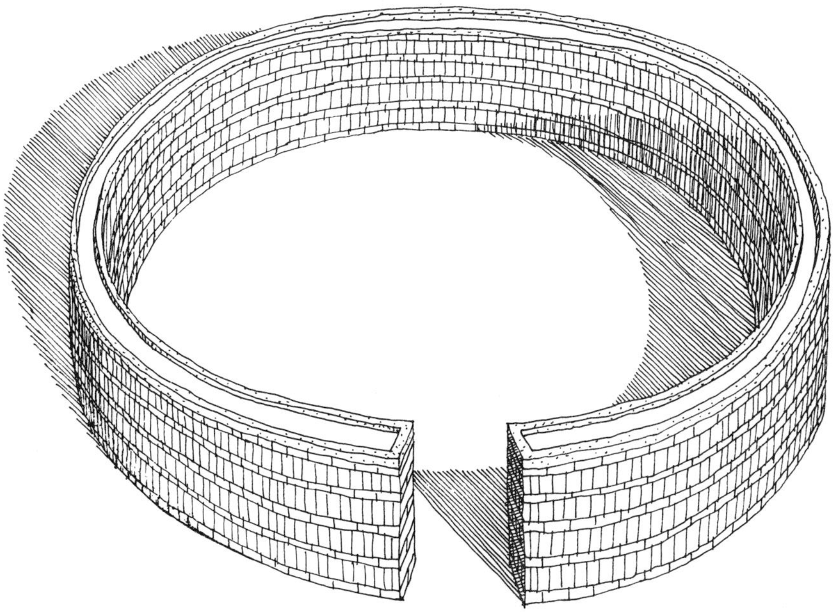

Before the building process could begin, the location of true north had to be determined, so that the pyramid could be accurately oriented. A circular wall was built approximately in the center of the site. It was built high enough to block a view of the surrounding hills and the top was made level. This created a perfect horizon line.

In the evening a priest stood in the center of the circle and watched for the appearance of a star in the east. Its position was marked as it rose above the wall and a line was drawn from that point on the wall to the center of the circle.

Figure 18. Marking Eastern Appearance of a Star

He watched the star as it moved in an arc through the sky and finally set in the west. As it dropped behind the wall its position was marked again and another line was drawn to the center of the circle.

Figure 19. Marking Western Disappearance of a Star

Because stars appear to rotate around the north pole, the priests knew that a third line drawn from the center of the circle through the center of the space between the first two lines would point directly north.[7]

From *Pyramid* by David Macaulay. Copyright © 1975 by David Macaulay. Reprinted by permission of Houghton Mifflin Company.

Figure 20. Determining North

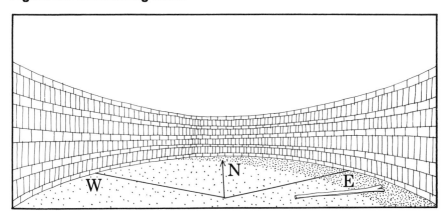

This series of explanations accent Macaulay's clear vision—that humankind will be remembered by the structures left behind—by defining architecture and building as the masterful culmination of art and science.

Often one incident brings a concept into focus and allows readers to move from the concrete to the abstract. Brent Ashabranner's individualizing example of a small boy gently depositing one glass marble at the base of the Vietnam Veterans Memorial poignantly reminds us that our heritage is as vast as the 58,176 names inscribed in granite and as simple as a single toddler. Not only does history define our past, it also shapes our future.

Muddled, unfocused, rambling, and oversimplified works not only provide poor explications of a discipline, they also contribute to unsatisfactory experiences with books. Such works only cheat young adults from participating in the thrill of discovery, the excitement of learning, and the power of knowledge.

LANGUAGE LEVELS

The language a writer uses must be appropriate to the audience. Language—including vocabulary, sentence structure, literary devices, and concept demands—that is too simple will insult a mature reader. On the other hand, language that is too sophisticated will bewilder the neophyte. We don't suggest that adults laboriously count the words and syllables in any given passage and assign an artificial reading level to the entire work. What we do suggest, however, is that adults keep language complexity in mind, alerting themselves to gross problems with readability. The following two authors writing on the same subject, for example, clearly have two different audiences in mind.

From *Pyramid* by David Macaulay. Copyright © 1975 by David Macaulay. Reprinted by permission of Houghton Mifflin Company.

David C. Knight, in *Robotics: Past, Present & Future*, explains to an unsophisticated young adult audience the origin of the word *robot*:

> The word that springs to most people's minds for such helpful mechanical creatures is *robot*. It was coined by the Czechoslovakian dramatist Karel Capek in his 1921 play called *R. U. R.* The play was about artificial men, and Capek took the name from the Czech word, *robota*, which means "compulsory service" or "work." So popular was *R.U.R.* in Europe and America that *robot* stuck in peoples' minds as standing for any mechanical man possessing human characteristics, and the word entered most of the world's languages.[8]

Now look at T. A. Heppenheimer's explanation.

> In this meager technological progress in robotics, the main contributions were literary: Mary Shelley's *Frankenstein* in 1817 and Karel Capek's 1921 play *R. U. R.* . . .
>
> If *Frankenstein* was a novel of ambivalence, *R. U. R.* was a cry of despair, an echo of the agony of World War I, which had brought all the evils Mary Shelley could ever have dreamed of. That war had started conventionally enough, with columns of German foot-soldiers marching into France, accompanied by horse-calvary and artillery. Very soon, however, it degenerated into a bloodbath, a massacre, made possible by such inventions as the machine gun, the submarine, and poison gas. Such technology not only intensified the carnage but prolonged the conflict, which tore Europe apart more thoroughly than any conflict since the Thirty Years War (three centuries earlier). In its wake, *R. U. R.* gave us the word *robot*—a name, an image, and a reputation to live down.
>
> The name *robot* came from Capek's Czech language, from *robota*, meaning labor or work. Other Slavic tongues have similar words (the Russian *rabota*, for example); they can be traced to the Indo-European and are cognate to such words as the German *arbeit*. In Czech, however, *robot* carried connotations of slavery or forced labor.[9]

Although both authors outline the derivation of the word "robot," important differences mark the two discussions. First of all, Heppenheimer includes more background material. Not only does he put the play in its historical setting, but he also offers etymological clues that allow readers to look beyond the simple definition to the strong connotations inherent in the word. We can reasonably expect older teenagers to process this information. They should already have the factual background—what *Frankenstein* was, at least a passing acquaintance with the First World War, and an understanding that few words have simple definitions—on which to connect his points. On the other hand, the same claims do not hold true for Knight's younger audience. Wisely, he chooses to stick to the basics—where the word originated, when Capek wrote the play, and what "robot" generally means.

Besides these differences in concept demands, the two authors also offer a definite contrast in their use of language. Vocabulary and sentence structure in Knight's passage are more appropriate for inexperienced readers. His sentences follow regular patterns well within the syntactical cueing system of his audience. Additionally, his simple, but not simplified vocabulary—he doesn't substitute one-syllable words like "fake " for the more precise "artificial"—falls well within the range of being difficult enough to challenge but not so elementary as to insult younger junior high students.

Heppenheimer's more sophisticated style speaks to the mature high school student. His sentences are longer, but it is primarily in their complexity—the liberal use of phrases, clauses, and appositives—that they differ from Knight's. And while younger readers might well be able to phonetically "sound out" words such as meager, wake, and cognate, it is doubtful that they could successfully attach meaning to them.

These examples illustrate the acceptable language extremes for most young adult readers. If a selection proves any simpler than the first example, it will insult; decidedly more sophisticated than the second, and it will overwhelm. In either case, teenagers will close the book and communication will be lost.

Writers must also take special care when introducing specialized or technical vocabulary. Words inherent in a particular content provide the language of that discipline and must be introduced, defined, and used repeatedly. Computer monitors must retain that particular label rather than the lay term "television screens," scientists should hypothesize rather than guess, and pets ought to be neutered instead of fixed.

Simply italicizing a particular word won't do the trick, although boldface type and italics, if used sparingly, will set a word apart and trigger the idea that this term is worth noting. In *Recent Revolutions in Anthropology*, Maxine P. Fisher uses this particular technique. When readers first meet the word "primate," a crucial term in anthropology, Fisher italicizes it and deliberately defines it in context. But she doesn't let the word drop there. She continues to use it when appropriate, thus allowing young adult readers many chances to get used to this important term. In addition, by using the language of her science, rather than more familiar but less precise terms, Fisher treats her audience with the respect that expects them to speak, and by extension think, like anthropologists.

In *Throwing Things Away: From Middens to Resource Recovery*, Laurence Pringle employs a particularly effective strategy for introducing the unfamiliar term "garbageology." Young adults can probably use root and affix clues to come up with a limited definition of this particular word, but, for most readers, that definition would hold little meaning beyond the technical. So, before introducing the term, Pringle cites several examples of garbage research, thus providing some background for the new word, which he additionally defines in context. These well-chosen case histories, plus a subsequent one concerning a fraternity house's refuse, provide concrete associations for his readers.

Yet, for all its importance—defining unfamiliar words, choosing words with precision, and using crucial words repeatedly—this process simply reflects the science of writing. The artistry occurs when writers use these tools to produce sentences that also sound right. Although mature readers consistently read silently, they nonetheless alert themselves to the way words and sentences sound. Consider all the references we make to what authors are *saying* or what they are *telling* us, and the connection between silent reading and hearing becomes clear. In *The Elements of Style*, Strunk and White point out this feature by mentioning, "When we speak of Fitzgerald's style, we don't mean his command of the relative pronoun, we mean the sound his words make on paper."[10] Think of the certainty inherent in Robert Frost's "good fences make good neighbors"[11]; or the despair of Jacob Riis's "The first tenement New York knew bore the mark of Cain from its birth"[12]; or the growing wonder in Loren Eiseley's "we stared a little blankly at each other, the skull and I"[13]; or the anguish in Martin Luther King, Jr.'s "Daddy, why do white people treat colored people so mean?"[14] and you'll hear the sound of the written word.

The sound of a sentence holds as much power to influence the reader as does the definition of each word. Thus, beyond meaning and metaphor, the cadence of the ancient storytellers that flows through Carl Sagan's "The cosmos is all that is or ever was or ever will be"[15] lets us know we are encountering a master of style. How writers weave these spells remains a mystery; that they do so reaffirms the triumph of art over science in their craft.

TONE

Even limited experience with young adults reaffirms the implications of an old adage: "It's not *what* you say, but *how* you say it that matters." It doesn't take the acting skills of a Meryl Streep or a Dustin Hoffman for a teenager to turn a simple response—"Sure, everybody's doing it"—from the acquiescent into the adversarial. Tone, not vocabulary, allows them to express these moods. Authors use the same tool in their writing.

Although tone can reflect any position on the emotional spectrum, five broad descriptors generally subdivide the range: condescending, conversational, humorous, neutral, and partisan. Within this grouping only a condescending voice emerges as inappropriate in informational books aimed at young adults. This tone defines the writer as a patronizing authority figure who employs the tools of oversimplification, didacticism, and authoritarianism to talk down to the reader. In the following example, which makes up one-fourth of a subsection entitled "The Scourge of Drugs" and comes from an encyclopedic volume on Latin America, the author politicizes the issue of drugs by declaring that those who buy drugs abdicate the qualities of reason and thought:

> It is difficult to understand the interest in this drug [crack]. The difference between man and the rest of life on earth is well-known: man can think, reason and largely control his environment and future under appropriate circumstances such as generally prevail in the U. S. Why will people with these vastly superior powers surrender themselves to a world of incomprehensible unreality? The ultimate destination is humiliation, degradation, and *total control by others*. Notwithstanding this, people pay large sums of money in order to obtain senselessness.[16]

While the author is obviously opposed to crack, he nonetheless owes it to young adults to give specific reasons, draw examples from the population, and quote reliable sources. Just to state that the destination of crack users is "humiliation, degradation and *total control by others*," falls on deaf ears to the teenager who sees joining the drug scene as a way out of the ghetto or the means to acceptance within a peer group. By patronizing, the author dismisses the very real perceptions, whether true or false, that this adolescent brings to the reading process. Through association, the writer simultaneously rejects the young adult reader.

By contrast authors who employ a conversational tone directly address the reader through questions, and write as if they were settling down to a discussion—a talk that can range anywhere from a chat to a more formal discourse. Notice how adroitly Daniel and Susan Cohen use this voice in the following excerpt from *A Six-Pack and a Fake I.D.: Teens Look at the Drinking Question*:

> If you feel that you are being discriminated against simply because you are young, what can you do? Well, you can bring the subject up for discussion in your school. You can write your state legislators. You can even get up a delegation to see your legislators. Frankly, we can't hold out much hope for success. Just recently a group of high school students who tried to talk to legislators on the subject was dismissed, quite contemptuously, as simply participating in a "civics lesson." Other legislators might be smoother or more polite, but they won't listen either. You haven't got much clout on this subject. Twenty-one, like motherhood, is a popular issue with most voters who happen to be over twenty-one and won't be personally affected anymore.[17]

The Cohens display a friendly attitude, but they do not try to become overly chummy with the reader. Their informal concern reinforces the manner of interested adults, a much more acceptable role for advisors than those who try to ingratiate themselves with teenagers by trying to become "one of the gang."

On the other hand, in *The Daywatchers*, Peter Parnell deliberately uses an informal, conversational tone to underscore his role of silent partnership with the reader who wants to observe and record hawks, owls, falcons, and eagles. Parnell writes of how he first became interested in these birds of prey as a teenager, how he initially collected and then simply observed the animals, and how he finally realized that his pleasure came from watching the majesty of one creature in its natural habitat. He describes these experiences in both words and illustrations, allowing the attentive reader a peripatetic walk through nature. Still, he challenges his audience to go out on their own, reminding them that their observations will be equally valid, but ultimately more satisfying to them than his.

Humor also finds a place in fine informational books, and as it does when it appears in fiction, wit and cleverness draws an audience. When a book on computers, particularly an introductory volume addressed to the person who perceives computer science as a high-tech, rarefied field, adopts a humorous tone, the author deliberately begins to tear down the reader's fears and awe. Such is the case in Michael Crichton's *Electronic Life: How to Think about Computers,* where the levity in both the following definition of "retrofit" and the concluding paragraph exemplify the strong voice that led the 1984 Best Books for Young Adults Committee to include this work on its annual list.

> Certain terms are chosen to disguise their real meaning. "Retrofit" is engineering jargon that sounds high-tech and scientific. But in computer terms, it usually means correcting what wasn't done right in the first place.
>
> "Enhancement" is a similar word. Additions to a computer system can modify or improve it, but when something is added to make the machine competitive with other computers in its class, that's called an enhancement.
>
> Whenever enhancements are retrofitted at no charge, or very slight charge, you can be pretty sure what's really going on.[18]

A neutral voice doesn't presuppose dryness, but rather presents material dispassionately and matter-of-factly. When Alvin and Virginia Silverstein published *AIDS: Deadly Threat* in 1986, a time when frenzied rumors made up much of the knowledge about the disease, their calm, neutral tone defused the sensationalism, allowing young adults an unemotional picture of the known medical facts. In less able hands, the following type of discussion could have fed irrational fears and prejudices:

> Now that blood banks are screening donor blood with tests such as these, medical experts say that our blood supply is safe. However, some doctors add a note of caution. They point out that it takes two to eight weeks after exposure to the AIDS virus before detectable antibodies appear in a person's blood—and some infected people never produce antibodies at all. So a person who has recently been exposed may be infectious but still pass an AIDS blood-screening test. That is why blood banks request people to refrain from giving blood if they are in a high-risk group for AIDS. With these precautions, there is now only a very small risk of getting AIDS from a blood transfusion—far smaller than the risks to life and health from *not* having a needed blood transfusion.[19]

All books about AIDS do not need to reflect this tone, although most works intended to provide medical facts and personal cautions do. Literature allows the scope for Randy Shilts's passionate and partisan *And the Band Played On: Politics, People, and the AIDS Epidemic* to look at information beyond the medical. Although Shilts covers this aspect in his book, his thesis clearly states that "these first five years of AIDS in America is a drama of national failure, played out against a backdrop of needless death."[20] To develop this argument, however, Shilts doesn't take pot shots at the government, scientists, researchers, doctors, victims, or political leaders but, instead, systematically and professionally documents the events from 1980–85 that led him to this conclusion. His stance is obvious, but his respect for the reader remains intact, for Shilts lists his numerous sources for the curious and never demeans the nonsympathetic reader. Undeniably Shilts shows the reader why he believes as he does. Never does he demand that his stance be adopted.

Similarly, Susan Kuklin's highly personal *Fighting Back: What Some People Are Doing about AIDS* shuns neutrality. The author, who became involved with a volunteer group established to help people with AIDS, interviews members of the group and details their roles as caregivers. She then uses her growing admiration for Michael, one of the group's clients, as the focal point for her story. These two books suggest that a writer's vision rather than his or her subject defines tone.

Just as a neutral tone doesn't necessarily indicate insipidness, a conversational tone frivolity, or a humorous tone slapstick comedy, a partisan tone doesn't have to translate into propaganda. It merely signals a writer who wishes to explain his or her deep, passionate position on certain issues. Partisan authors may persuade, but they shouldn't proselytize.

The concluding paragraph from Milton Meltzer's *Ain't Gonna Study War No More* reiterates his point of view, as well as his partisan tone, in this plea for readers to speak out when government challenges their own value systems:

> Surely the American people have that concern in mind—survival. And happily for the pursuit of peace, a sizable part of the American public no longer stays silent when it sees its government make mistakes in foreign policy. They react to the danger of repeating past errors. They know American leaders can be guilty of intrigue, deception, secretiveness, lawlessness. They learned that dissent has its positive side and should never be crushed. It was only when dissent over Vietnam rolled high enough to reach into Congress and change many minds there that the policy of Presidents was obliged to change. We rediscovered the old belief that the truth will make us free. We must continue to say how we see things, and speak out for what we believe.[21]

This paragraph represents the culmination, not the totality, of Meltzer's arguments. For over two hundred pages he thoughtfully explains that many of our ancestors were conscientious objectors, or nonresistants, who refused to bear arms against one another, although they established a country born of revolution—a country that has averaged one military conflict every year since its inception. He outlines how those who refused to fight often defended their principles with sacrifices as bloody as those found on any battlefield. He wrestles with the degrees of their faith: Were there times when the ends justified the means? Were the evils of slavery or Nazism so overwhelming that war was the only way to eradicate them? Meltzer doesn't demand a reader's compliance with his views, but he does demand the reader's thought.

No matter what language levels, scope, subjects, or voices authors choose, if they display passion and enthusiasm for their contents, then they hold the potential of showing young adults that the subjects they read about embrace exciting ideas and issues that matter.

Passion may also be a subdued emotion, intense, although not necessarily zealous. In *Flies in the Water, Fish in the Air,* Jim Arnosky quietly reveals that tone. He begins his discussion of fly rods with a sense of reverence, "The fly rod is the instrument that makes casting a fly an act of beauty and grace." After examining the features of several rods, Arnosky focuses his feelings in this closing: "I do most of my trout fishing with a bamboo fly rod made for a 6-weight line. Its bamboo has turned nut brown with the seasons. Its silk windings are wine red. The cork handle is sculptured to match the contours of my right hand's grip. This is more than a fishing rod. It is something of myself and my days astream that I can leave to my grandchildren."[22]

A writer's style goes beyond using appropriate language, providing the meanings of technical vocabulary, and selecting a proper tone. Style is really the vision that guides a work from inception to completion. A masterful style draws an audience into a book and compels them to keep reading. And style is what allows young adults to leave a book, not with a sense of finality, but rather, "a sense of joy—indeed celebration—about something they have sensed of the world in which they live."[23]

NOTES

1. Purves, Alan C. and Monson, Dianne L. (1984). *Experiencing Children's Literature.* Glenview, IL: Scott, Foresman, p. 60.

2. Meltzer, Milton (1976). Where Do All the Prizes Go? The Case for Nonfiction. *Horn Book, 52,* p. 21.

3. Ardley, Neil (1983). *Computers.* New York: Warwick Press, p. 36.

4. Ashabranner, Brent (1988). Did You Really Write That for Children? *The Horn Book, 64,* p. 751.

5. Katz, William Loren and Crawford, Mark (1989). *The Lincoln Brigade: A Picture History.* New York: Atheneum, p. 14.

6. Fritz, Jean (1988). *China's Long March: 6,000 Miles of Danger.* New York: G. P. Putnam's Sons, p. 20.

7. Macaulay, David (1985). *Pyramid.* Boston: Houghton Mifflin, pp. 22–23.

8. Knight, David C. (1983). *Robotics: Past, Present & Future.* New York: William Morrow, pp. 1–2.

9. Heppenheimer, T. A. (1985). "Man Makes Man." In Marvin Minsky, *Robotics.* Garden City, NY: Anchor Press/Doubleday, pp. 43–44.

10. Strunk, William, Jr., and White, E. B. (1972). *The Elements of Style.* Second ed. New York: Macmillan, p. 59.

11. Frost, Robert (1969). *The Poetry of Robert Frost.* Edited by Edward Connery Lathem. New York: Holt, Rinehart & Winston, p. 33.

12. Riis, Jacob A. (1957). *How the Other Half Lives.* New York: Hill and Wang, p. 5.

13. Eisley, Loren (1957). *The Immense Journey.* New York: Time, p. 2.

14. King, Martin Luther, Jr. (1964). *Why We Can't Wait.* New York: New American Library, p. 81.

15. Sagan, Carl (1980). *Cosmos.* New York: Random House, p. 4.

16. Dostert, Pierre Etienne (1988). *Latin America, 1988.* 22nd Annual Edition. Washington, DC: Stryker-Post Publications, p. 5.

17. Cohen, Susan and Cohen, Daniel (1985). *A Six-Pack and a Fake I.D.: Teens Look at the Drinking Question.* New York: M. Evans, pp. 105–06.

18. Crichton, Michael (1983). *Electronic Life: How to Think about Computers.* New York: Alfred A. Knopf, p. 119.

19. Silverstein, Alvin and Silverstein, Virginia (1986). *AIDS: Deadly Threat.* Hillside, NJ: Enslow Publishers, pp. 45–46.

20. Shilts, Randy (1987). *And the Band Played On: Politics, People, and the AIDS Epidemic.* New York: St. Martin's, p. xxii.

21. Meltzer, Milton (1985). *Ain't Gonna Study War No More: The Story of America's Peaceseekers.* New York: Thomas Y. Crowell, p. 268.

22. Arnosky, Jim (1986). *Flies in the Water, Fish in the Air.* New York: Lothrop Lee & Shepard, pp. 46–47.

23. Lasky, Kathryn (1985). Reflections on Nonfiction. *Horn Book, 61,* p. 532.

CHAPTER 8
A Conversation with
Brent Ashabranner

Brent Ashabranner says, "When I was in high school I won fourth prize in a Scholastic Magazine *national short story writing contest, and I never stopped writing after that." A world traveler, Ashabranner has lived in Ethiopia, and Libya and headed the Peace Corps program in India. He later served as deputy director of the Peace Corps in Washington, DC. Whether he's writing about the adjustment of unaccompanied refugee children coming to America or the plight of migrant farm workers, he manages to make complex cross-cultural issues interesting to young adult readers by focusing on "real people trying to cope with very real and serious problems."*

Brent Ashabranner

A&C We know that during your years of teaching English at Oklahoma State and later while working in several foreign countries you wrote some fiction, but today you're noted primarily as a writer of nonfiction. Why did you choose nonfiction for young people as your area in which to concentrate?

BA I thought of myself for many years as a fiction writer. At Oklahoma State I wrote mainly short fiction. I wrote a few articles, and overseas I continued to write fiction. While in Nigeria, I wrote a novel about Indians from the Oklahoma Territory, of all things. Then came a novel called *Strangers in*

Photograph by Jennifer Ashabranner. Used by permission.

Africa. But, I was beginning even then to write some nonfiction. The first nonfiction book I wrote was *Land in the Sun: The Story of West Africa Today.* It was a book for elementary school readers and was written while I was in Nigeria. My very first book, written with Russell Davis, was *The Lion's Whiskers: Tales of High Africa.* It's a book of Ethiopian folktales, but it also has a good deal of nonfiction material about Ethiopians. So even with the first book, I was beginning to take a hand at nonfiction writing.

My real concentration on nonfiction during the last decade started after I retired from the Ford Foundation in 1980 and decided it was time to devote all of my time to writing. My wife and I came back to the States knowing that we would now live here permanently. I felt I was going to write fiction again, but an old friend of mine, Paul Conklin, who's a fine professional photographer, came to me with an idea for a book about the Northern Cheyenne Indians of today and the struggles they were having to preserve their reservation from the big power companies that wanted their rich storehouse of coal found on reservation land. Paul wanted me to write the book, and the more I dug into the research material, the more interested I became. I couldn't quite decide that I wanted to do the book until I came across an ancient prophesy by one of the culture heroes of the Cheyenne tribe named Sweet Medicine. He predicted that the time would come when people with white skins would try to take the Indian land and keep it. He believed that the white skins would tear up the earth; the Indians would help them do it; then the Indians would disappear. That was a frightful prophesy and it tied in with my long-standing interest in folklore. So I teamed up with Paul and that book became *Morning Star, Black Sun.* Out of my talk with the young Cheyenne Indians came a realization of how much they wanted to retain their culture and yet how much they wanted to succeed in the dominant culture of today. Those two, often conflicting, desires led to another book—*To Live in Two Worlds.* So before I knew it I was a nonfiction writer.

A&C Most of your books deal with minorities and different cultures. We're wondering how your years in the Peace Corps and the U.S. Agency for International Development influence the subjects you choose to write about.

BA I think they influence my decision almost completely, because I learned from living in other countries how hard it is to step into a new culture that is alien and sometimes hostile and try to understand and make your way in that new world. I had to try to learn a half dozen languages, and I know how hard that is. When I came back to the United States, it really struck me that we are entering a new era in America. It's an era in which new immigrants from different parts of the world—Asia and Latin America—are here in large numbers. They are going to be very important in the future of our country. I had lived in some of the countries that these new immigrants once called home. During my years in the Peace Corps I had learned something about understanding other cultures and how people of other cultures can or should try to understand each other, so that's why I've turned to these subjects.

A&C Would you talk us through the creation of one of your books, from the original idea through the research to the finished product? We don't want to choose the book to focus on, but we think one of your finest books is *Always to Remember: The Story of the Vietnam Veterans Memorial.*

BA I will talk just a little bit about *Always to Remember.* It is my current favorite partly because it's still very close to me and also because my daughter Jennifer took the pictures for it. *Always to Remember* began accidentally. I was living in Washington then. I was out walking on the mall one day and had not visited the Vietnam Veterans Memorial. I knew it was there in the mall, in a part called Constitution Gardens. I just stumbled on it by accident. I walked down and looked at those names on the wall stretching east toward the Washington Monument, west toward the Lincoln Memorial—a seemingly endless litany of names in stone. Tears came to my eyes. I did not know it then, but *Always to Remember* was born at that moment. That book was truly born in my heart, whereas I believe all of my other books have been born in my head.

If I could take a few minutes to talk about another book that is a bit more typical of my process, I'd pick *Into a Strange Land.* This book was written in collaboration with my other daughter, Melissa, and that's a wonderful bonus for my life, that I could work with my daughters. When I was overseas Vietnam fell to the Communist North. Cambodia and Laos collapsed, and I began to see the refugees pouring out even at that time. In fact, I visited refugee camps in Thailand and in Indonesia where I was working and I began to understand what was happening. Hundreds of thousands of those refugees were then pouring into the United States. These were refugees not only from Southeast Asia but, at about the same time, Cuban refugees and tens of thousands from Central America. Refugees were becoming a very important new aspect of immigration to the United States.

When I came back to the States I had that personal background. I was very much interested in what was happening to the refugees and how our own population was changing in terms of these new immigrants. For two or three years I collected material about refugees. I've always remembered something Henry Moore said about the sculptor's task. He said you begin with a block and you have to find the sculpture that's inside it. You have to overcome the resistance of the material by sheer determination and hard work. I think the nonfiction writer's task is very much the same. I had the personal experience and notes that I had made. I had collected stacks of books, reports, special studies, newspaper and magazine clippings. By that time I had decided I would write a book about refugees, so I had begun to actually talk with and interview refugees. In a sense that was my block. I had all that material stacked around me and had to find the story that was inside it. I knew I wanted to write for teenagers about refugees today. About this time my daughter came into the process. We looked at my block of material and tried to find the story within. As we talked, we kept returning to the stories about refugee children who had come into this country by themselves—without their parents. Some of their parents had died en route, in the perilous escape journey; in some cases, parents had actually put their children on escape boats and sent them off. Often these parents could usually afford to send only one child, so the oldest boy was usually selected. We began to see young unaccompanied refugees as the best—and certainly most poignant—focus for the book. After that decision, we interviewed scores of teenaged Vietnamese, Cambodians, and Laotians who had arrived in America, from refugee camps, without their parents or any family members. We interviewed young unaccompanied refugees from other parts of the world: Ethiopia and Central America. We interviewed their American foster parents and the refugee agency people who work with these difficult cases. After we collected all of the materials it was a matter of deciding what aspects to treat: the escape, life in the refugee camps, the first entry into America, the battles with depression, the adjustment, and the eventual emancipation, as it is called by the refugee agencies. That focus on other young people made all of the difference in the success of that book and the way that book has been accepted and understood by the readers we wanted to reach and by the teachers and librarians who use the book.

A&C How much time does it take you to write a book?

BA I try to write two books a year. The collecting of the materials and the interviews for all of my books take as much time as the actual writing. Roughly I'd say three months for going around and talking to the people and three months for the writing itself. I keep emphasizing people because I know of no other way to make the complex social issues that I write about clear, understandable, and interesting to adolescent readers except to concentrate on people—tell of these issues through their eyes. Essentially all of my field work is talking with the people I'm going to be writing about. For *Dark Harvest*, my book about migrant farm workers in America, I actually got out in the fields and picked cucumbers and apples as I talked with them. In one sense the most interesting and exciting part of the books for me is to get out and be with the people I'm writing about.

A&C You're a writer who likes to collaborate. We've mentioned your early work with Russell Davis and the collaborations with your daughters. Many of your books feature wonderful photographs by Paul Conklin. Could you tell us about the importance of Paul's photographs, and do you have those pictures in front of you as you write the text? How do you two work together?

BA I'd be delighted to talk about that because Paul doesn't get nearly as much credit as he should. I believe that most nonfiction today must include photographs or illustrations. Good photographs help to tell the story, enhance the story, and help the writer. I don't have to describe what a person looks like. The picture is there. I do have Paul's pictures around me when I write. Essentially he has finished his work on a book when mine is just starting. The pictures are wonderful to help keep the memory and mood alive for me as I write the text. Paul and I always talk a book idea over, and sometimes the idea originates with him as it did with *Morning Star, Black Sun*. Usually, however, it originates with me, but his interest in the books is just as deep as mine. Whether I'm working with Paul or my daughter Jennifer, photographer and writer refine each other's concept of the book we're working on. I do believe that for our teenaged audience, the books just wouldn't be the same without photographs.

A&C You just talked a bit about *Into a Strange Land*, and when you hear the next question, you'll know how much we were affected by it. One of the most gripping beginnings in any of your books is the story that opens *Into a Strange Land* where you write about the young Vietnamese boy, Tran, who thinks he's going fishing and then in horror, realizes that his father's put him on a boat to the refugee camp. It's a gripping piece of writing—kind of a short story with flashbacks, dialogue, and other fiction techniques. Would you comment on using fictional techniques in writing nonfiction?

BA I agree with you about the opening of *Into a Strange Land*. I think it is the best opening I have ever written for a book. I had the opportunity to read that section to several classes when Melissa and I were still writing the book. Once when I was reading that opening, I looked up and saw a boy in the back of the room crying. That really shook me, but I knew I was reaching my audience. I never intentionally use fictional techniques or think a lot about them, but the opening story we've just been discussing could indeed have been fiction and yet it actually happened. In fact, we talked with many unaccompanied refugee children who had that experience. If you can put some of your material into story form and yet it is still true, I think

Figure 22. Jacket cover illustration from *Into a Strange Land*.

that's fine for a nonfiction book. Nonfiction for any reader might very well have episodes that read like fictional short stories. The only difference is that you can document the things you're writing. Nonfiction certainly doesn't need to be straight expository prose. I let the people

From *Into a Strange Land: Unaccompanied Refugee Youth in America* by Brent Ashabranner and Melissa Ashabranner. Published by Dodd, Mead, 1987. Used by permission.

that I'm writing about speak for themselves. They tell their own fascinating stories as they discuss personal fears, hopes, and ambitions. The last thing I want to write is an accumulation of dry facts.

A&C You're a successful writer of nonfiction and you often lecture about the genre. What are the hallmarks of a good piece of nonfiction for adolescents?

BA A good nonfiction book for teenagers explores an important subject and makes the subject clear and interesting. The book makes the young reader both think and feel.

A&C Book reviews are pretty important in the juvenile book field. We wonder what you look for in a well-done review of a nonfiction book.

BA I agree that reviews are exceedingly important in the juvenile book field. Many librarians and teachers rely on those reviews in making purchasing decisions. I like a review that tells, as fully as possible, what the book is about—one in which the reviewer tries to keep himself/herself out of the review as much as possible. I must say that the reviewers writing for *School Library Journal, Booklist, The Horn Book Magazine, Kirkus Review*, and the *Bulletin of the Center for Children's Books* are good at doing that. They are better than some of the reviewers for the *New York Times Book Review* and the *Washington Post*. Those reviewers seem to have a need to get themselves and their views into the piece so extensively that you're often left wondering just what the book is about. The review writer ought to keep the emphasis on the book itself. An author likes to feel that when negative comments appear in a review that those negative things are clear and substantiated.

I have benefited from reviews. I am happy to say that most of the reviews of my books have been favorable, but occasionally a reviewer points out something that helps me in future books. For example, I learned early on that reviewers of books for teenage readers take documentation of what the writers says very seriously. I wasn't paying sufficient attention to documentation, and after the first book or two that I wrote, I've been much more careful about letting my readers know where I got my information. I put it into the text in a way that doesn't interfere with the prose but assures the reader that I didn't just make things up. I've been much more careful with my bibliographies. Thoughtful reviews help me be a better writer.

A&C For years, textbooks on juvenile literature have said that the writer of nonfiction needs to be objective—show no bias and deliver an even-handed presentation of the subject. We suspect that that criterion has led to some rather dull nonfiction books. Your books certainly aren't bland. We think the reader knows where you stand on the issue of migrant farm workers or the plight of the American Indian or the difficulties unaccompanied refugee youth face when they come to the United States. Can a nonfiction writer be totally objective? Do you try not to show your feelings on an issue or do you take the opposite stance?

BA This is something I have thought about a lot. Most of the subjects I write about have an element of controversy in them—immigration, refugees, migrant farm workers, the treatment of American Indians, the Vietnam Veterans Memorial, even our national census. Reasonable people have different thoughts on and feelings about such subjects. Before I write a book, I know a great deal about my subject, I care about it, and I have developed a point of view about it. I think it would be wrong for me not to let my reader know what that point of view is. I must support my view with facts and documentation, and if there are other valid points of view—there usually are—I must let my reader know what they are. But to attempt complete objectivity on the kinds of subjects I write about would, to me, make no sense.

A&C Your books often deal with very complex economic and cultural issues like the Arab-Israeli problems or the shrinking number of family farms in America. You've said that you think these topics can be made interesting to young people because your books deal, at base, with conflicts. Would you talk a little bit about that idea of conflict in your books?

BA There are three kinds or levels of conflict: man against man, man against nature, and man in conflict with himself. All good fiction is based on one or more of these levels of conflict. The same is true of many nonfiction books. Every nonfiction book I have written contains some or all of these conflicts. The Vietnamese immigrant fishermen in *The New Americans* come into conflict with native-born fishermen in the Gulf of Mexico who resent the intrusion of the newcomers. The rancher in *Born to the Land* is in a life-and-death struggle against drought. The poverty-stricken Cheyenne Indian in *Morning Star, Black Sun* must decide whether to sell the sacred land of his ancestors to a coal mining company for a great deal of money. The lives of the people I write about are filled with such conflicts; seeing how they come to grips with them and overcome the obstacles they face makes for interesting and, I think, worthwhile reading.

A&C Why do you think youngsters read your books?

BA They read them because I write books about people who live hard but interesting lives. And they are not people I have read about or heard about but people I have met and talked with in their homes, at work, or wherever they may be. They are real people who are worth reading about. And there is another reason why students read my books: hard-working librarians and teachers get the books into young readers' hands. If those dedicated professionals weren't out there, many of my books wouldn't be published. I think that is the reality of the situation. I have watched teachers and librarians get students interested in books like mine, get them to check them out, take them home. Then, if I have done my job sufficiently well, the students will have a good reading experience.

A&C What title of yours seems to be the most popular with students?

BA *Into a Strange Land* has been very successful. There is evidence that *Always to Remember* is going to be quite successful as well. Those two seem to be the most popular.

A&C Does a nonfiction writer get letters from young readers?

BA Yes, I got a fair number of letters, but I'm sure I don't get nearly as many as the popular fiction writers. *Gavriel and Jemal: Two Boys of Jerusalem* seems to inspire quite a number of youngsters to write to me. As you know, it's the story of a young Jewish boy and an Arab boy. I've received a number of letters on this book from Jewish students and Arab-American youngsters. I always read and answer the letters because I'm delighted to receive them. Another book of mine that students write to me about is *Children of the Maya*. I received a letter from a boy who read it and he said, "I liked all of *Children of the Maya* except page 40. " Well, I knew even without looking what he was referring to on that page. He was referring to a story told by a refugee child in which the youngster talks about the death of his father. It reads like this:

> "Someone told the army that my father was helping the guerrillas, and one night four soldiers came to our house. When they banged on the door, my father knew what it was, and he climbed out the back window and ran. The soldiers said that they knew my father was helping guerrillas and that maybe he was with them now. They said they would find him, and they left.
>
> My father walked to San Miguel Acatan, and a friend hid him in his house. But the soldiers found him. They beat him and then shot him and cut off his head. They killed his friend, too, and threw them both in a ditch.
>
> The next day we found my father and carried him home. We washed him and put him in a coffin. I remember that his head did not fit very well with his body. It is something I wish I could forget, but I can't."[1]

Now that certainly is a terrible image of the head not seeming to fit on the body. I pondered for a long time about whether or nor to include it in the book. My editor also questioned whether or not it was too strong a story to put in the book. I decided to leave it in because that is exactly what the boy said to me. I have raised the issue with adolescent readers since the book came out and the verdict seems to be that the story ought to be there, but it is the kind of thing that a writer considers over and over again. As you can tell, I enjoy getting letters from my readers and really think about what they have to say.

A&C Are there three or four pieces of nonfiction for juvenile readers that you consider real quality touchstone books? Or if not books, Brent, are there authors that you think are top-notch?

BA Yes, there are. Jim Giblin's books come to mind first. Everything Jim writes, I read. He picks interesting subjects and makes them fascinating. I never thought of milk as anything more than something you drink until I read Giblin's *Milk: The Fight for Purity*. Milton Meltzer takes on some very tough subjects and does it beautifully in books like *Never to Forget: The Jews of the Holocaust* and *Ain't Gonna Study War No More*. Russell Freedman has written some fine nonfiction including his Newbery Award winner *Lincoln: A Photobiography*. Jim Arnosky writes a very different kind of nonfiction than I do, but I think his work is outstanding. All of these people are authors I admire.

A&C What can we expect next from the pen of Brent Ashabranner?

Figure 23. Jacket Illustration from *Always to Remember*.

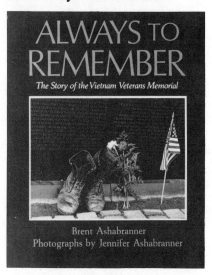

BA I've got a new book coming out called *People Who Make a Difference*. I have traveled around the country and met some folks who appear to be ordinary, run-of-the-mill people, but they are doing things that are making the world around them a little bit better. I've included fourteen people who are helping those around them live better and richer lives. One person in *People Who Make a Difference* is a karate master who is working with severely disabled children, children with Down's Syndrome, and youngsters with cerebral palsy. He's doing things that no one thought could be done to improve their motor skills, their attention span, and their self-image. It's a book of stories like that. It has given me enormous pleasure to write the book. I'm also working on a book about Arab Americans and this is very much in the vein of other things I have done. Then there's a book about Arlington National Cemetery. It's not exactly a companion to *Always to Remember* but along the same line. It will be called *A Grateful Nation*. I've always wanted to do a book about dogs so I'm working on one called *Crazy About German Shepherds*. Jennifer will be taking the photographs for the Arlington Cemetery and German shepherd books. My daughter Melissa and I are working on a book entitled *Counting America: The Story of the U.S. Census*. These books will keep me busy for a couple of years.

A&C As a writer of nonfiction for adolescents, what gives you the greatest satisfaction?

BA I think that I probably have two answers to that. I know that the most important reading that most human beings do is the reading done when they're young. I know that so vividly out of my personal experience. Even though I grew up in a small town many years ago, I was hooked on books about foreign places. I devoured Kipling, practically memorized *Beau Geste*, and read those wonderful true travel adventures by Richard Halliburton. I know that reading really affected the rest of my life and it is partly why I went into foreign development work. It's why I spent nine years in the Peace Corps. It's also one reason I now spend my time writing for readers in that age group. The other thing that gives me satisfaction is the same thing that gives any writer satisfaction. There's a special feeling when somebody comes up to you and says, "I really liked your book." Then you know you've connected with another human being.

NOTE

1. (1986). *Children of the Maya: A Guatemalan Indian Odyssey.* New York: G.P. Putnam's Sons, p. 39–40.

BOOKS BY BRENT ASHABRANNER

Always to Remember: The Story of the Vietnam Veterans Memorial. (1988). New York: G. P. Putnam's Sons.

Born to the Land. (1989). New York: G.P. Putnam's Sons.

Children of the Maya: A Guatemalan Indian Odyssey. (1986). New York: G. P. Putnam's Sons.

Dark Harvest: Migrant Farm Workers in America. (1985). New York: G. P. Putnam's Sons.

Gavriel and Jemal: Two Boys of Jerusalem. (1984). New York: G. P. Putnam's Sons.

******I'm in the Zoo*, Too! (1989). New York: Cobblehill/E. P. Dutton.

Morning Star, Black Sun: The Northern Cheyenne Indians and America's Energy Crisis. (1982). New York: G. P. Putnam's Sons.

The New Americans: Changing Patterns in U. S. Immigration. (1983). New York: G. P. Putnam's Sons.

People Who Make a Difference. (1989). New York: Cobblehill/ E. P. Dutton.

To Live in Two Worlds: American Indian Youth Today. (1984–o.p.). New York: Dodd, Mead.

The Vanishing Border: A Photographic Journey Along Our Frontier with Mexico. (1987). New York: G. P. Putnam's Sons.

Ashabranner, Brent and Ashabranner, Melissa. *Into a Strange Land: Unaccompanied Refugee Youth in America.* (1987). New York: G. P. Putnam's Sons.

Ashabranner, Brent and Ashabranner, Melissa. *Counting America: The Story of the United States Census.* (1989). New York: G. P. Putnam's Sons.

*** *Indicates a work of fiction*

CHAPTER 9
Organization

One newspaper cartoon from a few years back shows two old men, down on their luck, squatting alongside the railroad tracks sharing a can of beans over an open campfire. One man, shabbily dressed and with all his possessions tied up in a bandana on a stick, looks at the other and says, "Last year I was the CEO of a large corporation, but then I lost my list." Though the cartoonist clearly indicates that organization can make or break a business magnate, we want to extend the point: Organization, or the lack of it, can also lead to the success or failure of an informational book.

Proven writers must discover a unifying structure within which to present their information. Unlike style, tone, and purpose, organizational structure must not just mesh with content; it should also provide a clear context for understanding that content. Specific facts and opinions represent what the author wants to offer the reader; structure determines how the author wants the reader to process that information. Reference aids, such as a table of contents, an index, or appended matter, provide additional structure for the young adult who chooses to preview the book, find specific facts, or extend the basic text material. In this chapter we will discuss four distinct organizational schemes and how various authors apply these patterns. In addition, we'll examine four reference aids and the use and appropriateness of each in relation to specific works.

ORGANIZATIONAL PATTERNS

Although a variety of organizational structures exist, fine authors don't haphazardly choose one out of the air and then force their information into it. Brent Ashabranner admits that finding an appropriate "structure may take him almost as long to locate as the actual writing takes."[1] Respected science author Irving Adler defines the craft of writing nonfiction not only as the selection of key ideas, but also as the presentation of these ideas in a form readers can understand. Similarly, Jean Fritz, the 1986 recipient of the Wilder Award, reiterates the importance of structure when she writes: "The art of fiction is making up facts; the art of nonfiction is using facts to make up a form."[2]

Although each collection of data requires its own organization, several patterns emerge in book after book. It appears that mature readers either consciously or unconsciously look for these organizational patterns and structure their reading, and their thinking, around them. When reading a chronological history, for example, they key in on those reported events that happened first, then second, and then third. They are thus able to eliminate asides and appositives that have little relationship to the whole, while retaining more crucial information within a familiar perceptual frame. Sophisticated readers need works written in various patterns so that they may polish these skills; less facile readers require the same latitude in order to develop theirs. When recommending informational books to young adults, then, it is important that librarians and teachers take note of structure in addition to other features.

Enumeration

Enumeration, or topical outline, represents the most frequently used organizational pattern for informational books. In such works, writers describe their subjects by examining what they believe to be the relevant parts of that whole. Irene Kiefer, in *Nuclear Energy at the Crossroads*, explores the debate for and against the uses of nuclear power through five components of the controversy: the use of nuclear power; the generation of radiation; and the threats of nuclear accidents, low-level radiation, and radioactive waste disposal. Similarly, in *Taking On the Press: Constitutional Rights in Conflict*, author Melvyn Zerman examines the challenge to First Amendment rights from the four distinct points of view of the schools, individuals, law enforcement and the courts, and the federal government. In both books, the authors make complex subjects understandable by leading readers through distinct subtopics.

Some subtopics display an incredible similarity from one book to another. For instance, numerous books concerning pets cover a history of the animal, tips for choosing a pet, varieties of breeds, and first aid information. Many of the sports books also contain repetitive patterns that discuss a history of the sport, rules for playing the game, safety tips, necessary equipment, and a list of organizations and interest groups concerned with that sport. This tendency to address similar subjects within the same topic does not necessarily detract from the usefulness of these works. Young adults may find comfort in reading familiar material and security in a familiar format.

During the junior high years many younger teens are going through that stage of reading we call "unconscious delight," a time when they devour so many similar books that their reading matter appears almost interchangeable and when they often turn to series offerings such as *Alfred Hitchcock and the Three Investigators, Sweet Dreams, Choose Your Own Adventure,* and *Sweet Valley High.* The sameness of series seems to provide a comfortable sanctuary for young adult readers. But we suspect that many other teenagers encounter their unconscious delight not in story, but through information books. While subject or topic may first hook these informational readers in much the same way genre pulls their classmates into fictional series, the predictable enumerative patterning facilitates their reading process.

Just as readers of Nancy Drew know that the matchbook she finds on her airplane seat will become an important clue in solving her latest mystery, readers of topical works enjoy the certainty that after reading about the history of cycling, baseball, or volleyball, they will find out the rules and equipment necessary for competing in that particular sport. These readers develop patterns of thinking and reading about relationships among topics as surely as do other young adults who discover how a story works through a fictional series.

Chronological Order

The second most common pattern found in informational books is that of time or chronological order. Like Alice describing her adventures in Wonderland, many authors find it's best to "begin at the beginning" when explaining a concept, and to develop that explanation through its natural progression. Predictably, this pattern occurs repeatedly in historical books. Milton Meltzer's *Ain't Gonna Study War No More,* for example, sequentially outlines the history of pacifists from the writings of Lao-tzu in the sixth century B.C. to the peace movement during the Vietnam conflict. This historical focus allows Meltzer to use the weight of the entire heritage of pacifism to underscore his theme that a refusal to bear arms represents a viable, respectable alternative to war.

Chronological sequence does not automatically appear in all historical accounts. Albert Marrin's *The Yanks Are Coming* covers World War I from several different perspectives, from politicians to foot soldiers to pilots to those remaining on the home front. Marrin orders his book topically, allowing each interest group separate chapters that chronologically overlap the others.

Many authors use simple time sequence to structure books on topics far removed from traditional political histories, and frequently these works prove quite popular with young adults. Almost half of the books chosen by the junior high students in our 1986 study consisted of selections from the 700s on recreation and the performing arts. Not only was there sameness in subject, but there was also familiarity in structure: The majority of these books were written as historical accounts.

These teenagers showed a definite preference for history when it chronicled sports, film, and comics rather than when applied to nations.

Teachers wishing to reinforce time order through literature, instead of with worksheets which demand that students number events in the order that they happened, might well prove more successful in choosing works like *Superman from the 30s to the 80s, The Story of American Photography, An Album of Great Science Fiction Films,* or *Dirt Bike Racing* than accounts of pure history. Not only do these books appeal to a great number of young adults, but their chronological organizations provide teenagers valid experiences with this important pattern.

Story Narrative

Often considered the exclusive domain of fiction, story narrative also emerges as a powerful and popular structure in nonfiction. Pulitzer prize recipient Barbara Tuchman defends her consistent choice of nonfiction narrative by admitting that "no one could possibly persuade me that telling a story is not the most desirable thing a writer can do."[3] Young adults who traditionally favor fiction over nonfiction may discover those informational books organized as a story the perfect introduction to factual accounts, while the teenagers for whom the reverse is true—those who read nonfiction to the exclusion of fiction—may accept teachers and librarians' recommendations for narrative nonfiction as the first step in broadening their reading preferences to include novels.

Whether working with fiction or nonfiction, narrative writers use identical techniques of setting, characterization, and pacing. In writing about the discovery of the body's natural painkillers, Jeff Goldberg opens *Anatomy of a Scientific Discovery* with a setting reminiscent of mystery writers describing the grim scenes of their latest potboilers: "In Aberdeen, on the northeast coast of Scotland, winter begins in early October and does not let up until May, or so it seems. On most days it rains."[4]

Likewise, complex, multifaceted characters make their well-timed appearances in nonfiction. Readers of Carolyn Meyer and Charles Gallenkamp's *The Mystery of the Ancient Maya* will encounter Diego de Landa, who in the sixteenth century unmercifully persecuted the Mayan Indians under the mantle of Christianity but whose penetrating account of the ancient Yucatan provides the basis for much of our knowledge about them; John Lloyd Stephens, the nineteenth-century adventurer who appeared to simply enjoy traveling to faraway places, but then grabbed the glory from fellow collaborator and skilled artist Frederick Catherwood with his widely read books on their explorations into Copan, Uxmal, and Tulum; and Edward Herbert Thompson, the early twentieth-century archaeologist who explored, as well as exploited, the ruins of Chichen Itza. And even though readers know the outcome of

Steven Callahan's *Adrift: Seventy-Six Days Lost at Sea*—after all, he had to live just to tell the tale—tension builds to climax as inexorably in this work as it does in the thrillers of Lois Duncan or Robert Ludlum.

While novelists find a story in the kinds of things that can happen, nonfiction writers discover it in the kinds of things that have happened. But in the hands of either kind of capable writer, the pull of a story exerts a powerful influence on readers. Jean Fritz, an acknowledged master of narrative in nonfiction, underscores the drama inherent in *China's Long March* with an introduction calculated to parallel the first act of a powerful play:

> This story opens in 1934. By this time Chiang Kai-shek's National-
> ist regime was recognized by most foreign countries as the legal
> government of China. But not by the Communists. In the interior of
> China they were building up their army and spreading their revolu-
> tion among the peasants. They were still determined to take over
> China.
>   The scene is Jiangxi, a remote mountainous province in south-
> ern China. The danger is about to begin.[5]

Story narrative allows writers not only the luxury of using tech-niques often reserved for fiction, but also of introducing fictional elements into their tales. Yet, it requires a gifted writer to juxtapose both fact and fantasy without confusing the reader. In *Mill*, David Macaulay succeeds admirably. He personalizes the evolution and impact of a series of mills on a single community by weaving stories of fictitious builders, workers, owners, and archaeologists into his tale of the construction and function of a prototypical group of New England textile factories. And by introducing Howard Carson, a for-ty-first-century archaeologist affectionately modeled after Howard Carter, in *Motel of the Mysteries,* Macaulay not only satirizes the "Tut Mania" that gripped the United States during the Tutankhaman exhibit of 1978, but the science of archaeology as well. Carson stumbles on what he supposes is an ancient burial ground of twentieth-century Yanks at the site of the Toot 'n Come On Motel. As he uncovers treasure after treasure, he digs his own theoretical hole by drawing completely outra-geous conclusions about this long-lost civilization. Thus, through Car-son's eyes, a plastic ice bucket is interpreted as a canopic urn, a plumber's friend as a percussion instrument, and a shower cap as a sacred burial garment. This masterful satire reminds readers that while life may well be a story, it's certainly open to interpretation.

Simple to Complex

The fourth frequently used organizational pattern allows writers to progress from the simple to the complex by moving the reader through increasingly complicated skills and concepts. Not surprisingly, this pattern most often materializes in how-to books, works that show young adults how to build a model airplane, draw a dinosaur, or kick a field goal.

The sports books employing this structure introduce adolescents to basic moves, encourage them to practice these maneuvers, and then sequentially add more sophisticated steps to their routines. Books on golf, for example, instruct in proper ways to grip the club and address the ball before introducing techniques to develop a rhythmic swing. Using the same process to create a tangible product, Irwin Math in *Bits and Pieces* first shows his readers how to build simple analog and digital computer systems, and then how to enhance these machines to perform specific functions.

One of the more popular incarnations of this simple-to-complex pattern consistently reappears in drawing books. In most of these books though, this technique characterizes chapter rather than total book organization. In the *Draw 50* series from Lee J. Ames, for instance, each book offers fifty objects as models for young adults to draw on their own. These subjects may be arranged topically, as in *Draw 50 Cars, Trucks, and Motorcycles*, in which like machines are grouped together, or with a combination of patterns, as in *Draw 50 Dogs*. This latter work orders the drawings first by class—hounds, terriers, setters—and then alphabetically within these categories. The heart work, though, is a six-to ten-step process of adding simple shapes and lines to a basic form in order to replicate his finished product. Figure 24, from *Draw 50 Famous Faces*, shows how Ames employs this strategy when sketching Abraham Lincoln.

With their emphasis on copying shapes rather than processing the written word, books like Ames's series are often not considered developmental reading material. One junior high youngster recently told us that when he went to the school library the teacher always let him check out one drawing book, but then she made him get something else "to read." We'd like to argue with this perception. Young adults who use these books respond to them by either faithfully copying the steps or using the sequences as a guides for producing their own creations. That process parallels ours when we pick up individual volumes on more sophisticated subjects and either accept the authors' conclusions and points of view or use that information to formulate our own. In both cases individuals are interacting with text and extracting meaning from it. In our minds, that constitutes reading.

Additional Patterns

Other distinct patterns, such as the encyclopedic, alphabetic organization utilized by Tom McGowen in *The Encyclopedia of Legendary Creatures* or transition from the familiar to the unfamiliar in Patricia Lauber's *Journey to the Planets,* appear with less frequency in informa-

Figure 24. Drawing Abraham Lincoln

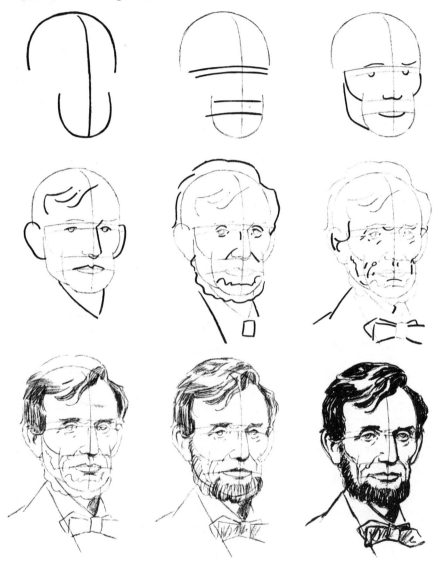

tional books. Quite often, though, books will employ a combination of patterns. For example, Betty Bacon suggests that informational books can be organized in terms of time and space. Time in this sense does not represent strict chronology, but rather "the cyclical patterns of the earth, the seasons, and life itself"[6] as detailed in, for example, *The Pond: The Life of Aquatic Plants, Fish, Amphibians, Reptiles, Mammals, and Birds that Inhabit the Pond and Its Surrounding Hillside and Swamp.* Gerald and Lee Durell's *The Amateur Naturalist,* on the other hand, employs space as both a unifying pattern and overall theme. Through this exceptional work, young naturalists can vicariously take nature walks from the beaches to the woodlands and observe the natural world based on the unique surroundings of these particular settings.

All of these organizational models serve as overall structures for content and do not restrict the use of additional text patterns, such as cause/effect, comparison/contrast, or chronological sequence, within their superstructures. Like several of the Ames books mentioned earlier, many such works employ enumeration as the unifying design for the whole.

Claudine G. Wirths and Mary Bowman-Kruhm's *I Hate School: How to Hang in & When to Drop Out* provides an apt example of thoughtful blending of two distinct patterns. Addressed to those young adults contemplating leaving school, this practical self-help book assumes that at least part of its audience will include poor readers. In the opening chapter Wirths and Bowman-Kruhm instruct young adults in efficient use of their topical outline by directing them to read just those chapters or topics related to their particular situations. By proposing this technique, the authors cut down on much unnecessary required reading. The format of each chapter further caters to their perceived audience, as information is presented through a series of questions and answers. Not only does this method automatically engage the reader in an active process, but it also breaks up large chunks of print into smaller, less intimidating sections. Through both organization and format, the authors have increased the probability that the very students they wish to reach will indeed read their book.

Efficient young adult readers are able to key in on organizational patterns and alter their reading accordingly. Other teenagers do not automatically make these connections between the structure of text and the process of reading. They can, however, learn such skills through teachers and librarians who are themselves aware of different organizational patterns and willing to help young adults exploit them.

REFERENCE AIDS

Book organization reaches beyond text patterns to include specific reference aids. Several of these features, such as an index, can potentially help young adults find specific facts, while others, like appendices, will frequently extend the text by showing teenagers where they can go to find further information. Although each is useful, none should be included in every informational book published for adolescent readers. Individual volumes that don't include these aids do not demand automatic rejection. Instead, their appropriateness has to be evaluated on a book-by-book basis.

One other issue concerning reference aids deserves comment. Although the vast majority of young adults understand the mechanics of utilizing these aids—like finding references in an index or entries in a glossary—frequently teenagers do not automatically turn to them or even capitalize on their power. Library lessons and classroom instruction that move beyond mere identification of book parts and extend to reinforcement and exploitation of these valuable reference aids provide worthwhile exercises for young adults.

Table of Contents

The table of contents serves as a particularly helpful tool for previewing subject, scope, and overall presentation. The table of contents provides page numbers for chapter and topical divisions, and as such helps readers find their place. But beyond this basic use, it can serve either as a straightforward preview for what's inside a book or as a series of tantalizing teasers to draw readers into a particular volume.

In *The 60s Reader*, authors James Haskins and Kathleen Benson use the table of contents to preview the material in the book. (see Figure 25).

Figure 25. Table of Contents from *The 60s Reader*.

CONTENTS

First of all, this table of contents provides a broad picture of the book's scope, showing that Haskins and Benson appear to stress political, social, and cultural protest during the sixties. Second, it outlines general content—material on the civil rights and peace movements as well as the music of the decade. It reveals that beyond the ten individual chapters, the book contains an introduction, a bibliography, and an index. Third, the table of contents directs readers to specific points in the text. Someone wanting to know about the drug culture, for example, can turn to page 200 for the chapter on that topic. And fourth, it presents Haskins and Benson's dual organizational patterns whereby the book is structured both chronologically, through the two chapters on the early and later sixties, and topically, through the remaining subject-oriented chapters.

On the other hand, the table of contents in Carolyn Meyer and Charles Gallenkamp's *The Mystery of the Ancient Maya*, piques the reader's interest while still indicating organizational structure, chapter divisions, page numbers, and the presence of a glossary and an index. (see Figure 26).

The questions that define parts 3 and 4, and chapter titles like "The Secrets of a Tomb" and "The Puzzle of the Deserted Cities," with their accompanying teasers, immediately engage readers in speculation about the Maya and serve to pull them into the text. Meyer and Gallenkamp hint at excitement, mysteries, puzzles, and adventure. That they deliver on these elements is a tribute to their vision and their craft.

Occasionally nonfiction works for young adults, like Judith St. George's *The Panama Canal*, do not contain a table of contents. Here, its omission underscores the narrative quality of the overall book, and other aids cover its obligations. The detailed index proves adequate for finding specific information, while other features allow for reasonable previewing. The cover photograph clearly indicates construction, the frontispiece diagram explains the lock system, and text illustrations show individuals struggling with the hostile terrain and the living conditions in a nontechnological tropical country at the beginning of the twentieth century. These prominent graphics highlight important pieces in the complex task of building the canal, providing an adequate preview of the historical focus of this particular work.

Young adults may not know the various formats tables of contents can take or their usefulness in previewing and indicating the presence of additional reference aids. The best chances for acquiring this knowledge come from librarians and teachers who provide direct instruction and deliberate encounters with these tools.

Figure 26. Table of Contents from *The Mystery of the Ancient Maya*.

CONTENTS

Chapters

Chapter divisions represent the conventional way authors of informational books organize text. Such separations not only help readers structure their thinking, but they also provide natural breaks in the reading process. Chapter breaks should appear as natural segments of the overall organization pattern rather than be dictated by an arbitrarily predetermined number of pages.

Beyond considering appropriate subject division, authors of informational books encounter further challenges when writing and designing chapters. First, each chapter should quickly engage the reader in the material. Second, many readers will look at only a portion or single chapter, so chapters should stand reasonably well as separate units. Third, authors must also view the book as a whole, and provide adequate transition from chapter to chapter. With this apparent dichotomy of providing both continuous text and self-sustaining chapters, writers face a tricky task. We will examine the ways they meet it first by looking at readers and then by spotlighting individual authors who have solved the problem.

There is no set way to read an information book. Unlike fiction writers, who have the luxury of assuming that most readers—except for those few who always look at the last page first—will read their books from beginning to end, authors of informational works must take into account the varied approaches of their readers. Sometimes young adults will start at the first page and continue until the end. At other times they will read just one portion and then stop, while on occasion they will read a chapter in the middle, and then work to either end until they have, in a roundabout fashion, completed the book. Therefore, writers need to engage young adults not only at the beginning of their books, but at the beginning of each individual chapter. And to keep these readers going, they will often employ some end-of-the-chapter techniques used by their fictional counterparts.

One of the surest ways to immediately draw readers into a text is by posing a question. This practice engages their attention and also focuses their thoughts on what is going to be discussed. Rita Golden Gelman effectively uses such a ploy in *Inside Nicaragua*:

"Oh, wait a minute," she says, when I tell her I have just returned from Nicaragua. "We studied those countries in my Spanish class. Is Nicaragua the one where the good government is fighting the bad guerrillas? Or is it the one where the bad government is fighting the good guerillas?"
Depends who you ask.[7]

Gelman immediately encourages readers to sort out the "good guys" from the "bad guys," a process she continues to develop throughout her discussion of the effects of civil war on the citizens of Nicaragua. Finally, she brings the book full circle by ending with the same question, and with the same answer: "Depends who you ask." Not only does Gelman begin her book by asking readers to think, but she also concludes in the same manner, offering no easy answers nor any simple resolutions.

Melvyn Zerman provides an equally effective hook at the beginning of *Taking On the Press: Constitutional Rights in Conflict*. He places the issue of First Amendment freedoms squarely into a teenager's own life and experiential background with a discussion of the censorship of student newspapers and the disciplinary action directed toward one student editor. After reading his opening line, "It came as no great surprise when Charlie Quarterman was slapped with his second suspension,"[8] readers naturally want to know what happened to this fellow teenager.

Other authors, like Laurence Pringle in *Throwing Things Away: From Middens to Resource Recovery*, develop small fictional episodes as chapter openings. In his discussion of waste disposal, Pringle not only emphasizes the historical nature of the problem, but he also begins in terms young adults can readily understand:

> "Remember to take out the trash, dear," Mother said to her son. He groaned, then reluctantly gathered up the deer bones, oyster shells, and a broken clay pot and carried them from the cave.[9]

John Langone uses two actual case studies to introduce *Dead End: A Book about Suicide*. In the first, a sixteen-year-old girl describes her own suicide attempt; in the second, another teenager talks about a friend who tried to kill herself. Both segments effectively personalize Langone's topic, allowing readers to compare their own thoughts and actions with those of two very real young adults.

Straightforward and less personal beginnings also work. In *Mass Extinctions: One Theory of Why the Dinosaurs Vanished*, Christopher Lampton satisfactorily sets his scene:

> Buried within the earth is a book that will reveal the secrets of the ages to anyone who knows how to read it.
> It is not written on paper, nor is it written in any language spoken on earth today. It is called the *fossil* record, and it is made up of the bones, footprints, and petrified remains of plants and animals that lived in the prehistoric past. The story told by the fossil record stretches over more than half a billion years. It is one of the most important stories ever told and one of the most fascinating. It is the story of life on earth. In some ways, it is a mystery story.[10]

And in writing *Living in Space*, James S. Trefil masterfully employs the speechmaker's adage: Tell them what you're going to say, say it, and then tell them what you said. He previews each chapter, delivers what he promised in the overview, and then uses the concluding paragraphs to summarize the main points. Trefil accomplishes this task without ponderous repetition and without evoking unpleasant memories of classroom textbooks.

When writing a book, capable authors introduce facts, concepts, and background material, and build on this information throughout the text. Such a technique gives a book cohesion and unity. Yet, these authors must also recognize that many of their readers will look at only a portion of the text. This audience has to be taken into consideration, and they pose a special problem for writers of nonfiction. For example, authors wouldn't include the background material they do unless they think it's important. Without undue repetition for continuous text readers, they must make references to this previously mentioned material so that those who dip into their books will be able to clarify confusing points by checking salient passages accessible through the index.

We suspect, however, that most writers would agree with the 1987 Newbery Award winner, Russell Freedman, who said in a speech to the American Library Association that his aim is always to write "a book that will be willingly read by someone from beginning to end."[11] And although authors can't prevent young adults from looking for specific information in the middle of the book, they can encourage further reading by leading them into subsequent chapters. In *Cosmic Quest: Searching for Intelligent Life among the Stars*, Margaret Poynter and Michael J. Klein borrow the technique of questioning to conclude their second chapter:

> It's difficult for human minds to grasp the idea of a black hole. Such objects are far beyond the realm of our experience. They are, however, only one of the fascinating puzzles that abound in our galactic neighborhood. What new riddles will appear? And which of them will we solve as we continue to explore the Milky Way? Will we find the clues that will eventually lead us to the discovery of extraterrestrial life?[12]

Such questions lead to thinking, thinking leads to reading, and many young adults will move to the third chapter not because they have to satisfy a school assignment, but because they want to satisfy their own curiosity.

In *Vietnam There and Here*, a well-researched account of the Vietnam conflict, author Margot C. J. Mabie encourages continuous reading with her chapter endings. In concluding the chapter on the Geneva accords, which politically divided Vietnam in 1954, she piques curiosity with this bit of foreshadowing: "But the soothsayers were wrong; there were bad years ahead for everyone."[13] Interested readers begin wondering what exactly did happen, and they turn the page and continue with her tale. Through such stylistic techniques these authors fulfill Barbara

Tuchman's goal for writing good nonfiction: "The writer's objective is—or should be—to hold the reader's attention."[14]

Some authors employ headings and subheadings to further subdivide their chapters, although these can interrupt a narrative flow and may put off readers who equate headings and subheadings with less popular textbooks. But since they are frequently used, young adults need to know how to take advantage of them. Comprehension techniques, which instruct readers to use headings and subheadings for chapter previewing and to turn the topics into questions while reading, can be reinforced not just in content-area classes, but in library and literature lessons as well.

Index

An index can prove an indispensable tool, and in most cases informational books should include indexes. Exceptions are alphabetic volumes like Tom McGowen's *Encyclopedia of Legendary Creatures* that contain collections of single and unique entries that show little potential for cross-referencing. Otherwise, indexes are important. They help young adults to find specific information, examine the amount of coverage for a particular topic, and identify related subjects and subtopics.

In terms of classroom and library instruction, young adults should encounter opportunities to find information in both alphabetical and analytical indexes. An alphabetical index, like the example below, lists all information alphabetically, and each entry receives identical placement:

Figure 27. Alphabetical Index.

Ames, Lee J., 73, 100
Arnosky, Jim, 65, 98, 119
Artists and Illustrators, 62 - 75
Bolognese, Don, 73, 115, 116
Drawing Books, 54, 87 - 123
Drawing From Nature, 98
Drawing Horses and Foals,115
Drawing Dinosaurs and Other Prehistoric Animals, 116
Draw 50 Dogs, 100.

An analytical index, on the other hand, groups pertinent subtopics under major subject headings:

Figure 28. Analytical Index.

The two indexes above serve only as simple illustrations and as such suggest the base, rather than the totality, of instruction. In addition to these designs, young adults need to use cross-references—entries like "Book Design, *see* Artists" and "Illustrators or Cartoonists, *see* Artists and Illustrators"—as well as indexes with special features like those that differentiate between text and pictorial references. Beyond introducing these mechanical features, teachers and librarians can also act as models by repeatedly using indexes to locate information, thereby reinforcing this reference.

Glossary

All subject areas contain their own specialized, technical vocabularies of words, terms, and jargon that may well prove unfamiliar to young adults. Sometimes context clues provide insufficient information for particular readers to figure out the meaning of unfamiliar terms. At other times, text explanations seem adequate when words or phrases first appear, but young adults easily forget or confuse these meanings when new vocabulary is subsequently mentioned or used out of context. At this point in their reading, teenagers may well want to check the definition of such questionable terms. Glossaries can prove a real boon to untutored readers looking to understand the language of a new discipline.

Unlike dictionaries, glossaries don't offer complete definitions of words and phrases. They only provide those explanations that pertain to the subject matter under discussion. A book on racing will define the term *trial* as a contest, while one on law will offer a completely different emphasis. In addition, parts of speech and pronunciation guides appear less frequently in glossaries than in other lexicons. So, while young adults should be encouraged to use glossaries, they need to be aware of their limitations.

Above all, glossaries should contain clear and succinct definitions. To define an "artery" as a muscular tube carrying blood in the opposite direction from a "vein," and a vein as a muscular tube carrying blood in the opposite direction from an artery, does little to clarify the function of these parts of the circulation system. If words are defined through other potentially unfamiliar terms, then their definitions must not mirror one another. It is reasonable to expect that readers will occasionally consult more than one definition when looking up unfamiliar words, but this cross-referencing should not turn into an exercise in frustration. Even though young adults reading Maxine Fisher's *Recent Revolutions in Anthropology* may have to check the entry for *Homo erectus* in order to understand the definition of *Acheulian industry*, this process will eventually provide a workable understanding of the original term.

Figure 29. Glossary Excerpt from *Recent Revolutions in Anthropology*.

Glossary

Acheulian industry: the stone tools associated with *Homo erectus*

Homo erectus: an extinct species of our genus which lived in Java, China, Africa, and Europe for one million years

Generally, glossaries should provide only brief definitions and allow text to expand the meaning. Joan Elma Rahn provides such a service in her book about the regulation of animal temperature, *Keeping Warm, Keeping Cool*. In the body of this book Rahn gives a thorough explanation for the term *arteriovenous anastomoses*:

> If the temperature of the limb begins to fall lower than 1° C, more blood is allowed to circulate to the tip of the limb—just enough, but no more than necessary, to maintain a temperature of 1° C. This blood circulates through a system of small blood vessels that connect *arteries and veins directly; it bypasses the capillaries. These small blood vessels are called arteriovenous anastomoses* (which means a union of arteries and veins); they are also known as *AVAs* for short. The AVAs are larger than capillaries, and so blood moves through them much more rapidly. As long as the temperature of the tissues in flippers or feet of arctic and antarctic animals remains above 1° C, the capillaries remain dilated (open wide) and the AVAs are constricted. When the temperature begins to fall below 1° C, the capillaries constrict and AVAs dilate. This brings a rush of warm blood through the limbs, and then the capillaries dilate again and the AVAs constrict. The temperature of the limbs is kept from falling below 1° C by repeated dilations of the AVAs. Dilations of AVAs do not occur any more frequently than is necessary to keep tissue temperature from falling below 1° C.[15]

Yet even with this clear and detailed discussion, Rahn finds it necessary to include the term, with the following succinct definition, in her glossary.

ARTERIOVENOUS ANASTOMOSIS (AVA): a type of fine blood vessel found especially in animals adapted to survival in very cold climates; AVAs connect arteries and veins directly; when arteriovenous anastomoses are dilated they release a great deal of heat to the tissues in which they are located and keep them from freezing.[16]

Recently, glossaries have taken on lives of their own as writers exploit them for specialized purposes. In *Inside Nicaragua*, Rita Golden Gelman devotes hers to the translation of the Spanish slang that she retains throughout her conversational interviews. And in *China's Long March*, Jean Fritz condenses her glossary-like entries to simple pronunciation guides for the unfamiliar Chinese names which appear in the body of the book.

Incidentally, in this particular work, Fritz positions her glossary at the beginning of the text. Several other authors, book designers, or editors have adopted similar locations for their glossaries. Such a prominent placement can remind young adults that this reference aid is available and worthy of special focus.

Appended Matter

As Yogi Berra said, "It ain't over till it's over," and nowhere is that statement truer than in information books. Authors frequently extend text by offering suggestions for further reading, addresses of special organizations, and even full-text documents. The variety of appended matter is as great as the topics they choose to write about.

A Young Woman's Guide to Sex by Jacqueline Voss and Jay Gale offers three separate, but equally valuable, appendixes. The first, entitled "Finding Help," discusses locating appropriate agencies in a telephone book and deciphering the indexing system used in most yellow pages; an annotated list of national organizations, with their addresses and telephone numbers, that answer questions about such topics as abortion, AIDS, breast-feeding, fertility, sexually transmitted diseases, and transsexuality; and an extensive, topical bibliography of recommended readings. The second appendix, "Suggestions for Security," lists safety tips to consider while at home, in the car, or outside. And the third, "Responding to an Attack," outlines the issue of passive versus active resistance during a sexual assault.

Herma Silverstein's *Teenage and Pregnant: What You Can Do* lives up to its title through a well-organized and accessible text, as well as in the complete appendix which lists, with addresses and telephone numbers, organizations located in every state "whose purpose is to help pregnant adolescents find programs in prenatal care, childbirth, and parenting; free or inexpensive birth control; help with staying in school, including day care facilities for infants and young children; low-cost medical care; sources for job opportunities; and assistance in locating housing, clothing, and infant supplies."[17]

In *Looking the Tiger in the Eye: Confronting the Nuclear Threat*, Carl B. Feldbaum and Ronald J. Bee include a time line that lists events that span one hundred years, from 1895, when Wilhelm Roentgen discovered the X ray, to 1987, when Ronald Reagan and Mikhail Gorbachev signed the INF treaty. This chronology reminds readers of the historical context of key events in the development of nuclear weapons and serves as a simple, factual overview for Feldbaum and Bee's complex topic.

What authors choose to add to their books can only be dictated by the subjects they cover. The full text of the Constitution and its twenty-six amendments makes a fitting appendage to Margot C. J. Mabie's *The Constitution: Reflection of a Changing Nation*, which analyzes that document in terms of its beginnings, its ratification, and its amendments. Philip Heckman not only offers a list of places to view holograms in his *Magic of Holography*, but he also includes in a separate appendix a particularly clear and valuable explanation of scientific notation. And in *The Public Ivys*, Richard Moll ends his guide to the best state-supported undergraduate colleges and universities on a light note with an appendix comparing the graffiti from eight campuses. Thus readers can expect to be greeted at the University of Texas with phrases like "*Repeat* your sins before it is too late"; at the College of William and Mary with "Physics majors die young"; and at the University of North Carolina, which claims the distinction of receiving Richard Moll's Grand Graffiti Award, with "I dream of giving birth to a child who will say, 'Mother what was war?'"[18]

Young adults are not born knowing about this lagniappe found in books. Like all the reference aids mentioned in this chapter, appendixes deserve special attention. Teachers and librarians can best provide that service by pointing them out when booktalking, referring to them in lessons, and using them when working with adolescent readers.

NOTES

1. Ashabranner, Brent (1988). Did You Really Write That for Children? *The Horn Book, 64*, p. 751.

2. Fritz, Jean (1988). Biography: Readability Plus Responsibility. *The Horn Book, 64*, p. 759.

3. Tuchman, Barbara W. (1981). *Practicing History: Selected Essays*. New York: Alfred A. Knopf, pp. 48–49.

4. Goldberg, Jeff (1989). *Anatomy of a Scientific Discovery*. New York: Bantam Books, p. 1.

5. Fritz, Jean (1988). *China's Long March: 6,000 Miles of Danger*. New York: G. P. Putnam's Sons, p. 12.

6. Baskin, Barbara and Harris, Karen (1980). *Books for the Gifted Child*. New York: R. R. Bowker, p. 227.

7. Gelman, Rita Golden (1988). *Inside Nicaragua: Young People's Dreams and Fears*. New York: Franklin Watts, p. 15 and 178.

8. Zerman, Melvyn Bernard (1986). *Taking On the Press: Constitutional Rights in Conflict*. New York: Thomas Y. Crowell, p. 3.

9. Pringle, Laurence (1986). *Throwing Things Away: From Middens to Resource Recovery.* New York: Thomas Y. Crowell, p. 1.

10. Lampton, Christopher (1986). *Mass Extinctions: One Theory of Why the Dinosaurs Vanished.* New York: Franklin Watts/An Impact Book, p. 9.

11. Freedman, Russell (1985). The Pleasure Principle: A Lively Look at the New Nonfiction. Program presented by the Children's Book Council/ALA Joint Committee at the American Library Association's 104th Annual Conference, Chicago, Illinois.

12. Poynter, Margaret and Klein, Michael J. (1984). *Cosmic Quest: Searching for Intelligent Life among the Stars.* New York: Atheneum, p. 21.

13, Mabie, Margot C. J. (1985). *Vietnam: There and Here.* New York: Holt, Rinehart and Winston, p. 37.

14. Tuchman, Barbara (1989). *The Dallas Morning News,* February 7, Section A, p. 10.

15. Rahn, Joan Elma (1983). *Keeping Warm, Keeping Cool.* New York: Atheneum, p. 109.

16. Rahn, Joan Elma (1983), p. 199.

17. Silverstein, Herma (1989). *Teenage and Pregnant: What You Can Do.* Englewood Cliffs, NJ: Julian Messner, p. 140.

18. Moll, Richard (1985). *The Public Ivys: A Guide to America's Best Public Undergraduate Colleges and Universities.* New York: Viking, pp. 280–81.

CHAPTER 10
A Conversation with
James Cross Giblin

James Cross Giblin is a respected editor of children's books as well as an award-winning writer of nonfiction. His books have won the American Book Award, the Golden Kite Award, and a Boston Globe—Horn Book Honor Award. Whether he's writing about milk, windows, skyscrapers, or chimney sweeps, his enthusiasm for the subjects he chooses shines through in the books. Giblin says, "I only hope my pleasure communicates itself to young readers, and makes them want to read more books. If it does, I'll be repaying the debt I owe all the fine writers who nurtured my love of reading when I was a child."

James Cross Giblin

A&C How did *Let There Be Light: A Book about Windows* become a book? What was the process, Jim? Could you take us from idea to finished book?

JCG I say in the beginning of the book that the idea came from looking out the windows of my apartment. I have a broad city view, not of a park or either of the rivers here in New York, but I can see from my apartment about fifty blocks down to the towers of the World Trade Center with a few other tall buildings in between. It's a nice view with lots of light.

Photo used by permission of William C. Morris, Harper Junior Books Group.

Windows have always been very important to me. I'm affected by light and views, and I know whenever I've looked for an apartment I've always taken light very much into consideration. One of my earliest memories as a child is of sitting in the kitchen of a house we lived in only until 1 was three and seeing the sun slant in through the kitchen window and hit a box of Ritz crackers. I remember the orange color. I was two or three years old, but I still remember the light coming through those ruffled kitchen curtains. Anyway, maybe that's where my interest in windows started. In a more general sense, I can tell you that an idea for a nonfiction book has got to strike me emotionally first. Now that startles some people, because they think of nonfiction as being written in a rather cold, objective manner where you organize research and lay out the facts about something. Maybe some writers work that way, but I can't. All the subjects I've written about have started with an emotional feeling on my part that made me want to pursue the subject further.

The interesting thing about *Let There Be Light* is that I never wrote a proposal to do that book. One day I was having lunch with my editor at Crowell, Barbara Fenton. I had just delivered the revision of *Milk: The Fight for Purity*, and we were celebrating. Barbara asked me what I wanted to do next, so I mentioned that I was toying with the subject of windows. Barbara liked the idea and said, "You know, of course, what the book should be called—*Let There Be Light*." That's one of the reasons the book is dedicated to her. The other reason is that, as you can see, she had faith in the idea from the beginning. It triggered something in her too.

As I focused on the subject of windows, I realized that there were lots of different strands in the material. Probably the most obvious was the technological strand. What were early windows made of? When did glass first begin to be used in them? How did we get from little slits in castle walls to the skyscraper walls of glass today? This whole technological strand also involved architecture. Then I began to consider the sociological strand. The subject became a kind of plant that kept sending out new shoots and leaves, and that made the writing much more fun. Unfortunately, all subjects for books don't grow the way the one for windows did. Sometimes an idea just withers. I've had a number of ideas like that I've put down in my notebook only to start thinking about them, and I just haven't been able to see the extensions, or maybe levels of the subject is a better way to put it. These levels are not only fun to explore, but they also make a book a more colorful tapestry.

In *Let There Be Light*, there's an interesting sociological level. I found myself wondering why ancient people didn't have windows facing the street but only facing inner-courtyards. It is the type of thing we've gone back to these days in many inner city neighborhoods. Was it done for protection? Were those early people afraid, and if so, what where they afraid of? These questions sent me off in another research direction. There's an early stage in nonfiction writing when the author raises a lot of questions. When you start to do the research, you really set out to answer the questions you've raised during this stage.

Of course with a subject like windows there's an aesthetic strand to develop as well. That led to stained-glass windows. On a technological level this meant research into how the windows were made. But on an artistic level the question became, Why did people feel so compelled during the Middle Ages to create these beautiful windows? Many stained glass windows were like medieval comic strips that tell a tale through pictures of Christ's final journey to Jerusalem, the whole agony of Holy Week, and then Resurrection. In my research I discovered that this was because most of the people who went to the cathedrals couldn't read, and windows like these were how they learned the great religious stories. Now that's interesting. It only resulted in a sentence or two in the book, but it's the sort of information that gives a nonfiction book depth.

Anyway, the research truly begins for me after I've posed these questions and found the levels inherent in the subject matter. I began the research for *Let There Be Light* in the most obvious way, by going to the *Encyclopedia Britannica* and looking up windows. Encyclopedia entries often give you a basis to begin your research, and they also provide a bibliography of other books to read. As you know, I also have a full-time job as an editor, so I have to do my research and writing after work, on weekends, and during vacations. I carried on concentrated research for this book in the summer and fall of 1986 and continued it through March of 1987. The research involved visits to various libraries, museums, field trips to Washington during vacations, and attendance at a workshop on stained-glass making. At any rate, I began writing the book at the end of March 1987, and finished it right after Labor Day, doing additional research as I went along.

Your readers might be interested to know that besides doing the text research for *Let There Be Light*, I also gathered the illustrations for it. Some of my earlier books had illustrations by artists. For example, Margot Tomes did wonderful drawings for *Chimney Sweeps*, since there was no way I could have gotten photographs of children cleaning chimneys in nineteenth-century England. That book was illustrated with a mix of modern photographs and drawings for all the chapters set in the past. *Fireworks, Picnics, and Flags: The Story of the Fourth of July Symbols* was illustrated with drawings, too, as were Edna Barth's titles in the Clarion Holiday Book series that I'd edited previously. But for my later books, starting with *Walls: Defenses throughout History* and going on to *The Truth about Santa Claus, Milk, From Hand to Mouth,* and *Let There Be Light*, I've found the pictures, and that's a big job. I've gotten more experienced at it over the years and know better where to go. I always start with museums, and the Metropolitan contributed a great deal to *Let There Be Light*. So did the National Gallery in

Washington and the Museum of Modern Art for the twentieth-century chapters.

The visual aspect of a juvenile nonfiction book is more important these days than it has ever been. Whether you're talking about color photos like those in Patricia Lauber's *Volcano: The Eruption and Healing of Mt. St. Helens,* the full-color reproductions in Rhoda Blumberg's *Commodore Perry in the Land of the Shogun,* Seymour Simon's books about the planets, with their spectacular photos, or Russell Freedman's Newbery Award-winning *Lincoln: A Photobiography,* all of these books depend to a great extent on the visual impact of their illustrations. Nonfiction today is more than just good writing, it's tied in with handsome design and outstanding graphics.

Most nonfiction authors have to pay for the pictures that go into their books. That means time invested to research the photos and then reduced royalties to pay for the chosen pictures. In *Let There Be Light,* I knew that if the book was really going to make an impression, it had to have color in it, and my editor agreed. Generally I can do a book like *Milk* spending less than $500 for photo fees. But in the case of *Let There Be Light,* each full-color stained-glass transparency cost me $125, and there are eight of those in the book. My picture budget on the book fell somewhere in the $1,500 to $2,000 range. A writer has to gamble that the extra money put out will pay off in sales because you've produced a more beautiful book. It's a gamble that I feel paid off in this case.

So let's see. I delivered the last of the photographs for *Let There Be Light* to Crowell in early December 1987, a little more than two years after I'd first mentioned the idea for the book to Barbara. Then the book took another nine months to go through production, including copy editing, designing, scaling of illustrations, the jacket design and copy, the index, all those elements. The finished book appeared in early September 1988, just three years after the lunch with Barbara when she and I first talked about it. And I hope it'll be in print for a long time.

A&C How did the editing process go on *Let There Be Light?*

JCG Barbara Fenton only gave me a few revision suggestions on that book. She made one major suggestion, though, that shows the importance of the editor's role. The original manuscript did not have the prologue, where I talk about looking out my own windows at a stormy night. That was Barbara's idea, not what was in it specifically, but she said, "Why don't you write a prologue to let us know why you wanted to write the book?" This led to something that I believe makes the book more personal and brings the reader in. That's what I consider a good editorial suggestion. It's not line-by-line nit-picking, but something more conceptual, and I think suggestions like it can make a big difference in any book.

Something else I tried with this book was in answer to a speech I heard Hazel Rochman give a few years ago. She was talking about the need for more complete source information in today's nonfiction for children and young adults. I thought her point was a good one, not just to authenticate the author's research but also to serve as a guide for a youngster who wanted to explore the topic further. But I don't like footnotes; they annoy me. However, I decided to try something in *Let There Be Light* that I hadn't done before: I provided a chapter-by-chapter listing of sources. Reviewers have commented on these source notes and so have others in the juvenile book world, so I guess they were appreciated.

A&C You've written and talked about the importance of fictional techniques in nonfiction books. Could you talk to us about this, and has your own background with an MFA in creative writing and an interest in play-writing helped you as a writer of nonfiction?

JCG Yes, I feel that my creative writing background has helped me, not only as a writer of nonfiction but also as an editor. Incidentally, I don't think the use of fiction techniques in nonfiction is anything very new, but not many people have talked about it in terms of juvenile nonfiction, at least not in the way I have. I should make one thing clear: I certainly don't mean fictionalized dialogue in biography or any other kind of nonfiction book. That was a trend of past decades but not now. I believe in fictional techniques, but not in fictionalization. What do I mean by fictional techniques? The opening chapter in *From Hand to Mouth*, about eating utensils and table manners is a good example. It shows a group of cave people in Southern France eating meat after a hunt. The details I included are based on descriptions of prehistoric life that I'd read—the clothing, the setting and so forth. I know that these people cooked meat on spits or open fires. I guessed that somebody may have stuck a forked stick into the meat to bring a piece away from the hot fire in order not burn his fingers. But I say it's a guess, and go on to speculate that this may have been the first fork, because it's a fact that people in remote parts of the world still eat with forked sticks today. Sometimes we use them ourselves when eating hot dogs at a picnic. So there's an example of a fictional scene that opens a chapter. When I'm writing a scene like that, I feel like a movie camera coming in for a closeup or pulling back for a longer shot in order to involve the reader.

I think it helps any reader, young or old, to get more interested in a nonfiction book if you focus on people doing things. For example, in *Let There Be Light* I could have written an expository piece detailing how glass was made years ago and left the people out of the process. Instead, I found out that during the Middle Ages men wore leather helmets to protect themselves from the intense heat of the glass-making process. So I have these leather-helmeted men actually making the glass.

The verbs become active instead of passive, and I believe the reader becomes more involved.

A&C How about the hooks that you have at the end of almost all your chapters? Would you call that a fictional technique?

JCG Yes, that's definitely a fictional technique. In my books the hook is usually a question. In *From Hand to Mouth*, for instance, there's one chapter that ends by discussing how the British and people of the Continent developed a way of eating with the fork. I conclude the chapter by saying that on the other side of the Atlantic, in the American colonies, people were developing a very different style of eating. Now that's not a big suspenseful Alfred Hitchcock type of hook, but it sets up a question. If you want to find the answer then you've got to go on to the next chapter. I learned this technique years ago from editing adventure stories by a British author named Arthur Catherall, who was a grand old guy. He's dead now, but kept on writing well into his seventies. Arthur literally had a cliff-hanging ending for every chapter, and it was fun to see how he did it. I'd trim back some of the pounding hearts and blood rushing to people's heads, but you really couldn't wait to go to the next chapter to find out what happened. Arthur had learned how to write that kind of story when he knocked out one adventure yarn after another for *The Boy's Own Paper* and other British magazines in the 1930s and 1940s.

A&C You've got a real knack for finding the humorous anecdote. Could you talk a little about humor and nonfiction? In *From Hand to Mouth*, for example, you include a wonderfully funny section about proper rules for conduct while eating, written by Erasmus in the 1500s. That was a terrific part of the book.

JCG I remember the day I came across that. I was doing research at the Library of Congress in Washington and was making my way through a seemingly endless book on table manners that had been translated from the German. It was terribly dense, but all of a sudden I came to a chapter on early etiquette. When I found those bits of advice from Erasmus, I was sitting by myself in the main reading room of the Library under that great dome and I suddenly began to giggle and several people turned around to stare at me. I tried to stop laughing, but the advice kept getting funnier, and I knew I'd found a little gem. (see Figure 31). The problem comes later when you wonder if other people will think something is as funny as you did. In the end, you have to trust your instincts.

From Hand to Mouth has more humor in it than any of my other books. The subject just seemed to lend itself naturally to humorous incidents. I'm working on a book now that will look at the truth about unicorns. It will also have some marvelously funny material that comes out of the Middle Ages. As far as humor goes, I don't think you can ever force humor in any art form, whether it's a play, a movie, or a novel. I never try to force-feed it into something where it doesn't seem appropriate. At the same time though, I do believe strongly that in any kind of writing, if you're going to have sections that you hope will reach some kind of serious or even tragic peak, you have to set them off, just as life is set off by something amusing, even ludicrous. There can be a pratfall in the middle of disaster, and often is. I think readers appreciate this because it makes what you're writing about seem all the more real.

Figure 31. From Erasmus's *On Civility In Children*.

Erasmus went on to list specific rules for proper conduct while eating. These may seem obvious to us today, but many were new to Erasmus' readers. Here are a few examples:

Take care to cut and clean your fingernails before dining. Otherwise dirt from under the nails may get in the food.

Don't be the first to reach into the pot; only wolves and gluttons do that. And don't put your whole hand into it -- use only three fingers at most.

Take the first piece of meat or fish that you touch, and don't poke around in the pot for a bigger one.

Don't pick your nose while eating and then reach for more food.

Don't throw bones you have chewed back in the pot. Put them on the table or toss them on the floor.

Don't clean your teeth with your knife.

If your fingers become greasy, it is not polite to lick them or wipe them on your coat. Bring a cloth along for this purpose if your host does not provide one. Or else wipe them on the tablecloth.

A&C We're interested in how you verify a fact. For example, in talking about the book *Fireworks, Picnics, and Flags*, you said that you read a story about an old bell ringer who sat in the tower of Independence Hall

---

From *From Hand to Mouth* by James Cross Giblin. Published by Thomas Y. Crowell, 1987, pp. 30–32. Used by permission of William C. Morris, Harper Junior Books Group.

waiting for word that independence had been declared so he could ring the bell. You found that story in two sources, but a third source said that the story wasn't true. You put the tale in the book and called it a good story but not the truth. How do you decide what's true—verification in three sources?

JCG It's a series of spot judgments. I can't really be more specific than that. A nonfiction writer spends a good deal of time weighing facts carefully and bringing all his instincts to bear on the decision of whether or not to believe a particular source. In the case of my book *Chimney Sweeps*, I used several primary sources. I drew a lot of the material about the lives of nineteenth-century British chimney sweeps from actual testimony of climbing boys and master sweeps given before a committee of the House of Lords. I didn't put it all in direct quotes, but it came from primary source material.

The story you referred to about the bell ringer in *Fireworks, Picnics, and Flags* came from secondary sources. I read two or three books that recounted it as fact, but something about it didn't ring true to me. When the American Library Association had their meeting in Philadelphia I used the opportunity to stay over an extra day and do some research. At the Free Library there I found a folder of articles published for the bicentennial. One of them was from the Sunday supplement of the *Philadelphia Inquirer*. A reporter had traced the story of the old bell ringer to a textbook published in 1857 called *Myths and Legends of the Revolution*. The story turned out to be a fictional one written for this anthology directed at upper elementary students. What made me mistrust the story from the beginning, even though two other writers of nonfiction called it fact? It just seemed too neat, and in this instance, my instincts were right.

I will say that it is entirely conceivable that there are things presented as facts in some of my books that aren't true. Perhaps I trusted a source that I shouldn't have. In a book like *Let There Be Light* you will find thousands of facts. An author does the best job he can with the materials available to him and he uses all his instincts. I've developed a kind of second sense over the years, first as an editor and now as a writer of nonfiction. I can pretty well spot it when an author is waffling. You start to be suspicious when you read a passage and find the author uses lots of adjectives and qualifiers and the dates are vague. Whenever I hit a stretch like that I head immediately for another source to fill in the gap and check the facts. When you write books like mine that depend on secondary sources a good deal you are always to some extent dependent on translations and summaries, so you do the best you can to check one source against another if you are suspicious.

A&C Why do you think youngsters read your books? Is it because there's some tie to the curriculum or is it for pleasure?

JCG Probably a combination of the two. I suppose you could say I've been a bit self-indulgent because I start with a subject that appeals to me instead of thinking about the school curriculum. I write for the boy I once was and children like him because I had a great time when I was in the upper elementary grades. The world opened up for me then. I became aware of history, and read avidly. This was during World War II, and of course I read everything I could about what was happening on the various battle fronts. But I also became aware of ancient Egypt and castles at that time. In fact, I find I'm usually drawn to ideas and subjects that I first read about as a child of eleven or twelve. I'm trusting that youngsters like the one I was are still out there. I hope that they'll pick up my books because they want to know more about the Great Wall of China or the plight of chimney sweeps. Then I hope that the illustrations I've gathered for the books will catch the reader's eye and make him want to read the text.

In terms of the school curriculum, I hope that imaginative elementary, junior high, and high school teachers will find various ways to tie my books to the curriculum. A chapter from *Walls* might fit into a unit on war and peace. A chapter from *Milk* might be part of a science or history lesson. *Let There Be Light* recently got a very nice review in the Sunday edition of my hometown paper, *The Cleveland Plain Dealer*. The reviewer spoke to the issue you raise here. Here's a paragraph from the review. "This is a book that does not have to be read from cover to cover to be appreciated. Children can use the index to look up information on everything from African dwellings to Frank Lloyd Wright to learn more about a particular interest or research a topic for school. Or they can just look at pictures and illustrations, pausing to read more about any that catch their eye." I hope all of my books can be used in this way.

A&C Do awards given to nonfiction books lead to increased sales?

JCG Certainly the Newbery Award that went to Freedman's *Lincoln* led to much greater sales than that book would have enjoyed without the award. In general, though, I think most awards have more of a subliminal than a sales effect, and that's true for fiction as well as nonfiction. What does help sales directly is to have a book named to a master list for a state award. It's a truism in the publishing world that if a juvenile book makes the Texas Bluebonnet list it will sell two thousand more copies in Texas. *Chimney Sweeps* was on the Bluebonnet List two years after publication and I can tell you that my royalties for that six-month period were bigger than the period before or after. I've won awards, including the American Book Award for *Chimney Sweeps*, that I don't believe had a direct sales impact. However, an award creates an aura around the book and the author, so that the next book you write is often taken more seriously. That's what I mean by a subliminal effect—and it's a very positive one.

A&C Do you think nonfiction is marketed differently than fiction is?

JCG Yes, because most nonfiction still is bought by school and public libraries. Large chain stores and dozens of new children's bookstores across the country are stocking picture books and fiction, but few nonfiction books for children and young adults are represented in these stores, with the possible exception of some full-color, nonfiction picture books. The kind of books that I write don't seem to have much of a bookstore market. So yes, the marketing efforts for nonfiction are different in that they are still aimed largely at the institutional market. Now we may see this change because of programs like the National Reading Initiative and the trend to teach reading through trade books, including nonfiction. I've heard someone is doing a teacher's guide to go with *Chimney Sweeps*, which is to be used with other paperback trade books in fifth-grade reading classes. I suspect we'd see more of this if we could get other nonfiction books into a paperback format. Up until now, that has seldom happened.

A&C Based on what you just said, could you use your crystal ball and discuss what you see as new trends in nonfiction for the nineties?

JCG I think we're going to see more packaging of all kinds of juvenile trade books for classroom libraries to be used in the teaching of reading and language arts. This trend should help the nonfiction genre by expanding the reading audience. There is a sense that the nineties are going to be *the* decade for children's and young adult trade books. Certainly, Barbara Bush's interest in literacy is encouraging. One friend of mine remarked that, having had eight years of "Just say no to drugs" with Nancy Reagan, maybe we're going to have four or eight years of "Just say yes to literacy" with Barbara Bush. Let's hope it turns out that way.

A&C Are there three or four pieces of nonfiction for juveniles that you consider real touchstone, quality pieces?

JCG Yes, I can think of special nonfiction books at different age levels. For instance on the picture book level, Betsy and Giulio Maestro's book, *The Story of the Statue of Liberty* is very simple and very accessible. Then at the back of the book there's a list of dates connected with the statue and other information for a youngster who's especially interested in the subject. It's very well done and helps to set a standard for nonfiction picture books. Jean Fritz's biographies of our revolutionary leaders from Patrick Henry to Benjamin Franklin are marvelous in the way they focus in on one lively, often humorous facet of the person's life. I'm sure they inspire kids to want to go on later and read more about these people. Russell Freedman's *Lincoln* points in some very interesting directions. First of all, it is very well written and very well and extensively illustrated. *Lincoln* does something else that I hope we can see more of in the nineties; it's a book for adolescents that can be read and enjoyed by adults. A bright ten-year-old can appreciate it, but it also was named a Best Book for Young Adults by A.L.A. Thinking of *Lincoln* and my own book, *Let There Be Light*, I would hope that some of the old boundaries that up until now pigeonholed nonfiction books for various age groups can be broken down in the next ten years. A lot of adults do not want to read nine hundred pages with footnotes on the subject of windows, but they might like my book.

A&C Which of your books are you proudest of, Jim?

JCG The book that I'm always most concerned about is the one that I'm currently working on. That's the one that's most alive to me. To be honest with you, I'm proud of different elements in a lot of my books. Yet, with each book there are things that if I went back I would do differently or I'd try a little harder. The one that pleases me the most in terms of the way all the elements came together—text, pictures, jacket, and design—is *Let There Be Light*.

A&C What do you look for in a good review of a nonfiction book?

JCG I guess first of all what any author hopes for is a reviewer who understands and appreciates what the author was trying to do, what the author tried to build into the book. Like most nonfiction authors, I can respect constructive criticism, both from an editor and a reviewer. That's the way you learn.

With the very visual books that I've been doing lately, I also hope reviewers will appreciate and comment to some degree on the pictures. It's amazing to me in the children's and young adult field how many reviewers comment exclusively on the text, ignoring photos and illustrations even in picture books. A few weeks ago, the *New York Times* reviewed *Let There Be Light*. The three-column review was basically good, but never once did the reviewer mention that the book was illustrated. I didn't consider that a good review, despite the complimentary things said about the

Figure 32. Jacket Illustration from *Let There Be Light*.

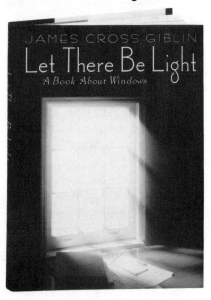

text, because I felt the reviewer should have let the readers know that the book had over seventy illustrations, and commented on them also.

A&C You've recently done a book for adults—*Writing Books for Young People*. In your chapter on nonfiction, you say that when an author writes a nonfiction book for juveniles, the writer ought to have a close focus on a significant aspect of a topic. Does that mean you dismiss books that have a more global focus? What about a book like David Macaulay's *The Way Things Work*?

JCG No, I would never dismiss any type of book, and I think there are always exceptions to every rule. But I do feel my advice is generally valid for today's nonfiction scene. Along with the emphasis on more visual books has come a trend toward a closer focus on one significant aspect of a topic. It used to be that if you wrote a book about explorers for sixth-grade readers, the book might include ten short biographies. Today you'd probably write a separate biography on each explorer. In the case of *The Way Things Work*, I believe the focus in that book is on how a selection of items works. It doesn't pretend to be all-encompassing. And, as I understand it, Macaulay was recently signed to do a series of nonfiction books for younger readers. He'll focus on a single topic in each book.

A&C Did you enjoy writing *Writing Books for Young People*?

JCG Yes, but that book was a real challenge for me. Whether I was writing about how to write nonfiction for juveniles or doing the chapters on fiction and picture books, I wanted to be specific enough to be helpful while at the same time general enough to cover a wide range of topics. It wasn't an easy book to do. As a matter of fact, I found it harder to write *Writing Books for Young People* than any of my non-fiction books for children and young adults. In many ways, it was like writing a novel, because all of the research came out of me and my thirty years' experience as an editor. Along the way, I discovered it was far easier to look up something in a library than to dig down into myself and my memories and shape a book from them.

A&C As a writer of nonfiction for juveniles, what gives you the greatest satisfaction?

JCG Picking a topic that interests and excites me and then exploring and struggling with it to make it clear and interesting to readers—young and old alike. It's tremendously rewarding when the book comes out and you get a sense that readers are finding their interest and curiosity piqued by the subject much as yours were when you began to delve into it. That's what gives me the greatest satisfaction.

BOOKS BY JAMES CROSS GIBLIN

**Chimney Sweeps: Yesterday and Today.* (1982). New York: Thomas Y. Crowell.

Fireworks, Picnics, and Flags: The Story of the Fourth of July Symbols. (1983). New York: Clarion Books.

From Hand to Mouth, Or, How We Invented Knives, Forks, Spoons, and Chopsticks & the Table Manners to Go with Them. (1987). York: Thomas Y. Crowell.

Let There Be Light: A Book about Windows. (1988). New York: Thomas Y. Crowell.

Milk: The Fight for Purity. (1986). New York: Thomas Y. Crowell.

The Skyscraper Book. (1981). New York: Thomas Y. Crowell.

The Truth about Santa Claus. (1985). New York: Thomas Y. Crowell.

Walls: Defenses throughout History. (1984). Boston: Little, Brown.

Writing Books for Young People. (1990). Boston: The Writer.

Giblin, James Cross and Ferguson, Dale. *The Scarecrow Book.* (1980–o.p.) New York: Crown Publishers.

** *Indicates a paperback edition also available*

CHAPTER 11
Format

Up until this point we've stressed purely textual matters—accuracy, style, content, and organization. But books exist as more than extended collections of words. Increasing attention is being given to visuals in the production of outstanding information books. Illustrations, including photographs, line drawings, charts, diagrams, and graphs, are not considered afterthoughts and yanked from available files for last-minute inclusion but, rather, are investigated and printed or commissioned with as much care and forethought as goes into the researching and writing of text. In addition, other physical features—size, pagination, leading, and typeface—all matter in overall appeal and need to be considered when evaluating information books.

ILLUSTRATIONS

After examining the popular information books circulated by local junior high school students, we discovered one salient feature among their selections. All but one, Margaret O. Hyde and Alice D. Outwater's *Addictions: Gambling, Smoking, Cocaine Use and Others*, contain illustrations. While this observation does not presuppose that the presence of illustrations necessarily constitutes a criterion for choice among young adult readers, it, along with the publishing trend to consider graphics as an integral part of a work, does determine that teenagers will encounter illustrations in the information books they read.

But do young adults notice these illustrations? We believe they do. In reporting on the preferences of junior high students involved in the International Reading Association's 1981 Children's Choices's program, Carter and Harris note that positive comments about graphics emerged as the second most frequently mentioned component (after subject) of information books.[1] Similarly, Barbara Samuels' analysis of ballots from the 1987 Young Adult Choices' list concludes that illustrated volumes received favorable reactions on individual ballots as well as in the overall voting. In fact, Samuels notes that the "number one vote getter" in the southwest region was Timothy Ferris's handsomely illustrated

Spaceshots: The Beauty of Nature beyond Earth, a book students enthusiastically described as "superb," "stupendous," "great," "beautiful," and "incredible."[2]

Yet, unlike mountains, illustrations inspire and challenge for reasons other than the declarative "because they're there." Not just any picture will do. The photographs in *Spaceshots*, for instance, represent stunning graphics carefully selected, artistically and thematically arranged into a coherent whole, and expertly printed on high-quality paper. This favored book serves as a reminder that illustrations require evaluation not just in terms of their existence, but rather through their effectiveness: their relationship to text, position on the page, presence of captions, and appropriateness of content.

Photographs

Black-and-white photographs appear more frequently in informational books than any other kind of graphic. Sometimes they materialize as routine filler that provides a diversionary break in the reading process, but are placed in a book with little forethought or attention to overall design, vision, or content. At other times, the photographs overpower the text. We've found dramatic illustrations of erupting volcanoes, gritty goal line defenses, and daring rescues at sea accompanied by insipid, factually laden prose. Neither kind of book works as a unit. Like the components of picture storybooks, text and illustrations in information books should fuse to produce a total far superior to its individual parts.

In *Journey to the Planets* Patricia Lauber creates that near-perfect partnership between text and illustrations. The photograph of Callisto, one of the moons of Jupiter, shows a weathered sphere which, through its craters and imperfections, resembles an ancient Roman coin. Reference to the moon's "battered face" and primordial origins complement the photograph, while the picture, in turn, extends these archaeological metaphors from the text. Similarly, Lauber's description of Ganymede, another of Jupiter's sixteen satellites, with "groves and ridges that look as if they had been made by a giant rake,"[3] comes alive through the accompanying *Voyager* photograph of the moon's surface, an uneven landscape that conjures up images of the tortured swirls on a van Gogh canvas. (see Figure 33). Yet these stunning illustrations would lose their power in other contexts. Lauber has gone far beyond the mechanical task of placing a picture in a book simply to break up chunks of text or to provide identification. In these two instances, she has unerringly chosen the precise illustrations to illuminate her elegant prose.

Effective, carefully selected photographs offer more than simple identification of objects and people. They hold the potential of underscoring themes, activating emotions, suggesting tangential knowledge, and challenging readers to think about and question the images they see

Figure 33. Voyager 1 Photographs of Jovian Satellites Callisto and Ganymede

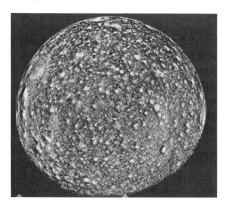

before them. James Cross Giblin's talent for choosing such multifaceted graphics is clearly evident in Figure 34, a photograph reproduced from *Let There Be Light: A Book about Windows*. Showing an extended frontier family of numerous wives and youngsters, along with a hodge-podge of their possessions arranged in front of a tiny, log dwelling, this picture invites the reader to contemplate the physical and social consequences of the family's day-to-day living. In addition, Giblin's understated caption—"A Mormon family in frontier Utah gathers in front of their log cabin, which boasts a large, new glass window"[4]—allows a glimpse of his sly wit and provides a delightful reward for careful readers.

Captions prove just as important as photographs, and writers and book designers will elect to deal with them in one of three ways. They can use simple descriptive or identifying phrases, detailed explanations, or eliminate them all together. Depending on the circumstances—topic, text, and selection of photographs—their choices may turn out either brilliantly or dreadfully. Book selectors will have to form their own opinions concerning the effectiveness of the resulting captions and the appropriateness of their placement in each individual book they encounter.

Generally, captions should appear with illustrations. The endearing photograph of two young boys that appears in Russell Freedman's *Children of the Wild West* needs, and has, a caption explaining what they are doing. In this case, the simple, declarative phrase—"Gathering cow chips"[5]—clears up ambiguities in the illustration by telling readers exactly what the boys are carrying (see Figure 35). The caption concentrates on one salient feature, and doesn't elaborate or overwhelm

Used by permission of NASA.

Figure 34. A Mormon family in frontier Utah, gathers in front of their log cabin, which boasts a large, new glass window.

readers with irrelevant minutiae by noting that the tub handles are made of rope, that the boys are the sons of Mr. and Mrs. George Dew, or that their ranch is located in Cherry County, Nebraska.

Since their attention isn't diverted by such detail, adolescents are free to use their own perceptions to draw historical, cultural, and sociological inferences concerning the boys' dress, surroundings, and responsibilities. That the children must contribute to household chores at an early age and have jobs, which include what for them is heavy labor, suggests that the family is one of limited means. Their broad-brimmed hats indicate that the sun beats down on the hot, Kansas plain, while the absolute desolation of their surroundings provides a stark example of the monotonous terrain that marked the early home-steads of many of our ancestors. That Freedman doesn't try to block such speculation through a detailed, explanatory caption underscores his gift of understanding what to point out and what to leave alone. He tells readers what they need to know, but doesn't intrude on their observations.

Rather than adopting a standard form and strictly adhering to it throughout her book, author Barbara Rogasky wisely allows each photograph and map to dictate its own caption in *Smoke and Ashes: The*

Figure 35. Gathering Cow Chips.

Story of the Holocaust. Some illustrations, like the full portrait of Adolf Hitler, merely require simple phrases for identification. Others demand more detailed background explanations. For example, Rogasky includes photographs of two teenagers involved in Hitler Youth whose features are perfectly clear, but whose motivations need further amplification, which she provides in two expanded captions. In still other instances, Rogasky eliminates captions altogether, and indirectly asks young adults to really look at her stark black-and-white illustrations and ask themselves "What's happening here?" A sense of the terror, cruelty, misery, and violence that was the Holocaust begins to register as readers reconstruct the action while turning page after page. And even those photographs that we've seen innumerable times before, like the haunting image of that innocent youngster raising his hands in surrender in the Warsaw ghetto, still force us to examine them anew. If that is our reaction, imagine how much more powerfully these illustrations must affect young adults encountering them for the first time.

While Philip M. Isaacson consecutively numbers the ninety-three color photographs appearing in *Round Buildings, Square Buildings, &*

Buildings that Wiggle Like a Fish, he does not intend for these numerals to stand as the sole descriptors for his illustrations. He devotes the body of his book to detailed and pointed explanations of key features found in each photograph, and uses the numbers merely for referencing a particular picture. In this case, captions do not appear in their normal positions underneath or adjacent to the photographs themselves but, rather, serve as the text for Isaacson's book. The combination of prose and illustrations suggests a lecture accompanied by carefully chosen slides.

On the surface, it would seem reasonable to demand that all photographs meet minimal standards and contain sharp lines, focused images, and perfectly arranged subjects. Yet, when looking at book after book depicting airplanes in cloudless skies, animals in stereotypical poses, and workers hovering around office computers with no evident deadline pressures, one longs for a little discord. Where are the thunder clouds, the remnants of last night's dinner, or the paper wads and disposable coffee cups? These elements reflect reality, and should surely appear in some of the books recommended to young adults. In addition, to demand that photographers use the perfect f-stop or the most exact light meter or the steadiest hand would eliminate some of history's most powerful images, such as the stills reproduced from the 8mm footage of the Kennedy assassination fortuitously taken by a tense amateur, or the murky images from World War II concentration camps obtained surreptitiously by daring observers. In these cases the immediacy of the photographs far outweighs their technical flaws.

Yet books that contain photographs from situations in which photographers have control over their settings should unquestionably reflect professional standards. Mathew Brady's studio portrait of Abraham Lincoln would not have been chosen by Russell Freedman for the cover of *Lincoln: A Photobiography* had Brady jiggled the camera or failed to include the top of Lincoln's head in his picture.

In most cases, photographs of unknown or unusual subjects should establish a sense of size by including familiar, relational objects in the visual field. Figure 36 from Sue Burchard's *The Statue of Liberty: Birth to Rebirth*, not only shows how the head of the Statue of Liberty was displayed at the 1878 Paris Exposition, but also allows the young adult who has never seen the statue a feeling for its enormity by including trees in the background and a park bench in the foreground as elements for comparison. Even those books that employ microphotography, like Lisa Grillone and Joseph Gennaro's *Small Worlds Close Up*, aid the curious reader by first photographing the object in its natural size and then offering a magnification for comparison.

Figure 36. Enormous Head of Statue of Liberty Photographed in Relation to Familiar Objects.

Drawings

Line drawings and reproductions of original art provide another dimension to graphics in information books. In order to be effective, they must function not as mere decoration but, rather, serve to clarify, extend, or personalize the text. Such standards cause one to dismiss inappropriate or generic drawings, like the all-purpose navigator decked out in Elizabethan finery that accompanies many text and trade books on early exploration. Evaluators must also address nonfunctional as well as nonspecific drawings, rendering useless, for example, a detailed Sioux teepee inserted in a chapter describing the Battle of Little Big Horn.

Occasionally, however, illustrations that do not clarify, extend, or personalize text may still function as vital elements in informational books. The cartoon-like figures that accompany Claudine G. Wirths and Mary Bowman-Kruhm's *I Hate School* neither magnify nor interpret the information presented. At best they spotlight certain, although not necessarily crucial, points in the text. They still serve an important purpose. As was pointed out in Chapter 9, the primary audience for this particular work consists of less able readers. If these young adults feel intimidated by the task of reading this book, then they will never pick it up in the first place, and one avenue of communication on a vital subject will remain closed to them. The more nonthreatening the book appears, the more quickly the possibilities increase that these targeted readers will indeed open it. In this case, the illustrations, along with the question/answer organizational structure, parallel the authors' vision and intent. Together these features serve as formatting tools by breaking up potentially intimidating prose and suggesting an inoffensive assignment for the reluctant reader.

Figure 37. Both placement and design of Patti Stren's illustrations in *I Hate School* contribute to the nonthreatening format.

Illustrations must always complement young adults' experiential backgrounds rather than supplement adult knowledge. Cartoons in computer books that relate to the world of business lose their punch when delivered to a teenage audience. Similarly, political cartoons, like the masterly satires of Thomas Nast, serve as fillers rather than pointed

From *I Hate School* by Claudine G. Wirths and Mary Bowman-Kruhm. Illus. Copyright © 1987 by Patti Stren. Published by Thomas Y. Crowell, 1987. Used by permission of William C. Morris, Harper Junior Books Group.

examples, unless they are accompanied by extended explication when included in books aimed at younger adolescents.

Artists' illustrations that consider both audience and text, however, prove invaluable. Books on the prehistoric world, for instance, often rely on a visual recreation and interpretation of events in order to portray cave dwellings, dinosaurs, or early humans. Frequently book designers will mix media in such works and include accompanying photographs of fossils or archaeological sites. These supplementary illustrations serve an important function, for they begin to show young adult readers the raw materials from which archaeologists and artists draw their conclusions, and by either implication or direct instruction, part of the process of reconstructing the past. If such photographs do not appear with drawings and paintings in these books, then the text should oblige the curious by providing similar information.

A few outstanding works, like David Macaulay's *Mill* and Peter Parnell's *The Daywatchers*, remind readers that some authors need search no further than their own studios in order to find a gifted illustrator whose artistic vision and skill will perfectly balance their texts. These fine author/illustrators set the standards for others in the field, and their unique contributions need to be examined separately, for their illustrations solicit an aesthetic response from the reader and thus expand their function far beyond the informative. That is what art should do, and it is what these artists do well. Their books provide young adults with more than vehicles for identifying buildings or birds. Instead, they accent the drama and passion in knowing and seeing.

These two books attract potential readers from the moment they pick them up. Both dust jackets make powerful statements. The cover of Macaulay's work shows a nineteenth-century stone mill undergoing renovation. This drawing invites the curious to tour the construction site, while the size of the volume (9½ x 12¼″) hints at the majesty of this production. Similarly, the jacket on Peter Parnell's *The Daywatchers* dramatically showcases a peregrine falcon rising above a gold disk. Is it the sun? Is he outside it, above it, part of it, or is this golden orb part of him? Clearly Parnell implies that this extraordinary creature embodies greatness, demands respect, and excites passion.

These books don't simply tantalize. They promise readers drama, excitement, pleasure, and beauty, and they deliver it. The illustrations inside emphasize point of view, purpose, and feeling as surely as does text. Macaulay's aerial perspective in some drawings indicates the mills' settings and relationship to the surrounding countryside, while the detailed construction plans and notations show the union of raw materials, technology, and design, and their corresponding relationships to the buildings. The purpose of this work is not to show young adults about bricks and boards but, rather, to demonstrate the impact of a structure on a community, and its resulting place in history.

**Figure 38. Jacket Cover
Illustration from *Mill*.**

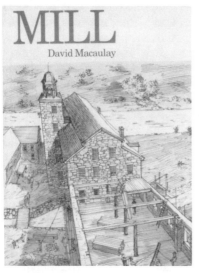

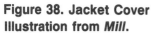

David Macaulay

Parnell eloquently sets his goals in the introduction, stating that his purpose in writing and illustrating is to convey his impressions about nature in general and birds of prey in particular, "portraying this feeling—not every feather, but the character, the aura, of the creatures, whatever those qualities are that set them apart from the chicken and the mole."[6] His detailed drawings of beaks, feathers, and talons reveal the various evolutionary differences between each species, while the sprawling portraits of eagles, falcons, owls, and hawks show off these animals in their natural habitat. Able to impart both the concrete and the conceptual through his illustrations, Parnell encourages young adults to look at his birds, not to see, but to behold, to wonder about their characteristics and their place in nature, and finally to begin to understand the communication in art as well as the power of ornithology.

If we wanted teenagers to know what a prototypical mill looks like, we could provide them with a photograph; they could locate the building and make numerous generalizations about it. If we wanted young adults to correctly identify various birds, we could give them an appropriate field guide. But, to paraphrase a Chinese proverb, *Mill* and *The Daywatchers* allow them to see not the building or the bird in the picture, but rather the picture, with all its corresponding drama, excitement and passion, in the mill and the animal.[7]

Like their photographic counterparts, illustrations of unknown subjects should include some familiar background objects so readers can determine their relative size. In most cases, this factor is addressed through an artist's sense of proportion. Occasionally, it's not. In Helen Roney Sattler's *Dinosaurs of North America*, for example, artist Anthony Rao draws some of his animals in isolation, without including local flora and fauna to provide clues as to relative size. Although Sattler painstakingly describes the general measurements of these creatures, like Euoplocephalus, which averaged 18 feet or 5.5 meters tall and 8 feet or 2.5 meters wide, young adults may well need the additional visual anchors in order to really understand the size of Euoplocephalus.

On the other hand, David Peters' *Giants of Land, Sea & Air: Past and Present* masterfully treats size as both topic and theme. The book concerns giants: the largest species of extinct animals and the biggest individual on record for those creatures of the modern world. Peters draws all his objects to the same scale, 1 inch = 22½ inches. But even in this oversized book, measuring 9½ x 13," Peters cannot retain his scale and fit all of his animals on a single page, or even on a full double-page spread. To show these giants, Peters visually and physically extends his pages. In drawing the giant squid and the whale shark, he not only covers both the left- and right-hand pages of a double-page spread with a single figure, but he allows the tail of each animal to wrap around the right-hand side, continuing on the following page. The overlapping figures form a horizontal line which runs throughout the book. Some of his figures are so big that even this design proves inadequate, and in order to showcase exceptionally large animals, Peters further manipulates the book's design. For the illustrations of the gargantuan blue whale and Apatosaurus, he introduces accordion pull-out pages, thereby extending the size of his canvas by an additional book width.

Peters also recognizes that even with this attention to design and detail readers may well encounter difficulties in comprehending the largeness of some animals, so he visually anchors every double-page spread with a man and a woman, both drawn to the same scale as the animals are. Readers can thus begin to understand the relationship of the size of the animals to themselves.

Paper Engineering

In *Giants*, David Peters manipulates format by introducing pull-out pages in order to accommodate his drawings. Once such a device was thought to be the province of the playroom. In 1983, with the publication of Jonathan Miller's *The Human Body* and Patrick Moore's *The Space Shuttle*, "movable books" began appearing in young adult classrooms and library collections. At that time, these two well-known and respected authors meshed their talents with book designers and utilized state-of-the-art paper engineering to produce movable books aimed at young adult readers. Teenagers could simulate the movement of the parts of the body, not by flipping transparencies like they once did with high school biology texts, but by pulling tabs, turning wheels, and maneuvering overlays of substance. They could read about the parts of the ear, and they could also produce sound. In the same way they could recreate liftoff, docking, and orbiting of the space shuttle. Using both print and tactical experimentation, they were able to simulate the building of a colony in space.

Figure 39. Human divers provide perspective for the giant squid drawn by David Peters in *Giants*. Note that some tentacles wrap around the following page.

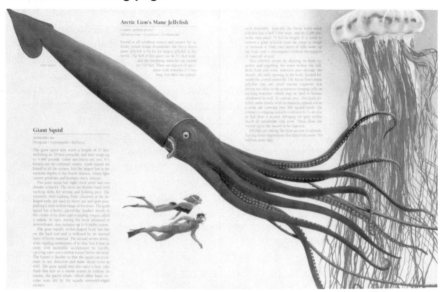

That's what they *could* do. The question is, though: Is that how young adults actually respond to these books, or do they merely use them as convenient outlets for diversion? That's precisely what the two of us wondered in 1985, after numerous movable books targeted for teenagers began to appear on publishers' lists. In order to find out, we placed eighteen such works in one junior high school, and asked the students to fill out response forms on the books they circulated.

What did these youngsters tell us? Some of the student responses focused on the illustrations, describing them as "realistic and nicely detailed"; "interesting from the fact that you can see what a person is talking about"; and that they "showed detail and perspective better than normal paper pictures could."

Others rejected books like *The Royal Family Pop-up Book* that merely use paper engineering to enliven otherwise dull volumes. They characterized such works as "silly" or, most damning of all, "maybe O.K. for younger kids." The fact that design needed to complement and expand subject in order to produce an interesting work didn't go unnoticed. Comments such as "I never knew the eye worked that way"; "It shows the computer and tells what each part does"; and "It shows how frogs use their powerful legs" clearly indicate that both content and form triggered favorable reaction.

Content matters. No amount of drama in the illustrations can rescue trivial subjects. The main reason *The Facts of Life* and *The Universe* have received both critical and popular acclaim—they appeared as Best Books for Young Adults in 1985—is that the graphics exist for a reason: They help explain difficult concepts such as DNA or the Big Bang theory.

Although paper engineering may well overshadow the text, it must always supplement it. Because of space restrictions in such works, text exists as little more than expanded captions. Therefore, this explanatory prose must be concise and abbreviated. Clever formatting, like the pull-out wedges hidden between the pages of *The Universe*, may allow additional space for further text, but they don't substitute for rambling or unfocused explanations.

Figure 40. Pull out wedges in *The Universe* allow for extra text without compromising the dramatic paper mechanics.

Well-constructed pop-up books are not toys. For some young adults they unquestionably spell reading motivation, while for others they provide just the right mode for explaining a difficult concept. One youngster summed up both features with this comment: "The book's real neat, and the best learning book I have ever seen."

Layout

Layout positively or negatively influences a potential reader's initial perceptions of a book. Artfully spaced graphics, generous margins, and lined borders invite browsing, while small type, minimal margins, and

From the *Universe* by Heather Couper and David Pelham. Reprinted by permission of Random House, Inc.

poorly placed or nonexistent illustrations suggest a utilitarian presentation of material. That these perceptions may prove false doesn't matter, for they nonetheless shape young adults' initial attitudes toward the books they choose to read and may well decide whether a book circulates or remains forever on the library shelf. A well-laid-out book delivers a subtle message: A lot of time and care has gone into producing this book. As a reader, it's worth your consideration.

The size of the photograph and its placement on the page also determine the overall visual effect. A postage-stamp picture of the Grand Canyon or Mount Rushmore certainly fails to capture the grandeur of these wonders, while a full-page close-up of an ordinary paper clip seems a pointless waste of space. But when size and subject correspond, the resulting illustration can make a powerful statement.

The expert eye that designed Knopf's new nonfiction series, *Eyewitness Books*, deserves special mention in this section. Line drawings, artistic reproductions, diagrams, and sharp color photographs are all artfully arranged on the pages for visual appeal as shown in Figure 41. Designed as a series of single- and double-page spreads, with each covering one facet of an overall topic, these books offer an enticing introduction to a variety of subjects, including shells, early humans, mammals, birds, trees, music, butterflies and moths, ponds and rivers, arms and armor, and the skeleton. The combination of colors, shapes, and textures makes each book a pleasure to look at, while the minimal text entries add interesting and informative details.

The very layout of Jim Arnosky's *Flies in the Water, Fish in the Air: A Personal Introduction to Fly Fishing* reinforces the word "personal" in the subtitle. In his text, Arnosky lovingly recreates his days astream and introduces young adults to his favorite sport as well as his genuine pleasure in the outdoor world. But it is through his margin illustrations—soft, flawlessly executed line drawings of fish, water, bugs, flies, and equipment—that readers best get a feel for the diary-like qualities of this particular book. These sketches, depicted in Figure 42, personalize Arnosky's experiences, subtly reminding the reader that he really saw that northern water-thrush, indeed blew on the wings of a waterlogged bumblebee, and certainly observed mayflies emerging as adult "duns" and later molting into sexually mature "spinners."

In some instances, book designers will group illustrations together into several, special sections spaced throughout the book or as a single, center signature. Whatever the design, the reason for it is usually technical, for more often than not, such groupings are printed on high-gloss pages which differ from the materials used in the body of the book. Different types of paper serve different functions. Text glares when printed on vellum, and photographic originals lose their luster

Figure 41. Taken from the *Eyewitness* book *Sports*, this layout is typical of the mixed media used throughout the series.

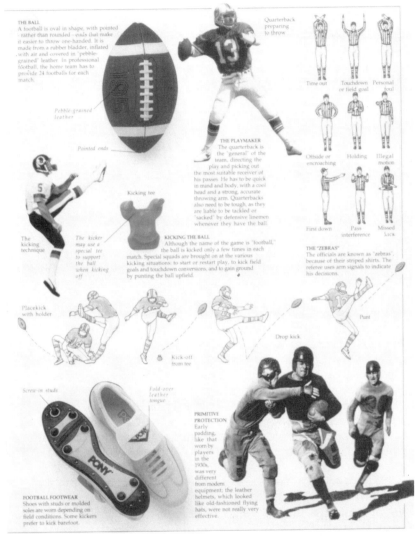

when reproduced on paper with the high rag content more suitable for text. In addition, plastic-based vellum doesn't stand up well to extended, hard use. It retains fingerprints and ballpoint pen marks, two by-products of heavy use by young adult readers. Thus, books dependent on text are most frequently printed on paper with a high rag content, and those more dependent on photographs on heavier, glossier surfaces. As a compromise—to best show off certain prints, or to inject color into a

From *Sports* by Tim Hammond. Copyright © 1988 Dorling Kindersley Limited, London. Reprinted by permission of Random House, Inc.

Figure 42. From *Flies in the Water, Fish in the Air* by Jim Arnosky.

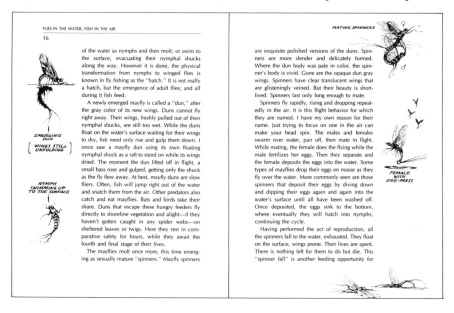

black-and-white text—publishers will often elect to use special plates. The resulting illustrations are frequently referenced in the text, making it awkward for readers to keep their place, as well as their train of thought, as they flip back and forth between illustrations and prose.

Occasionally, though, this grouping of illustrations works to the reader's advantage. In Feldbaum and Bee's *Looking the Tiger in the Eye: Confronting the Nuclear Threat*, the two illustrated sections serve as pictorial summations for previous chapters, and in Giblin's *Let There Be Light: A Book about Windows*, the special color sequence of stained-glass windows rewards the reader with a dramatic, visual treat.

Diagrams

Like studio photographs, diagrams should also contain sharp, clear lines. Since their very purpose is to represent specific facts, figures, or theories that authors feel need visual clarification, there's no room for abstract art or impressionistic interpretations. Figure 43, a representative diagram from the *Facts on File Visual Dictionary*, an unusual lexicon that relies on pictures rather than text for its definitions, adheres to these standards. The twenty-six components of a castle are clearly

---

From *Flies in the Water, Fish in the Air* by Jim Arnosky, copyright © 1986. Reprinted by permission of Lothrop, Lee & Shepard (a division of William Morrow & Co.).

labeled, the unadorned type is easy to read, and the simple illustration is devoid of unnecessary frills that might potentially confuse the reader. Like all the diagrams in the *Facts on File Visual Dictionary*, this one succeeds in illuminating points for readers rather than obscuring them.

Figure 43. The Parts of a Castle from *Facts on File Visual Dictionary*.

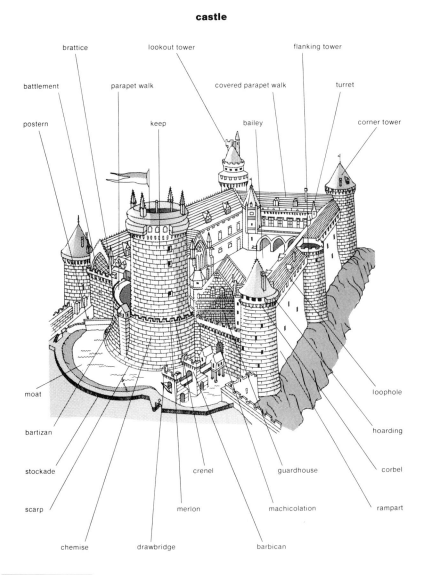

castle

From *The Facts on File Visual Dictionary* by Jean-Claude Corbeil. Copyright © 1988 by Editions Quebec/Amerique, Inc. Reprinted with the permission of Facts on File, Inc.

Charts

Charts function as efficient organizers of like information. The diameter, distance from the sun, and number of satellites of the planets in our solar system; the population figures, types of government, and major imports and exports of the countries of Africa; and the individual events, the names of the athletes, and the number of gold medals won by each nation competing in the Olympics, could all be displayed as three, separate charts. By using these aids, young adults can locate specific facts quickly and make comparisons between each planet, country, or Olympic team.

Charts also highlight factual information which might otherwise bog down the reader if presented in a series of sentences. Had Barbara Rogasky, author of *Smoke and Ashes: The Story of the Holocaust*, chosen to write about the death camps in the following manner, her readers might well gloss over this series of facts as they accustomed themselves to a repetitive pattern: At Chelmno there were 360,000 victims and 3 survivors; at Belzec there were 600,000 victims and 2 survivors; at Sobibor there were 250,000 victims and 64 survivors; at Treblinka there were 800,000 victims and fewer than 40 survivors; at Maidanek there were 500,000 victims and under 600 survivors; and at Auschwitz there were 1.5 million to 2 million victims and, because Auschwitz served as both a concentration and a death camp, several thousand survivors.

But, notice how powerfully the following chart (Figure 44) forces the reader's eye, and thoughts, on the same information.

Figure 44. Chart from *Smoke and Ashes: The Story of the Holocaust* by Barbara Rogasky.

CAMP	VICTIMS	SURVIVORS
Chelmno	360,000	3
Belzec	600,000	2
Sobibor	250,000	6 4
Treblinka	800,000	Under 40
Maidanek	500,000	Under 600
Auschwitz	1,500,000 to 2,000,000	Several thousand because it was both a concentration and a death camp

By organizing her material into a clear table centered on the page, Rogasky demands the reader's attention, allowing these potentially numbing facts to forcefully speak for themselves.

Graphs

Like charts, graphs organize information displaying comparisons between like elements. To do this effectively, however, each segment—whether a bar, a line, or a piece of the pie—must remain distinct from the others. Both the X and Y axes must be clearly labeled. And finally, the type of graph should reflect the best representation of subject matter. Bar graphs display distinct elements of a whole, pie graphs indicate unity, and line graphs connote trends.

One further point needs to be considered when evaluating the effectiveness of graphs: Does the subject really warrant pictorial treatment? A simple graph showing an aggregate total serves no purpose. In a bar graph, for example, the figure would translate into a single vertical line, looking for all the world like a giant monolith. That information is better presented as a factual statement.

Maps

The shocking results of the 1988 Gallup poll commissioned by the National Geographic Society clearly indicates that Americans demonstrate a disturbing lack of knowledge about landforms; place names; and the relative location of countries, continents, cities, towns, rivers, and oceans. When we consider the fact that even a United States President could confuse the geographical location of Poland, the importance of featuring maps in books for young adults becomes apparent. Therefore, the absence of a map in Carolyn Meyer and Charles Gallenkamp's *The Mystery of the Ancient Maya* is startling, for quite possibly part of the intended audience may not even be aware in which hemisphere the Maya lived.

Maps can serve one of two functions. First of all, they can identify place, size, and physical attributes of particular landforms. And second, they can act as distribution diagrams, indicating products, population figures, voting patterns, types of industries, social services, troop occupations, mean income of families, and the like. Whatever their purpose, maps must help, not hinder, the reading process. Therefore, artists should keep each map relatively simple and not crowd too many elements into a single design. In addition, maps should be drawn with clear lines; employ appropriate symbols for products; utilize legible marks for boundaries; and, considering the paucity of information concerning geographic details, indicate a scale of miles.

Although the map reproduced in Figure 45 lacks a scale, it effectively shows the cities and towns Rita Gelman visited for *Inside Nicaragua*. In addition, the inset indicates the relative position of this country to the United States. Its prominent placement at the beginning of the book further serves as a proper introduction for the text while also allowing for ready reference: Turning back to the beginning of the book to clarify a place name constitutes a much simpler task than searching for a map within the text.

Figure 45. Map showing relative location of Nicaragua from *Inside Nicaragua*.

By way of contrast, the map included in Judith St. George's *The Panama Canal* does not prove nearly as effective, even though it does include a scale of miles. It adequately shows Panama, the isthmus, and the neighboring countries of Costa Rica in Central America and Colombia in South America. But it shows Panama's position in the Caribbean only and fails to include the Pacific coast of either Mexico or the United States, a relationship young adults must visualize in order to understand why the site was selected for a canal in the first place. The map depicts Florida quite clearly, but not California, home of several ports equally important in the overall plan for northwestern South America.

Occasionally, location maps provide a touchstone for those books that cross geographical boundaries or cover unfamiliar territory. Milton Meltzer's *Rescue: The Story of How Gentiles Saved Jews in the Holocaust* contains a detailed frontispiece map of Europe under Nazi occupation. In addition to these political divisions, the map clearly labels the places Meltzer mentions in his text. Meltzer's tale travels from Germany to Poland to the Ukraine to France to Denmark to Hungary to Italy and on to Holland and Belgium. To help keep this journey straight in the minds of young adult readers, each chapter contains an appropriate inset from the original, larger map. Just as Meltzer's text discusses an important piece of history, his maps provide an equally important geography lesson.

Like graphs and charts, distribution maps allow readers to conceptually organize related information. Alan E. Nourse's revised edition of *AIDS* includes the following map showing the number of AIDS cases recorded by the Center of Disease Control through the end of October 1988.

In this case, the map emerges as the best medium for displaying the information. A chart would contain fifty-three vertical entries, and a graph depicting the same information would reproduce as a crowded mass of figures, much too complicated for quick comprehension. But the map not only presents the information clearly, it also allows for geographical comparisons. We suspect that most readers will first look at their home states to see the number of reported cases, but after that initial search they can also begin to answer questions like "Where are the most (or least) reported cases?" "What do these areas have in common?" and "Why does AIDS appear to cluster in some spots and not in others?"

Young adults encounter illustrations in the information books they read. By thoughtfully evaluating these graphics, teachers and librarians can help young adults exploit these valuable tools.

SIZE

Remember the old riddle that asks and answers the question: "How long does a piece of string have to be to reach to the moon? Just long enough to get there." Much of the same logic applies to the size of a particular book. Books need to be long enough to contain text and large

Figure 46. Map Showing Geographical Distribution of Reported AIDS Cases.

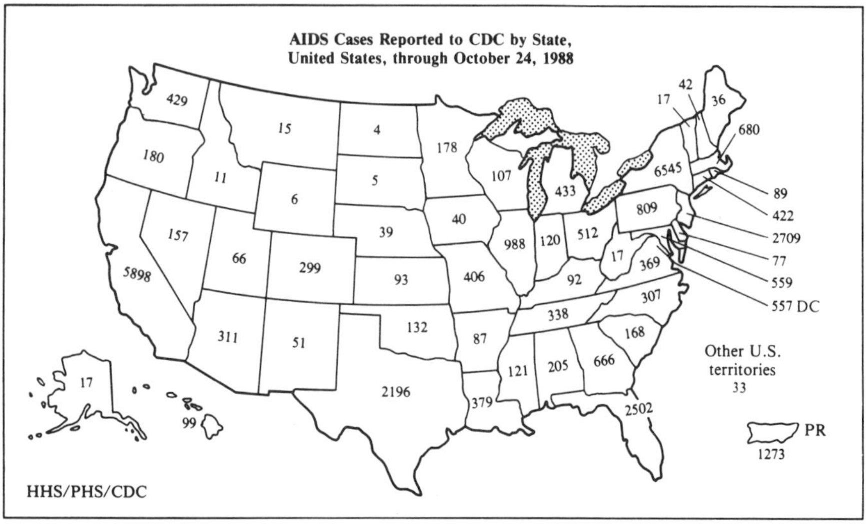

AIDS Cases Reported to CDC by State, United States, through October 24, 1988

429   15   4   178   17 42 36   680
180   11   5   107   6545
6   39   40   433   809   89
157   66   299   988 120 512   17   369   422
5898   93   406   92   2709
311   51   132   338   307   77
87   168   559
17   121 205 666   557 DC
2196   379   2502
99

Other U.S. territories 33

PR 1273

HHS/PHS/CDC

enough to showcase illustrations. But the question of size also involves further considerations. If a book is too long, will it discourage teenage readers? If it is too short, will it appear remedial? If a book is too wide, will it look like a "baby book?" If it is too narrow, will it resemble a toy? Like Goldilocks sampling the three bears' porridge, each book must find the size that is just right.

Except for series books, like the *Eyewitness Books* from Knopf or the *Impact Books* from Watts, where size must remain a constant, physical dimensions will differ from book to book. Although the variations found in any young adult library collection may pose shelving problems, they nonetheless strengthen the perception that individual books exist as distinct and unique works. Jane Steltenpohl, editorial director at Julian Messner, admits that she always considers these physical features from the beginning of a book's life, for knowing how a book will look constitutes as much a part of editing as finding an appropriate structure for the prose. When planning for Guido Dingerkus's book *The Shark Watchers' Guide*, for example, Steltenpohl retained a vision of the finished product as short and wide; she wanted it to suggest the rough dimensions of a fish. With measurements of 9 x 7½″ and a blackish-green cover that appears to come straight out of the ocean's depths, it does.

Similarly, the 10½x 9¼″ dimensions of Russell Freedman's *Buffalo Hunt* resemble an artist's portfolio, an appropriate metaphor considering the fact that the illustrations are reproductions of famous Western artists such as George Catlin, Karl Bodmer, and Charles Russell, as well as of Native American artists. Subject and size also correspond in David Peters' 9½ x 13″ book *Giants of Land, Sea & Air: Past & Present*. The large format emphasizes the giant animals, as design and subject complement one another.

Along with these design considerations emerges the all-important factor of audience: How will young adults perceive a particular work? Teenagers develop all sorts of built-in perceptions about books. Librarians and teachers know, for example, that adolescents prefer mass-market paperback editions to hardbacks, and they've all encountered those young adults who know—with that unshakable certainty of adolescence—that short books are easy and long books are hard to read. Yet, by examining the two hundred most frequently checked-out information books from among our three thousand junior high students, we could find absolutely no correlation between size and frequency of circulation, except in series books. Out of these two hundred books, eighty-six different sizes were represented. There were, however, some limits. The smallest book circulated measured 5⅓ x 7,¾″ while the largest was 9¼ x 11½.″ Smaller books were simply not available, while larger volumes, particularly outsized atlases, failed to circulate with enough regularity to appear on the list.

Falling on the low end of that range were *First Books*, from Franklin Watts, a series originally intended for upper elementary students. As this series evolved, several volumes began to contain content also appropriate for teenagers. But the size of the books, each measuring 7⅛ x 8½,″ presented a problem with older students. While these teenagers could well profit from the information, they couldn't gain any points with their peers when carrying a book with large type, box-like dimensions, and generous margins. Consequently, Franklin Watts decided to create a new series, *Venture Books*, to accommodate the titles appropriate for the junior/senior high student, packaging them in the same size (6 x 9″) and format of their more readily acceptable *Impact Books* series.

We offer no standards for pagination. Although the average number of pages for all volumes in our study was 124, this figure means little when we consider that the most frequently circulated book, *The Guinness Book of World Records*, contains over 600 pages, and books with a scant 64 pages circulated as frequently as did their longer counterparts. Possibly because of the illustrations, which break up continuous text; the certainty that they can choose to read selected portions of any given book; or high interest in a given subject matter, young adults do not shy away from long nonfiction books. It appears that overall length matters little in circulation patterns.

TYPE SIZE

Typography influences both the readability and appearance of a book. Books directed to young children, just developing their perceptual skills, frequently employ slightly outsized type, but such considerations aren't germane for young adults. According to early research by Miles Tinker and Donald Patterson, type size that falls between the ranges of nine and twelve points represents the standard and is the easiest to read. Deviations from this norm, even into the larger type sizes, hinder rather than help the reading process.

Although adults don't have to measure the type in every book they evaluate, a general frame of reference may help in deciding the appropriateness of individual books. Below are some examples of standard type sizes that should provide a point of reference for recognizing conventional typography:

This sentence is set in 9 point type.

This sentence is set in 10 point type.

This sentence is set in 11 point type.

This sentence is set in 12 point type.

Occasionally book designers will go outside these limits, but seldom does such a decision prove wise in nonillustrated volumes of continuous text. Books requiring extended reading should contain standard typography. The one exception to this rule occurs with books that provide directions. If young adults will be reading and simultaneously performing some task, like baking cookies, copying a computer program, or building a model rocket, then type size should be larger to facilitate both activities. There is nothing more distracting than to have to hunt around for the next step amid lines of prose when a reader is right in the middle of a project. Consequently, numbered, offset directions with enlarged type are perfectly acceptable elements in such books.

COVERS

Frequently little choice exists in bindings, for nonfiction books may be available only in trade paperbacks or paper-on-boards editions. The durability in publishers' library bindings render them preferable. On the other hand, sturdy, bound-to-stay-bound coverings are excessive. Despite their strength, in too many instances they will far outlive the usefulness of their contents. It is unfortunate that spiral-bound volumes receive apparent disfavor in library and classroom collections, because these prove particularly appropriate for how-to books. How much better it is to open a spiral-bound book that lies flat on the table and copy a computer program than to force open that book with a stack of weights and break the binding in the process.

Bindings for movable books deserve special mention, for many educators question the life of these volumes. Well-constructed books with sturdy covers and thick pages will stand up to continual use. Several of the movable books in our study enjoyed over fifty circulations without being discarded.

Whatever the binding, books with jackets or illustrated covers circulate more readily than books without them. Since books that stay on library shelves will not be read no matter how fine their content, we cannot ignore the importance of covers as effective enticements to the reader. Fine books wrapped in poor covers will require extra booktalking in order to circulate, while dramatic covers may well sell individual volumes without too much adult prodding.

Photographs appear more frequently on the jackets and covers of information books than any other medium. Effective ones provide clues as to content. The cover on Milton Meltzer's *Voices from the Civil War* (see Figure 12 in Chapter 4) shows two soldiers, one Confederate and one Union. They provide a fitting introduction to the book, because it focuses on people. Thoughts, feelings, concerns, bewilderment, disenchantment, and heroism are all revealed through various diary entries, letters, and public records. Through the words of actual historical figures readers can begin to see history as a culmination of personal records.

Photographs can also establish the tone of a book. The haunting picture of Chief Joseph on the cover of Russell Freedman's *Indian Chiefs* acts as a character sketch for the man whose memorable words, "I will fight no more forever," register both the pride and the futility of his once powerful nation. In this case, photography emerges as an art form, revealing the person and not just the visage.

Graphics and symbols frequently appear on book jackets. Occasionally they suggest negative connotations. The designer of the jacket on the first edition of Alan E. Nourse's *AIDS* provides an unfortunate example. A large red letter, an *A*, is sewn on a

Figure 47. Jacket Cover Illustration from *Indian Chiefs*.

From the book *Indian Chiefs* by Russell Friedman. Published by Holiday House, 1987. Used by permission.

grey background. While the *A* obviously stands for AIDS, it nonetheless conjures up images of Hester Prynne's shame, a particularly inappropriate symbol considering the book's nonhysterical tone. The jacket on the revised edition, released in 1989, has wisely substituted a photograph of the virus for the scarlet letter.

Color and typeface play an important part in cover design, particularly on those jackets that exclusively use words instead of pictorial art. Interesting fonts and vivid hues can entice the reader, while a standard typeface printed in bland colors will have little effect. James Haskins and Cathleen Benson's *The 60s Reader*, an outstanding book on that decade, may well require extra booktalking to move it off the library shelves, for the light-green words on a lavender jacket fail to entice, inspire, or even interest most readers.[8]

No one type of cover—photographs, original art, or a simple and pleasing design incorporating the book's name—is better than another. But since covers, no matter what their content, lead to increased circulation, they should be retained on books. Even during a budget crunch, libraries will realize few gains if they remove dust jackets and mark the spines rather than pay the few pennies necessary to provide protective plastic covers.

Format matters. In the case of graphic material, it matters in initial book selection. Other aspects, like typography and jackets, become important because of the impact they have on young adult readers. Fine works that have small type or dull jackets can't be dismissed automatically; but librarians and teachers can be aware of the impressions such works generate and deliberately try to counteract them when appropriate.

NOTES

1. Carter, Betty and Harris, Karen (1982). What Junior High Students Like in Books. *Journal of Reading, 26*, pp. 42–46.

2. Samuels, Barbara G. (1989). Young Adults' Choices: Why Do Students "Really Like" Particular Books? *Journal of Reading, 32*, pp. 714–19.

3. Lauber, Patricia (1987). *Journey to the Planets.* Rev. ed. New York: Crown Publishers, p. 63.

4. Giblin, James Cross (1988). *Let There Be Light: A Book about Windows.* New York: Thomas Y. Crowell, p. 86.

5. Freedman, Russell (1983). *Children of the Wild West.* New York: Clarion Books, p. 70.

6. Parnell, Peter (1984). *The Daywatchers.* New York: Macmillan, p. 11.

7. Moore, Janet Gaylord (1968). *The Many Ways of Seeing.* New York: World Publishing, p. 16.

8. Telephone conversation with Stephanie Zvrin, July 18, 1989.

CHAPTER 12
A Conversation with
Daniel and Susan Cohen

Daniel and Susan Cohen are two of the most prolific and popular writers of nonfiction for teenagers. Their mass-market paperbacks about wrestling superstars, rock videos, monsters, and UFOs sell hundreds of thousands of copies. Their hardback books on teenage stress, alcohol, drugs, and homosexuality have proven popular with teenage readers and have received solid critical praise. Reviewers describe their writing style as lucid, conversational, realistic, and personal.

Daniel and Susan Cohen

A&C One of the most interesting aspects of the nonfiction books you've done is the diversity of subjects you write about, from *Wrestling Superstars* to *When Someone You Know Is Gay*. How do you decide on a topic for a new book?

DC To a certain extent it depends on the circumstances surrounding each book. *Wrestling Superstars*, for example, was a strictly commercial venture. Pat MacDonald, our long-time editor at Simon and Schuster, called me. She hesitated for a while and finally said, "Dan, how much do you know about professional wrestling?" I said I'd learn, but in fact, I knew somewhat more about professional wrestling than I even cared to admit. In my teen years I'd been a real fan of wrestlers like Gorgeous George. I talked Susan into helping out, but she was not particularly enthusiastic. The book idea intrigued me because it had the sort of bizarre qualities that I enjoy in some books.

SC We thought of *Rock Superstars* ourselves because we know a lot of teenagers who are interested in rock. Seeing their interest gave us the idea. I spent many hours viewing MTV, watching rock bands, and going out asking kids in the town who their favorite rock stars were. We live in a small town, and it seems to be a good spot to get a kind of middle America view of life. Knowing these youngsters and seeing how interested they were in rock bands and rock stars led us into that book. Other titles like *When Someone You Know Is Gay* and *Teenage Stress* result in a different sort of book from the mass-market kinds we've been talking about. One major difference, of course, is that the mass-market books are paperback.

A&C It must be more difficult to get a book published if the idea comes from the writer and not the editor at a publishing house. Was it difficult finding a publisher for *When Someone You Know Is Gay?*

DC Yes, the book took a long time to do and a long time to sell. Evans finally did do the book, but we looked at a couple of other publishers who were, quite frankly, frightened of it. We heard it was too controversial or that it had been done before. It certainly hadn't been done before. I think the publishers liked our presentation but were afraid of the subject matter. If the publishers had a large backlist of children's books, I think they feared that a book like ours might attract hostile attention in some areas and that might hurt their other books. Since Evans has a very small children's backlist, consisting mostly of our books, they didn't run that kind of risk.

A&C It is often suggested that the author of a nonfiction book needs to be an expert on that subject in order to write about it or show enthusiasm for the topic. Is it possible to be an expert on Olympic stars, rock videos, and teenage stress?

SC No, and I don't think it is necessary. In some ways it's an asset not to be an expert. In fact, I think you probably come to the subject fresher, with fewer preconceived ideas. We talk to a lot of kids and know what kinds of questions they're asking. Those questions and the answers to them let us know what our readers are interested in and what they really want to know. We do the research and find out the answers. We are, after all, not writing books for experts. We are not writing technical books that would appeal to a limited group of people who have an enormous background on a subject.

DC Our primary responsibility is to be good communicators. We need to be able to take information which the experts have and write it in such a way that would interest teen readers. One of the problems with being an expert is that you're often out of touch with the person to whom your expertise is to be communicated. The true expert often writes above the reader's head, focusing on issues that the general reader is really not interested in. I've done some writing strictly in science, and I can tell you that the writing by people who are experts is often the worse kind of prose for young people. Now there are a few experts who write well, like Carl Sagan or Isaac Asimov. Most scientists who try to write for children and teenagers do a poor job not because they don't know their subject, but because they don't know their audience.

SC The audience needs to be pulled in. The writing has to be interesting and lively. If you can't ignite the spark that gets the reader interested, you're not going to reach him with any quantity of information.

A&C You're getting at the issue of what makes a good nonfiction book for adolescents. What are your criteria?

DC The basic hallmark is that teenagers will want to read it. No matter how good a book is, if it's not the sort of book that a significant number of kids are going to take off the shelf and read, then it's worthless.

SC One of the real questions with books for juvenile readers is Who is your audience? Is it parents and librarians? These adults often look for books that they want kids to read. Or, is your audience the kids themselves? Sometimes children and young adults have very different ideas about what they want to read. The whole issue of audience is one that people who write for adults don't have to deal with.

DC We try very hard to pitch our books toward the youngsters who are actually supposed to read them and not toward parents and librarians who put out the money to buy the books. As you can see, a writer for juveniles is in the position of having to serve two masters. I think whatever success we've had in the juvenile book field is because we always keep the "average" adolescent reader in mind when conceiving and writing these books.

SC But we do vary what Dan just said, based on the book we are doing. For instance, we know that when we do a book on something like rock superstars, it's going to be hitting a wide range of readers. On the other hand, when we do a book for teenagers like *When Someone You Know Is Gay* or *A Six-Pack and a Fake I.D.*, we know we're aiming at good middle-class readers. We're not always trying to reach the same group of readers; some of our books are meant for a wider audience, while others are targeted toward a more sophisticated audience.

A&C What title of yours seems to be the most popular with students?

DC I think *A Six-Pack and a Fake I.D.* is the most popular book.

SC It has the greatest appeal.

DC The wrestling books have sold half a million copies in paperback, but it's not comparable. A $2.25 paperback is not comparable to an $11.95 hardback.

A&C Several of the books you've done together like *A Six-Pack and a Fake I.D.* and *Teenage Stress* have been popular with teenagers and praised in the various review sources. Could you talk us through the process of creating one of those books, including a look at how the two of you work together?

DC In the case of the two books you've just mentioned, the ideas came from the two of us and the former editor-in-chief at Evans, Herb Katz. I had done some other young adult books for Evans. Herb knew of Susan's background in social work and suggested we collaborate on some books that focused on teenage behavior. We've been married for thirty years, and we work together well. I tend to handle the parts of a book that have the scientific or historical background while Susan handles the more personal issues. I often say that she writes all the things about sex because that embarrasses me.

SC That's sort of a sexist breakdown. I certainly would feel qualified to handle the historical part of a book, though I might not do the greatest job in a science section. I'm the one who does the interviews because I'm better at interviewing. I have a master's degree in social work and for a while I was a social worker and did a lot of interviews. So I've had more training in interviewing. I'm the one who talks to the kids and tells their stories. I can be more personal than Dan, but he is a much faster writer than I, and he's much better at organizing in his mind. I have to write things on paper and then redo them. That's just the way my mind works. It doesn't collect information and then structure it; I have to see it. Dan is the kind of writer who can organize lots of information inside his head, so he sometimes is able to do the historical or scientific research much more quickly than I could. I do the personal interviews much more effectively.

A&C Does the research process for *Sports' Newest Superstars* or *Heroes of the Challenger* differ from the research involved in *A Six-Pack and a Fake I.D.*?

SC It's much easier to do the research for *Sports' Newest Superstars* and *Heroes of the Challenger*. In the case of those two books, you contact places, get information, and put it together. The interviews involved in a book like *A Six-Pack and a Fake I.D.* are tougher to do.

DC We didn't have an interview with Mike Tyson for *Sports' Newest Superstars*. [If we can't get interviews with the stars] We talk to their press people and agents, get printed materials from other places, and reinterpret the information for a young audience. But for *Six-Pack and a Fake I.D.*, for example, the drinking stories that are told are all authentic and based on actual interviews. Books like *Six-Pack* are much more difficult and time-consuming. You don't have a body of pre-set information nor do you have publicity people you can go to for help.

A&C Your books on drugs and alcohol don't have the preachy, lecturing quality that is found so often in literature for teenagers.

SC We try not to moralize. In preparation for writing *A Six-Pack and a Fake I.D.* we read scores of books and pamphlets on the subject of teenagers and drinking. They were all so moralistic in tone that we knew perfectly well no kids were going to read them or take them seriously. We try to talk to the kids in a very straightforward way that builds a trust between author and reader. You can't sound like some sort of spy from the adult world trying to give them propaganda. You have to be honest, tell them the truth, and not moralize. That's what we try to do on subjects like drugs and alcohol.

DC You cannot talk to a group of junior high or high school students without noticing that on the one hand they are very sophisticated and on the other hand have a good deal of misinformation as well. A good many of the pamphlets handed out in health classes are wildly inappropriate and might just as well be burned. It's fine when you have fourth graders getting T-shirts that say "Just Say No to Drugs. " But if you continue that approach into junior high school and high school, you've lost your audience.

SC Or you have the kids who aren't going to do it anyway. You always have a certain group of kids who are not going to get involved with drugs. If you want to reach the other kids, the ones who possibly will experiment with drugs, you have to tell them the truth. You can't tell them that one drink is going to send them to hell. There are kids out there who are going to try some level of drug taking, and you can't lie. It doesn't mean you have to romanticize or push any of it. They need to know the truth about what will happen if they take drugs. You can't tell them that if they smoke pot once, they'll end up in the hospital for the rest of their lives. They know that's wrong just by looking around them at the kids who smoke pot.

DC One of the limitations we acknowledge up front is that our books aren't written for the ghetto teenager with all the problems of growing up in that world. We don't write the books for those teenagers because they are not going to read them. We're after the kids in the middle who are likely to experiment with drugs and even enjoy them for a time. They need the truth, and they are the teens we're trying to reach.

A&C Even if you're writing about alcohol or teenage stress, you manage to put things in there that make the reader smile. A lot of nonfiction books aren't like that. Could you tell us about the role of humor in a nonfiction book?

DC You almost have to have it in there. Many of the subjects we write about are sometimes grim and heavy. That tone has to be lightened with humor or we lose our readers. Also, from a writer's point of view, it's pretty boring to write the grim text page after page without some break. I think kids have a natural humor; they like the joke or the ironic comment. It appeals to them and to Susan and me as well. I'm not sure how conscious we are about using humor in the books, but it does seem to be a natural part of both of our writing styles.

A&C We notice that much of the prose in your books appears in short chunks. You provide some information, then do a short interview with a teenager. Is that approach a deliberate technique to make the book more accessible to adolescent readers?

SC Yes, that is correct. I think you have to realize that teenagers often don't read in the same way that many adults do. Serious, adult readers start on page one and read through the whole book. Adolescents tend to skip around a good deal. Too much information without a break may just stop them from continuing the book. When they are given some information followed with an interview or personal story, that tends to bring the information home and allows the reader to identify with the kids in the story. I think the technique you refer to makes its much easier for youngsters to understand what we're saying and makes the book more interesting to them.

DC In fact, it's really not just kids who read this way. Look at what the average adult reads. Books on the adult bestseller lists are not very intellectually challenging. I think some of the books we do are a lot more intellectually challenging than much of what you see on the bestseller shelves in bookstores.

SC Kids bear this terrible burden that adults are always after them wanting to push good things on them. Unfortunately most adults don't read the "good things," if you look at the bestseller lists. The same attitude is true of television. Parents don't want their kids to watch junk on television, but the parents view it. America is not a country made up of serious readers. Writers for teenagers need to be aware that even those who read also watch TV. Certainly the material shouldn't be presented in a condescending or patronizing way, but it does need to be presented in a way that youngsters raised on television can take it in.

A&C Several of your books feature a good many photographs. How do you feel about the importance of photos in nonfiction books for teenagers? How do you go about doing that part of the research?

DC Occasionally the photographs have been the hardest part of it. In the celebrity biographies we've done, photographs are enormously important, because teenagers want to see pictures of their idols. Getting pictures of these stars often depends on pure luck. Sometimes a celebrity's agent will give you more pictures than you could ever use. Other times, it's like trying to get an interview with Greta Garbo; they won't provide anything. We did some books on rock stars and couldn't include some very popular stars because they wouldn't give us permission to use the pictures. We have no idea why. There seems to be no logic in how this whole procedure works, at least as it relates to celebrities, but getting the pictures can be one of the toughest and most frustrating parts of writing some nonfiction books.

A&C A good deal has been written about the importance of documentation in nonfiction books. How important do you feel a bibliography, index, and footnotes are?

SC Here we have a disagreement, sometimes. Even when we get outstanding reviews, the reviewer will often point out that we don't have notes. Our feeling is that we're not writing technical books, and we want to give our readers bibliographies that will be meaningful to them. Over the last few years we've changed our bibliographies to include movies and television shows. Since so much is available on videocassette it makes these things more accessible to kids. This is a whole new area of bibliography that we think should be included in most nonfiction books because teen readers are going to be much more influenced by some of these films than they are by many books.

DC Even the books we list in the bibliographies are books we think young readers will find meaningful and accessible. I think including footnotes or citing studies in a nonfiction book for teenagers is deadly. It's deadly because most kids will pick up a book, see footnotes, and put the book down. That's it. It's too much like school.

A&C Dan, you've done several books on monsters such as *The Encyclopedia of Monsters.* In those books you talk about "cryptozoology." Are you a cryptozoologist?

Figure 49. Jacket Cover Illustration from *UFO's: The Third Wave.*

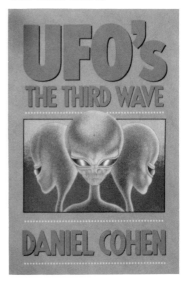

DC Yes, I'm a member of the International Cryptozoological Society. I like to think of cryptozoology as romantic zoology or monster hunting. It's a group of people who believe, or would like to believe, that there are large, strange, unknown animals out there that have not yet been defined or adequately discovered by science. I think we're reasonably serious people, but I like the term "romantic zoology" because the chances of finding the Loch Ness monster or Bigfoot are really quite small in my view. But the lure of it is enormous. So as long as you understand that the chances are small and you are honest in your quest—you don't fake pictures or anything like that—it's a great deal of fun, and who knows, maybe we'll find something.

A&C You've also done many books on UFOs. After spending so much time researching and talking with people on both sides of the issue, do you line up on the side of the believers?

DC No, I really don't. For over forty years I've been looking into this. I started when UFOs were still flying saucers, back in 1947. I have to say that today we're in exactly the same place we were in 1947. There are many very interesting stories around, but the solid evidence is still lacking. We don't have the incontrovertible photograph. We don't have the physical artifacts. What we have are a lot of stories. Certainly the possibility of extraterrestrial life is one that I fully acknowledge. But, it would seem to me that after all this time, if we're being visited as frequently as some people seem to believe, we should have better evidence of it, and we don't. So I have to say I'm not a believer, but I'm still interested because it's fascinating. People are still seeing things that they cannot explain, and there are terribly interesting people in this field. I have to say I've had a great deal of fun with it. It's not every day you meet people who've been to other planets, or say they have. And there's all kinds of wild speculations that go on and even that, intellectually, is fun. We're still waiting for the hard evidence. There's a phrase that goes around that states: Extraordinary claims require extraordinary proof. If the extraordinary claim is that you have been abducted and taken off into a space ship, you need extraordinary proof for that. I haven't seen that proof.

A&C What do you look for when you read a review of one of your books in the reviewing sources? How do you get a feel that the reviewers have done their jobs?

DC It's certainly obvious to a writer when a reviewer has written a review from the book cover flap, or if his every reference is to something within the first six pages of the book. You get a good idea of whether or not the reviewer has done his or her homework. You hope that the reviewer has picked up on the main focus of the book you've written. They may disagree with the focus, but at least they understand what you set out to do. We just got a couple of reviews of *When Someone You Know Is Gay*. They're quite good reviews and both the reviewers understood that this is a book meant primarily for straight kids. It's information for straight kids rather than for gays. That was the main thrust of the book. We both felt very good about that. The reviewers understood what we were trying to do with the book. That understanding is the main thing we look for in a review. We also look for nice quotes that might appear in ads to help book sales. That's part of what authors look for as well.

A&C What can we expect next from the pens, or is it word processors, of Susan and Daniel Cohen?

DC Not a word processor, but a forty-year-old Royal manual typewriter. We've got a book coming out on dogs. A little bit further down the line will be a book for younger kids on zoos. The whole idea of zoos is changing, what they should look like, what should be in them. Zoos of the future will be very different places from what they are today. We're also thinking about doing a book on the racial situation in America. It has changed a good deal since the sixties. Many problems have developed in high schools and colleges, and we think that has to be addressed forthrightly.

A&C How do you decide whose name goes first on a book?

DC We don't. The publisher does. We just wait until the cover comes out and see whose name is first.

SC Sometimes it's hard because you know that one or the other of us should have been listed first, but that's how it works. I had enough of a struggle getting some publishers to put my name on the books at all. It took almost two years before the publishers realized I wasn't just retyping his manuscripts. People still tend to think if you're the woman and you're a married couple, the woman just helps out with the typing and, perhaps, some background research. It's really not helping out at all. On some of our books I've done the majority of the work and on others Dan has taken the bulk of the work. Still, these days, some people continue to fall into old stereotypic ways of thinking.

Figure 50. Jacket Cover Illustration from *When Someone You Know Is Gay*.

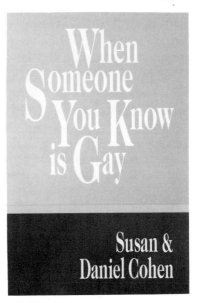

DC Speaking of stereotypes, let's talk about one of the real problems we have with the juvenile book publishing establishment. It's the issue of books for boys. I think that publishers believe that boys beyond the age of eleven don't read, or if they do, read only books about trucks or sports. So it's very hard to get books for boys. I think publishers, librarians, and teachers tend to give up on boys after a certain age. I really think that's awful.

SC We are among the few writers of nonfiction for kids who are read by both boys and girls. I think that's partly because of the subjects we take, but it is also because we don't direct our books specifically to girls or boys. We aim at both sexes. But, the issue Dan raises is a very real problem in the juvenile book field. I think good nonfiction for teenagers can cut across that male/female reading barrier better than fiction.

A&C Which book are you proudest of?

DC The book we're probably proudest of right now is, *When Someone You Know is Gay*. It was the most difficult book to do. It deals with a subject that just wasn't being covered. The book took more work than anything we've ever done.

SC Yes, as we've said, it was difficult to sell, involved an enormous amount of research, and took a great deal of rewriting. When we started, we didn't have a clear idea of where we would be going. I did more than fifty in-depth interviews with individual teenagers, parents, and teachers. I also worked with one large group of about seventy gay teens. I'm proud that we were able to take a tough subject and present it in an honest and sympathetic way to straight kids. I think it's a genuine contribution. There's nothing else out there like it.

A&C As writers of nonfiction for teenagers, what gives you the greatest satisfaction?

DC Cashing the royalty check or seeing the book. Really, I like working out the particular problems that go with each book. How are we going to present this particular piece of information? Where are we going to find the answers to these questions? Finding solutions to such problems are where my greatest satisfaction comes from.

SC I think taking this information and working it into a readable form is important. To feel that you've been honest with your readers, told the truth, and showed them the way things really are in such a way that they'll enjoy reading it and not lump your work in with some boring textbook is important and satisfying to me.

BOOKS BY DANIEL COHEN

Bigfoot: America's Number One Monster. (1982). New York: Archway/Archway Hi-Lo Books.

Biorhythms in Your Life. (1981). New York: Fawcett.

Carl Sagan: Superstar Scientist. (1987). York: G. P. Putnam's Sons.

A Close Look at Close Encounters. (1981). New York: G. P. Putnam's Sons.

Creativity: What Is It? (1977). New York: M. Evans.

Creatures from UFO's. (1978). New York: G. P. Putnam's Sons.

Curses, Hexes, & Spells. (1974). New York: J. B. Lippincott/Weird & Horrible Library.

**The Encyclopedia of Ghosts*. (1984). New York: Dodd, Mead.

The Encyclopedia of Monsters. (1983). New York: Dodd, Mead.

**The Encyclopedia of the Strange*. (1985). New York: Dodd, Mead.

The Encyclopedia of Unsolved Crimes. (1988). New York: Dodd, Mead.

ESP. (1986). Englewood Cliffs, NJ: Julian Messner.

Ghostly Terrors. (1981). New York: Archway.

Gold: The Fascinating Study of the Noble Metal through the Ages. (1976). New York: M. Evans.

The Great Airship Mystery: A UFO of the 1890's. (1981). New York: Dodd, Mead.

Great Mistakes. (1979). New York: M. Evans.

The Greatest Monsters in the World. (1984). New York: Archway.

The Headless Roommate & Other Tales of Terror. (1980). New York: M. Evans.

Henry Stanley and the Quest for the Source of the Nile. (1985). New York: M. Evans.

Hiram Bingham & the Dream of Gold. (1984). New York: M. Evans.

Hollywood Dinosaur. (1987). New York: Archway.

**Horror in the Movies*. (1982). New York: Clarion Books.

The Last Hundred Years: Household Technology. (1982). New York: M. Evans.

The Last Hundred Years: Medicine. (1981). New York: M. Evans.

Masters of Horror. (1984). New York: Clarion Books.

Missing: Stories of Strange Disappearances. (1980). New York: Archway.

Monster Hunting Today. (1983). New York: G. P. Putnam's Sons.

Monsters You Never Heard Of. (1980). New York: Archway.

The Monsters of Star Trek. (1984). New York: Archway.

Phone Call from a Ghost: Strange Tales from Modern America. (1987). New York: G. P. Putnam's Sons.

Re-Thinking: How to Succeed by Learning How to Think. (1982). New York: M. Evans.

Real Ghosts. (1984). New York: Archway.

Real Magic. (1982). New York: G. P. Putnam's Sons.

The Restless Dead: Ghostly Tales from around the World. (1987). New York: Archway.

**Science Fiction's Greatest Monsters*. (198). New York: G. P. Putnam's Sons.

The Simon & Schuster Question & Answer Book: Computers. (1983). New York: Simon & Schuster.

Southern Fried Rat and Other Gruesome Tales. (1983). New York: M. Evans.

Strange & Amazing Facts about Star Trek. (1986). New York: Archway.

**Supermonsters*. (1978). New York: G. P. Putnam's Sons.

The Tomb Robbers. (1980). New York: McGraw Hill.

UFOs: The Third Wave. (1988). New York: M. Evans.

Waiting for the Apocalypse: Doomsday Deferred. Rev. ed. (1983). New York: Prometheus Books.

World of UFO's. (1978). New York: J. B. Lippincott.

The World's Most Famous Ghosts. (1985). New York: Archway.

BOOKS BY DANIEL AND SUSAN COHEN

The Encyclopedia of Movie Stars . (1985). Smith.

*Going for the Gold. (1988). New York: Archway.

*Heroes of the Challenger. (1986). New York: Archway.

How to Get Started in Video. (1986). New York: Franklin Watts.

*Rock Video Superstars. (1985). New York: Archway.

*Rock Video Superstars II. (1987). New York: Archway.

Teenage Stress: Understanding the Tensions You Feel at Home, at School & among Your Friends. (1984). New York: M. Evans.

What You Can Believe About Drugs: An Honest & Unhysterical Guide for Teens. (1988). New York: Henry Holt.

When Someone You Know Is Gay. (1989). New York: M. Evans.

*Wrestling Superstars. (1985). New York: Archway.

*Wrestling Superstars II. (1986). New York: Archway.

*Young and Famous: Hollywood's (1987). Newest Superstars. New York: Archway.

*Young and Famous: Sport's Newest Superstars. (1987). New York: Archway.

*Zoo Superstars. (1989). New York: Pocket Books/A Minstrel Book.

BOOKS BY SUSAN AND DANIEL COHEN

A Six-Pack & a Fake I. D.: Teens Look at the Drinking Question. (1986). New York: M. Evans.

Teenage Competition: A Survival Guide. (1989). New York: M. Evans.

* Indicates edition is paperback

** Indicates a paperback edition also available

CHAPTER 13
Uses

Even the best nonfiction will often not get into the hands of readers without the help of professional librarians and teachers. Like any other materials, nonfiction books need to be introduced to teenagers in a variety of contexts. The following chapter will examine some of the ways teachers and librarians can effectively integrate nonfiction into established classroom and library programs.

CLASSROOM USES AND CURRICULUM CONNECTIONS

If secondary classrooms are to exist as learning laboratories where young adults encounter stimulating subject matter, diverse viewpoints, and challenging ideas, then it seems natural that informational books reflecting these elements would appear in daily lessons and curricular planning. All too often, however, state adopted texts and literature popular in centuries other than our own serve as the exclusive reading components for innumerable courses. While these materials contain value, alone they do not offer the enrichment, the variety, and the forums necessary for true learning to take place. Supplementary works, rich in content, language, and points of view, can reinforce these educational staples, offering young adults the very tools they will need to become independent learners.

Point of View

A single textbook frequently forms the nucleus of many secondary content classrooms.[1] Teachers often rely on the content presented and students—even those who dutifully read the assigned chapters—often find them uninspiring. Rarely do young adults refer to textbooks as the catalysts that propelled them into any lifelong interests. Helpful adults, the popular media, trade books, and life experiences perform these functions. Textbooks do not. All too often these publications consist of factually laden prose presented without style, theme, or point of view.

If point of view exists in textbooks, it does so as accepted dogma. In Texas, according to a 1983 mandate, for example, "positive aspects of the USA's history must be stressed in world history texts used in public schools."[2] Those negatives—the sorry mistakes that have dotted our past and may well affect our future—are either left out, glossed over, or presented in a favorable light. The Spanish-American War thus becomes little more than a dramatic charge up San Juan Hill, and America's unwillingness to accept the horrors of the Holocaust an easily dismissed failure to communicate with Eastern Europe. These and other equally as distorting fictions deftly turn the drama of history into a whitewash.

One of the important advantages of nonfiction is that it can challenge these comfortable but incorrect perceptions and offer young adults various points of view on the same topic. The Civil War comes across as one type of event when seen through the eyes of a scholar writing about the conflict. An adolescent reader gets a different perspective on the war by reading the letters from various Yankee and Confederate soldiers, as found in Meltzer's *Voices from the Civil War.*

Likewise, a science textbook that proclaims how wonderful our lives have become since the advent of computers might be countered with nonfiction selections that examine some of the negative aspects which accompany the computer revolution: the hundreds of Detroit workers who have lost their car manufacturing jobs to computers and robots, the many consumers who have had the experience of wanting to complain about an incorrect bill or order only to be told it couldn't be helped because it was a computer error, or the individuals who cite instances in which they are required to identify themselves by number rather than by name. With the computer revolution, some would argue, we are becoming a more faceless society. It is only in trade books that young adults will find those arguments discussed in any depth. For want of space, computer science and sociology texts only mention these peripheral concerns.

The well-researched illustrations that appear in informational books can additionally stimulate meaningful discussion and writing assignments as well as enrich course content. Figure 51, taken from Russell Freedman's *Children of the Wild West,* invites a thoughtful comparison of the merits and disadvantages of culturally based educational opportunities. Whether the teacher promotes a verbal discussion or a written response to these photographs will depend on a combination of educational objectives. No matter what the forum, these contrasting portraits ask young adults to think.

Even with such commanding graphics available, it is through the use of a variety of source material that teachers best challenge their students to think. Let's take one subject—the Vietnam War—and see the various points of view informational books can offer the teen reader.

Figure 51. Indian Youths before and after Schooling in Hampton, Virginia in 1878.

One of the most powerful books about the Vietnam War is a collection of letters sent from servicemen and women back home to their loved ones: *Dear America: Letters Home from Vietnam*. It appeared as a Best Book for Young Adults in 1986, and was also selected by thousands of adolescent readers as a favorite in the International Reading Association's Young Adults' Choices Project.

Here readers see the tragedy of Rick Carlsen, a medic killed just ten days after writing his mom about his plans for returning to the World and wanting to "keep the seventh day open to the Lord."[3] Further on in the book is a letter from Captain Rodney R. Chastant, who writes, "Some men choose to fight on the streets. Some choose to fight in the universities. Some choose to fight in the parliaments . . . I choose Vietnam."[4] Contrast these words with those from Sergeant Phillip Woodall: "This war is all wrong. I will continue to fight, win my medals and fight the elements and hardships of this country. But that is because I'm a soldier and it's my job. . . . "[5]

The letters from *Dear America* were all written by men and women serving in Vietnam. Journalist Laura Palmer approaches the war in a different way. She examined letters and mementos left at the Vietnam Veterans Memorial in Washington, D.C. Palmer went back and traced these remembrances to the people who left them at the wall. Her book includes letters written by and interviews with survivors who were moved to leave their expressions of love at the memorial. In Palmer's *Shrapnel in the Heart* teenagers can see the legacy of Vietnam through the eyes of survivors—friends, family, and loved ones left behind by fighting men and women. Extending beyond the political arena and the battlefield, *Shrapnel in the Heart* underscores the human cost in any war.

A more recent book provides an entirely different perspective. Journalist Bob Greene asked this question in one of his newspaper articles: "If you are a reader of this column, and you are a Vietnam veteran, were you ever spat upon when you returned to the United States?" For years Greene had heard the stories of vets who returned to America after the war and were spat upon by fellow citizens. He wanted to know if such incidents really happened. Greene received over one thousand responses, many of which he presents in his book *Homecoming: When the Soldiers Returned from Vietnam*.

What must it have been like to fight in Vietnam and return to America only to be spat upon? Ernest P. Huerta of Chicago describes such an incident, concluding his memory with the conditions he faced when returning to Vietnam: "The area was hot and humid and two-inch-long beetles would bite the hell out of you at night. . . But when I got back there I actually felt happy."[6]

For a quite different point of view, teenagers can read Gerald R. Gioglio's *Days of Decision: An Oral History of Conscientious Objectors in the Military during the Vietnam War*. Gioglio presents the stories of twenty-four American GIs who were conscientious objectors in uniform. Their experiences tell what it is like to fight the military from the inside. The three kinds of COs represented in Gioglio's book—those imprisoned for resistance, those who served as unarmed medics, and those who received CO status and were discharged without stints in prison or as medics—relate stories of harassment, social isolation, military justice, and stockades. *Days of Decision* provides teenagers with fine examples of oral history. In addition, it might lead readers to Meltzer's *Ain't Gonna Study War No More*, a history of pacifism and war resistance in the United States. In any case, what this oral history does is expose readers to an aspect of the war and a point of view not written about in traditional high school textbooks.

The list of related books continues. Margot C. J. Mabie's *Vietnam There and Here* offers a more detailed history of the war than any textbook with limited space can allow; Don Lawson's *An Album of the Vietnam War* may reach those students more attuned to learning through graphics than print; and Edward F. Dolan's *MIA: Missing in Action* explores the contemporary dilemma of determining the fate of the approximately three thousand service personnel still classified as missing. By introducing these and other related books teachers deliver a subtle message: Neither I nor your textbook stands as the authority on any given subject. This concept is the hallmark of critical thinking, an important attribute that characterizes the difference between a person who simply gets an education and an educated person.

Reading Aloud

In the last ten years, there has been a rebirth of interest in reading aloud to young people. Jim Trelease's *The Read-Aloud Handbook* has sold over one million copies and appeared in a 1989 revision entitled *The New Read-Aloud Handbook*. Margaret Mary Kimmel and Elizabeth Segel's fine book *For Reading Out Loud!* is now also in its second edition. These missionaries of read-aloud point to the joy of sharing books with young people, the intimate bond it builds between parent and child, the sense of a community of readers it inspires in the classroom, and the educational benefits derived from the experience. Study after study show that if youngsters are read aloud to on a consistent basis for fifteen or twenty minutes a day, they will increase their performance scores on reading tests, enrich their overall vocabularies, improve their reading comprehension, and be aided in their language development. Indeed, the highly quoted *Becoming a Nation of Readers* summarizes the educational importance of reading aloud this way, "The single most important activity for building the knowledge required for eventual success in reading is reading aloud to children."[7]

Equally as important as the educational benefits is the reading motivation benefit attached to reading aloud. When Mary Jett-Simpson surveyed 1,821 students to find out their reactions to specific reading motivation activities, she found that "teacher reads aloud in an exciting voice was one of the most preferred."[8] Reading aloud to students is one of the few activities that is pleasurable for reader and listener, provides research-supported educational benefits, and is selected by young people as one of the most motivating activities a teacher can do to encourage reading.

Many teachers and librarians have always known the pleasure and motivation power associated with reading good books aloud. Memories of our favorite teachers are often recollections of that professional reading aloud to us in school. In *Voices of Readers: How We Came to Love Books*, G. Robert Carlsen and Anne Sherrill report on thousands of "reading autobiographies," or descriptions of the reading lives of students, from Carlsen's college classes in young adult literature over the last three decades. In the final section of *Voices*, Carlsen and Sherrill summarize the "Conditions that Promote Reading" as reported in these autobiographical descriptions. Being read aloud to was found to be one of the most important conditions that promote reading:

> The writers of the protocols tell of their joy during elementary school when a teacher read books aloud. Sometimes they were afraid that school would end before the final chapter had been reached. Teenagers' appreciation of the classics seems to develop from the oral renditions by talented teachers. Even in college classrooms, students recall the pleasure of having a professor read passages aloud from the books under discussion. Oral reading is so successful a technique with most age groups that it can be called one of the "never-fail methods" for the teaching of literature[9]

Chapter 1 discusses the professional prejudice against and lack of attention given to nonfiction. Nowhere is that bias more obvious than in selecting and recommending books for teachers and librarians to read aloud. Trelease writes, "Of the two forms of literature (fiction and nonfiction), the one that brings us closest and presents the meaning of life most clearly to the child is fiction."[10] Later he says: "Nothing consistently holds the attention of a classroom of children with divergent interests quite like fiction."[11]

Quotations like the above continue the prejudice against nonfiction. We believe children and young adults ought to be exposed to fine read-alouds from both the fiction and nonfiction camps. A good nonfiction book can, indeed, present a youngster with a close look at the meaning of life.

Middle school and high school teachers and librarians who are interested in some good nonfiction read-alouds might start by examining the following, annotated list of ten titles. Our list, like any other, is personal and idiosyncratic. If your favorite nonfiction read-aloud does not appear here, write and let us know of your success. In any case, add your title to the list so that other professionals can see that a good read-aloud is not, by definition, only a work of fiction.

1. *Adrift: Seventy-Six Days Lost at Sea*, by Steven Callahan.
Steven Callahan's travel adventure moves quickly from dream-come-true to nightmare when his boat is hit, possibly by a whale, and Callahan is forced to endure seventy-six days in a raft as he clings to life. This young adventurer kept a diary of his fight for survival against sharks, starvation, and dehydration. His entries describe how he catches fish, collects rainwater, and keeps body and spirit alive. *Adrift* is an exciting read-aloud that speaks to teenagers of courage, resourcefulness, and an indomitable will to live.

2. *Anguished English*, by Richard Lederer.
Sometimes it's nice to have a funny book to dip into and read four or five minutes every day, get youngsters laughing, and then move on with the rest of the day's lessons. If you love examples of how students, politicians, journalists, and even some of the rest of us mangle the English language, then this is a book to consider. The author is a veteran high school English teacher who has spent years collecting these gems. Lederer includes hilarious examples of anguished English culled from student compositions, for-sale ads, newspaper headlines, and quotations from famous people. Reading this book aloud is the funniest way we know to teach teenagers about dangling participles, mixing metaphors, and the importance of proofreading what they write.

3. *China's Long March: 6,000 Miles of Danger*, by Jean Fritz.
In 1934, surrounded by the Nationalist Army of Chaing Kai-shek, Mao Zedong's First Front Army of the Chinese Communists retreated northward. Fritz's narrative recreates their six-thousand-mile journey across China over raging rivers, perilous mountains, and through vast, empty grasslands. Fighting nature, internal discontent, and the more sophisticated Nationalist Army, the men and women of the First Front were driven by the certainty that the only way to improve their lot was through the social, political, and economic revolution dictated by their leader. Teachers who keep a copy or transparency of the pronunciation guide in front of their students when reading will help them recognize and remember unfamiliar names and places. In addition, activities that chart this journey on a map help listeners retain a sense of the geographical locales.

4. *Dreams of Dragons: Riddles of Natural History*, by Lyall Watson.
Do plants have memories? Are our lives controlled by chance or design? Is the predominance of righthandedness in society a weakness or a strength in our evolutionary development? Through twelve thoughtfully developed essays, Watson explores these and other personal questions about the natural world. From his opening sentences ("Some of my best friends are cannibals," and "Nobody sees much of unicorns any more"), Watson alternately shocks and intrigues his listeners, challenging them to think, to contemplate, to wonder about the workings of a biological planet often taken for granted. These essays are more effectively presented in small doses, allowing about a week to pass before introducing each new one.

5. *Fighting Back: What Some People Are Doing about AIDS*, by Susan Kuklin.
Mention AIDS to a classroom of young adults and the reactions—fear, denial, revulsion, compassion, uneasiness, ignorance, rejection, and curiosity—will mirror those of the adult population. *Fighting Back* addresses these responses. By examining the volunteer work of a team of buddies organized by the Gay Men's Health Crisis (GMHC) to help Persons With AIDS (PWA), it concentrates on the individual support freely given by a cross-section of New

Yorkers. In dealing with real people and their human experiences, Kuklin effectively blends biography, story narrative, and exposition, introducing listeners to three powerful elements typical of informational books.

6. *Into a Strange Land: Unaccompanied Refugee Youth in America*, by Brent and Melissa Ashabranner.

Each year thousands of refugees from all over the world set their sights on freedom and flee their homelands for new lives in the United States. Whether these people come from Southeast Asia, Cuba, Haiti, or Central America, many of the refugees are children and young adults. This is the story of unaccompanied refugee youth in America. What's it like for these teenagers to enter a strange land without parents or other family members? The Ashabranners begin their book by telling the story of a Vietnamese youngster whose father places him on a boat headed for a refugee camp in Thailand and from there, hopefully, on to America. Young Tran's story is one of love, hope, and terror. It is one of the most gripping read-aloud scenes we've encountered.

7. *Magazine: Behind the Scenes at "Sports Illustrated,"* by William Jaspersohn.

Jaspersohn takes teen readers backstage at *Sports Illustrated* to show them how this popular magazine is created. He follows reporters as they cover major sporting events and interview famous sports stars. The excitement of the tennis playoffs and the basketball finals are coupled with the ever-present deadlines to produce copy and photos. This photo essay employs plenty of black-and-white pictures, making *Magazine* a good choice for young middle school readers who aren't ready for lengthy prose passages. While the names of many of the winning athletes have changed since the book first appeared, teenagers will be happy to provide the names of the newest stars in the sports world as they get a glimpse of all the aspects that go into creating a popular magazine.

8. *Never Cry Wolf*, by Farley Mowat.

Mowat's Robinson Crusoe adventure story has everything going for it: It's an animal story, a story of wilderness survival, and a chronicle of one man's evolving respect for wild wolves. Mowat is dropped alone on the frozen tundra to find out why wolves are killing all the caribou. As he observes and begins to understand the wolves, he realizes they are not the caribou killers but animals greatly misunderstood by humans and in danger of being massacred by bounty hunters and government programs. Mowat's days with the wolves are laced with humor, scientific observations, concern for the environment, and thoughts on the place of human beings in the world of nature. The movie made from this book remains one of the most popular videocassettes of recent years. It provides teachers with a chance to read the book aloud, show the movie, and encourage adolescents to compare and contrast the two.

9. *The Pond: The Life of Aquatic Plants, Fish, Amphibians, Reptiles, Mammals, and Birds that Inhabit the Pond and Its Surrounding Hillside and Swamp*, by John Sampson.

Let Sampson's exquisite prose capture listeners as he describes the cyclical patterns of nature through observations of the creatures inhabiting and visiting his family pond in the northeastern U.S. over the course of one year. Sampson clearly views his young adult audience as respected observers of the natural world as he describes for them, without anthropomorphism or sentimentality, the daily circumstances—the small triumphs and fatal failures—of turtles, fish, rodents, deer, and birds who inhabit his neighborhood. This book serves as a fine introduction to scientific writing as well as to participatory observation.

10. *Unbuilding*, by David Macaulay.
Through a masterful blend of factual expository prose and fictional story narrative, Macaulay outlines the process of dismantling the Empire State Building a scant sixty years after its dedication in 1931. His satirical premise—that an Arab oil prince purchases, demolishes, and removes the skyscraper—not only reminds listeners of the consequences of carelessly taking our culture for granted, but also provides an unusual perspective on the construction, design, and aesthetic value of this great structure. Teachers who choose this book will experience a greater success if they show and discuss the illustrations when reading aloud, and then allow students extended opportunities to examine the drawings in more detail.

Questioning Strategies

"I feel so inadequate when dealing with nonfiction," a high school reading specialist confessed to us. "When I'm talking to students about fiction, I have some standard questions I can fall back on to start them thinking. I can ask about plot, setting, characters, or a number of other features. But when it comes to nonfiction, I don't know what to ask beyond 'What was the book about?' or 'Did you enjoy it?'"

We suspect that her remarks could have been made by many teachers and librarians. Fiction and its structure traditionally form the core of our literary backgrounds in general and of young adult literature classes in particular. Many of us just aren't used to examining informational books, and we shy away from asking young adults to take a critical look at the genre. The following ten questions are intended to provide a starting point for initiating discussion about informational books. Not every question needs to be used for all books, and neither does ten represent a magic number of questions that should be asked after each reading experience. Instead, these questions, and the reasons for including them, are designed to help librarians and teachers begin to expand their own strategies for eliciting responses about nonfiction.

1. *How would this book be different if it had been written ten years earlier? Ten years later?* This question not only forces young adults to look at copyright date and consider its importance, but also to think about the changes that occur, have occurred, or may occur in the discipline they're reading about. In addition, it allows adolescents a chance to share their interests and thoughts about a particular subject with an interested adult. In those cases where contents will not be altered by date, teenagers can still discuss why such information apparently remains constant.

2. *Which illustrations do you wish you had taken or drawn yourself? Why?* Young adults are asked to examine the illustrations not in terms of content, but rather in terms of execution. It's frankly a blatant attempt to put the student in the role of artist or photographer and think about the circumstances under which the illustrations were executed: How did David Macaulay get that perspective from the top of a pyramid? What would it have been like to translate the first *Voyager* images of the storms on Jupiter? How dangerous was it to take photographs of men in battle?

3. *Compare this nonfiction book with another one written on the same topic. How do they differ? How are they alike? Which one do you like better (or believe more)? Why?* This series of questions allows teenagers to examine different sources; to look for conflicting information or points of view; to think about organizational patterns, scope, and depth of presentation; and to compare the veracity of each work. It also provides a natural opportunity for teachers and librarians to explore individual reading habits in order to make further recommendations.

4. *What segment, portion, or focus of this book would make a good documentary? Why?* Documentaries, like informational books, express a bias or point of view. Here young adults are encouraged to identify that focus and find incidents and facts that support the author's thesis. They can compare the tools available to an author with those of a filmmaker. Will some text examples have to be deleted, expanded, or added in order to make a compelling documentary?

5. *What steps do you think the author followed to research and write this book?* Rather than ask adolescents to merely check documentation and bibliographies, this question places them in the role of author and directs them to examine and evaluate source material from a more personal standpoint. In addition, it provides a chance for teachers to discuss the process of scholarship and writing.

6. *How would this book be different if it had been written for a fourth grader?* Scope and depth of presentation represent important, but difficult, concepts for young adults to grasp. To ask them to weigh these factors in a book they've just read tends to produce speculation about the book they wish the authors had written instead of the one they did, or a plea to expand a particularly interesting segment. This question addresses scope and depth of presentation but casts these in terms of another audience—an age group young adults all know about because they've already passed through that developmental stage.

7. *What kind of teacher do you think the author would make?* A consideration of style—including clarity, language levels, and tone—is the purpose here. Does the author explain concepts well? Is the material presented as a lecture, a conversation, or a sermon? Does the author write above, below, or at a general level of understanding? An alternative to questions 6 and 7—*In addition to length, how does this nonfiction book differ from an encyclopedia article on the same topic?*—combines the ideas of audience, purpose, style, scope, and depth of presentation.

8. *If you had a chance to interview the authors of this book, what would you ask them?* This question allows the reader to go beyond the information presented in the book—to speculate about theories, facts, or the writing and research process. A few young adults may well formulate insightful questions that they really want responses to. In such cases, teachers and librarians may want to encourage these individuals to write to the authors in care of their publishers.

9. *Tell me three facts, theories, or incidents that you found particularly interesting. Now, assume you haven't read the book. Can you find this information? Why or why not?* This task directs young adults to reference aids, and gives some practice in using them. Many of their responses, particularly those dealing with theme, points of view, or specific examples, will not be readily accessible through an index. Together teachers and students will have to try several several subject entries, or use the table of contents, the glossary, or an appendix, thereby modeling and discussing the use of these aids.

10. *Look at the title and the jacket of this book. What do they indicate the book will be about? Do they give a fair representation of the book's contents?[12]* The decision to read a book is often based on the way it's marketed—the jacket design, the title, the endorsements on the cover. Young adults need to be aware of these advertising tools and begin to make some judgments concerning their appropriateness. During this discussion, librarians and teachers can lead teenagers to previewing strategies like skimming and scanning and can suggest expanded uses for the table of contents.

LIBRARY PROGRAMMING AND COLLECTION DEVELOPMENT

Programming is loosely defined as those activities initiated and designed by a librarian with the intent of bringing young adults into the library and publicizing the physical plant, the resources, and the personnel available to them. Although each project will generate its own particular objectives, increased circulation generally emerges as one of the purposes of programming. The following section will address three familiar components of programming and the ways in which informational books can be highlighted in each. It will conclude with a discussion of weeding nonfiction from young adult library collections.

Bibliographies

Our experiences indicate that the generation and distribution of printed bibliographies on special subjects pays off in increased young adult reading. Thoughtfully developed annotated lists alert teenagers to new topics and resources, and frequently give them a purpose for visiting the library. Effective bibliographies include suggested, not required, reading. They should be used sparingly. To publish lists on any conceivable topic quickly results in overkill, exiling those carefully constructed bibliographies to the depths of a high school locker to join other discarded communiqués like open-house notifications, failed quizzes, and innumerable notes from classmates.

Topics for bibliographies emerge from community activities, interests, curriculum demands, holidays, news events, television programs, movies, and any other area that touches a young adult's life. The most successful bibliographies treat a topic loosely, by looking at its broadest possible limits. In that way, all genres of literature can be covered. A "Back to School" bibliography for example, suggests traditional school stories like Robert Cormier's *The Chocolate War*, Lois Duncan's *Killing Mr. Griffin*, and John Knowles' *A Separate Peace*. But poetry like Mel Glenn's *Class Dismissed!*, personal accounts like William Finnegan's *Crossing the Line: A Year in the Land of Apartheid*, and informational books like Claudine G. Wirths and Mary Bowman-Kruhm's *I Hate School: How to Hand In & When to Drop Out* also find comfortable slots in "Back to School" reading.

Effective bibliographies offer a range of recommendations thoughtfully selected from the library's holdings. Those that include every book on a given topic serve no purpose; the card catalog already performs that function. The inclusion of popular titles along with those books that push young adults beyond these comfortable boundaries recognizes that adolescents want familiarity as well as challenges in their outside reading. If teenagers find "good" books on these lists, then they'll begin to trust the librarian to offer further reading suggestions.

The most consistently outstanding bibliographies for adolescent readers appear in *Booklist*. Since 1982, the Books for Young Adults' Department has generated approximately fifty such retrospective lists, identifying topics from World Cultures to Humor to the Vietnam War. Librarians are free to duplicate them as well as to use them as models. These lists represent the wide range of reading interests characteristic of young adults, include suggestions from every point on the literary spectrum, and address the varying maturity levels of the intended teenage audience. Annually, in the

August issue, the *Booklist* staff publishes an index of all the fine bibliographies they've compiled over the preceding decade, making it easier for a librarian to find the exact location of a particular list.

With the advent of in-house publishing departments, especially in many public school systems, librarians can now produce publicity materials that they formerly ordered from large, commercial establishments. They can personalize these items, and use them for a variety of programming activities. Bookmarks, with a few well-chosen suggestions for outside reading, work as "Mini-Bibs" for special young adult patrons. Figure 52, for example, shows an in-house bookmark designed for distribution to students taking either band, orchestra, or chorus.

This simple bookmark serves two important functions: It reminds students of the existence and hours of operation of the school media center, and it highlights several fine books that may have particular appeal to those enrolled in music classes. Bibliographies often create a surge of interest in a topic. Therefore, it's wise to have some back-up books in mind for those patrons who can't immediately find what they've requested. But don't expect this interest to die. Months after distributing such lists, librarians have found teenagers wandering the stacks with well-worn sheets in their hands, searching for a particular book that looked like good reading when they first saw it on a bibliography.

Figure 52. Bibliographic Bookmark

Take note of
A Good Book:

Berger, Melvin. *The Science of Music.*

Brooks, Bruce. *Midnight Hour Encours.*

Haskins, James. *Black Music in America.*

Meigs, James B. and Stern, Jennifer. *Make Your Own Music Video.*

Turner, Tina. *I, Tina.*

Library Hours:

8:00 A. M. - 5:00 P. M.

Monday - Friday

Booktalking

At certain times both librarians and teachers booktalk. They catch students between classes and sneak in a quick preview of new releases, they watch young adults return books and mention other works that relate to this material, and they engage teenagers in short conversations about intriguing reading matter. The following discussion of booktalking, however, covers more formal presentations. If you haven't used booktalking as a motivational tool, then refer to the chapter bibliography for general works that provide detailed discussions of the potential in booktalking, sample booktalks, and general tips for developing powerful presentations. The purpose here is not to turn novice booktalkers into professionals but, rather, to suggest ways in which various literary genres can be introduced in traditional programs.

All literature—fiction, informational books, biography, poetry, drama, folklore—represents the appropriate raw materials for booktalking. Since booktalks function to "entice the listener into reading,"[13] broad themes and a wide variety of books will serve to expand a reader's tastes and interests. If a teacher requests a booktalk on reading to parallel a study of the American Revolution, the librarian will want to include such books as Milton Meltzer's *The American Revolutionaries* or Lila Perl's *Slumps, Grunts, and Snickerdoodles: What Colonial America Ate and Why* along with such traditional historical fiction as Christopher and James Lincoln Collier's *My Brother Sam Is Dead* or Esther Forbes' *Johnny Tremain*.

Even topics that highlight fictional genres have applicable slots for nonfiction. Brian Aldiss' *Trillion Year Spree: The History of Science Fiction; The Penguin Encyclopedia of Horror and the Supernatural;* Don Bolognese's *Drawing Spaceships and Other Spacecraft*; Peter Nicholls' *The World of Fantastic Films; William K. Hartmann's Cycles of Fire: Stars, Galaxies and the Wonder of Deep Space;* or *Straight on Till Morning: Poems of the Imaginary World*; are natural partners to imaginative literature. Likewise, the concept of mystery can effortlessly expand to one of finding solutions and thus include titles like David Macaulay's *The Way Things Work,* Jim Murphy's *Weird & Wacky Inventions,* or Christopher Lampton's *Mass Extinctions: One Theory of Why the Dinosaurs Vanished.*

The reverse is also true. Booktalks centering on science fair projects, for example, could encompass fictional works like Jane Louise Curry's *Me, Myself and I,* in which the results of an ill-planned science experiment form the base for this intriguing story of time travel, or Helen Plotz's *Imagination's Other Place: Poems of Science and Mathematics.* Such choices expand, rather than limit, young adults' reading interests.

There are several points to keep in mind when booktalking nonfiction. First of all, the audience will want information concerning the scope of each book. To advertise David Taft's introductory *Computer Programming* as "everything you ever wanted to know about BASIC," will disappoint sophisticated users who open it and discover that the text addresses only elementary operations. Similarly, booktalkers should avoid misleading the audience. Introducing Roy Gallant's *Private Lives of the Stars* with a knowing wink and a reference to the flamboyant Hollywood lifestyle will probably ensure that this book gets checked out, but it will also produce an unhappy reader who finds the contents concerning the life and death of major stars in our universe an unwelcome surprise. Young adults must trust the booktalker to give an honest and accurate preview of each discussed book.[14]

Second, booktalkers should give young adults some indication of a book's depth of presentation. John A. Garraty's *1,001 Things Everyone Should Know about American History* devotes only a few descriptive sentences to each entry. Readers looking for trends, sophisticated theories, or detailed discussions won't find them here. Instead, they'll discover tidbits of information. For example, Thomas Jefferson said "a little rebellion, now and then, is a good thing, and as necessary in the political world as storms are in the physical"[15]; in 1849 Elizabeth Blackwell became the first woman to earn her M.D.[16]; "Wobblies" refers to the Industrial Workers of the World[17]; and William Howard Taft was once described as "a large body, entirely surrounded by men who know exactly what they want."[18]

Just as young adults should know that the surface facts mentioned in *1,001 Things Everyone Should Know about American History* will ill-equip them for a junior high school research paper, they also need to be alerted to the sophistication of other titles, like David E. Fisher's *The Origin and Evolution of Our Own Particular Universe*. Not intended for the neoyphyte, Fisher's work explores complicated physical theories which require some background knowledge on the part of the untutored reader.

Third, the use of appropriate illustrations will enhance booktalks. This practice adds variety to the presentation and alerts young adults to the presence of powerful graphics. Highlighting well-chosen illustrations also accents theme, introduces content, and allows the booktalker to model the "reading" of pictures. Figure 53, from Russell Freedman's *Indian Chiefs*, for example, underscores the callousness with which individuals stripped Native Americans of their heritage. R. M. Wright, the purchaser of this vast pile of hides, carelessly sits atop the very symbols of the Plains Indians' way of life, seemingly oblivious to his exploitation. Hazel Rochman, author of *Tales of Love and Terror: Booktalking the Classics*, suggests that booktalkers first introduce this powerful photograph, discuss it in detail, and then juxtapose this scene with the reading aloud of one of the numerous quotations that reveal the pride, defiance, resignation, or acceptance from the Native Americans featured in the text. Books like Timothy Ferris's *Spaceshots* which stress visuals, should be introduced comparably.

Traditionally, booktalkers choose to handle graphics in one of three ways. They will show illustrations through slides, hold up the book for the audience to see the pictures, or describe them without using any props. No one style emerges as more effective than any other, and individuals will have to choose the one that best fits their particular situations or programs.

Carefully chosen, competently reproduced, and effectively presented slides dramatically enhance booktalks. Their very presence underscores preplanning, while the projection allows the entire audience to see details in each photograph. But the use of slides creates some problems.

Figure 53. Slaughter at Dodge City.

A nominal production cost will be incurred; the room where the booktalk is to be presented must accommodate the use of visuals; and the equipment must be tested before the presentation. Another potential problem exists beyond these technical considerations—the relationship between booktalker and audience. A darkened room distances the two when eye contact shifts from the book or booktalker to the screen.

Holding up a book and pointing to particular illustrations highlights the work itself, keeping the focus precisely where it belongs. This technique only works, though, if the audience can comfortably observe each picture. When young adults can't see a particular illustration, they quickly become frustrated and turn their attention elsewhere.

Occasionally booktalkers can describe a specific illustration without showing it immediately. This description from David Bodanis's *The Secret House* should entice readers even if they can't see the dramatic photograph: "The microscopic organisms that inhabit our environment, those nasty looking creatures that have 'sacs with legs, . . . a few loose armor plates, holes for breathing, eating, elimination, and copulation, and stubby little hairs sticking out all over to help feel what's going on.'"[19] At the conclusion of the presentation teenagers can come up to the booktalker and take a closer look at this particularly "gross" photograph. This time extends the pleasure, sharing, and rapport built up between the librarian and the young adults.[20]

The final point to remember when booktalking nonfiction is simply to transfer many of the techniques used in other kinds of presentations: Put the book in context, read aloud portions of the text, encourage

Used by permission of the Kansas State Historical Society.

audience participation, and spotlight particularly interesting vignettes. A booktalk on adventure or heroism that includes Don Lawson's *The Abraham Lincoln Brigade* will probably have to sketch the historical background of the Spanish Civil War so listeners can develop a frame of reference for the work, while Milton Meltzer's *The American Revolutionaries: A History in Their Own Words* might best be presented through the oral reading of the following excerpt from Gottfried Mittelberger's *Journey to Pennsylvania*:

> During the journey the ship is full of pitiful signs of distress—smells, fumes, horrors, vomiting, various kinds of sea sickness, fever, dysentery, headaches, heat, constipation, boils, scurvy, cancer, mouth-rot, and similar afflictions, all of them caused by the age and highly salted state of the food, especially of the meat, as well as by the very bad and filthy water, which brings about the miserable destruction and death of many. Add to all that shortage of food, hunger, thirst, frost, heat, dampness, fear, misery, vexation, and lamentation, as well as other troubles. Thus, for example, there are so many lice, especially on the sick people, that they have to be scraped off the bodies.[21]

Occasionally during a booktalk librarians will encourage verbal participation from the classroom audience. Jim Murphy's *Weird & Wacky Inventions* and *Guess Again: More Weird & Wacky Inventions* suggest such an interactive approach. In both works Murphy provides drawings of strange inventions throughout history—a scalp massager; a coffin with an escape hatch; a combination clothes brush, flask, and drinking cup—and asks readers to identify the function and purpose of these odd creations. After young adults brainstorm their ideas, the booktalker can read the accompanying short descriptions of each object, providing both a nonthreatening application of critical thinking skills and a pleasant introduction to expository prose.

Booktalking remains a powerful tool for librarians to introduce young adults to fine literature. In order to reach the widest possible audience, however, booktalks should cover as many literary genres as possible. The payoff in covering informational books, poetry, drama, biography, and fiction will be excited young adults who want to know about books, talk about books, find books, and read books, an appropriate return on the time invested.

Displays

Displays and bulletin boards afford the librarian additional opportunities to spotlight special projects, compelling subjects, and outstanding books. Like other programming tools, they can alert teenage patrons to informational books housed in the library, but again, like other programming tools, they need to be used wisely.

Bulletin boards with catchy titles like "Fall Back into Reading," signaling the start of a school year and consisting of several book jackets attractively stapled on a colorful backdrop, suffer from overuse and consequently lose their punch when seen—or ignored—by a well-seasoned young adult audience. Bulletin boards should not serve as mere decorations but, rather, as stimulants for library patrons to circulate targeted materials. In order to do so, the exhibit must catch their attention, a tricky objective when dealing with young adults who have matured in an age of media sell. One technique worth considering is the use of real testimonials from adolescent patrons to excite teenagers about the library's offerings. Nothing is wrong with the theme "Fall Back into Reading"; the problem lies in its clichéd presentation. For one alternative, the librarian could ask a variety of young adults to recommend books that relate to their school experiences: the team quarterback to recommend a football book, a cheerleader a book on gymnastics, a band member a book on music, a student council representative a book on politics, a Spanish Club member a book in another language, a Future Farmers of America enthusiast a book on agriculture, or a science club participant a book on projects for the science fair. The librarian could then take a close-up photograph of each of the participants, mount their pictures and recommendations on cut-outs representing their hobbies, and stand back and watch the other teenagers head to this bulletin board to see what their classmates have to say.

Like any other idea, this one won't last if it is overused, but the concept can expand to several exciting projects. Graffiti boards, in which young adults write book recommendations on plain butcher paper, likewise stimulate interest in peer reading. And a display of paper airplanes created by readers of Seymour Simon's *The Paper Airplane Book* or Ralph S. Barnaby's *How to Make and Fly Paper Airplanes*, containers of make-up produced by readers of Vicki Cobb's *The Secret Life of Cosmetics*, or drawings from nature inspired by the works of Jim Arnosky all act to encourage other young adults to check out these books.

Effective library displays will generate excitement and act as motivational tools to stimulate reading. Sometimes that curiosity is aroused by making the display less accessible rather than by overtly bombarding the patrons with stimulating graphics. When working as a librarian in New Orleans, Karen Harris wanted to focus attention on science books. She attractively arranged several on the tops of shelves, but these books went unnoticed. Then she tried a little reverse psychology. Harris cut out white butcher paper in the shape of a picket fence, cut several peepholes in the slats, put the books in a display case, and covered the glass with the paper. The junior high students were suddenly drawn to the cabinet, they jockeyed for positions so they could see the books inside, and quickly begin to ask if they could look at one of those books, or if it would be all right to take one home to read. As an inducement for reading, the display worked.

At other times, quiet, less publicized displays fulfill a need. Mike Printz, head librarian at Topeka West High School in Kansas, maintains a permanent book bin in one corner of the library. Entitled "Afraid to Ask?" this display houses material on personal topics such as divorce, drugs, and incest. In addition, Printz keeps a generous supply of pamphlets from the State Board of Health on such topics as AIDS and birth control and brochures from such agencies as Al-Ateen in the same location. Although Printz acknowledges that many of the materials are borrowed but never checked out, he also notes that they are generally returned to the display. Printz provides help for many troubled students, but wisely does so without attracting the curiosity of their peers.

When preparing both bulletin boards and other displays, librarians might want to take a tip from Madison Avenue: Less is sometimes better. Students studying the Middle Ages, for example, don't require an exhibition alerting them to every available title in order to generate interest in the topic. They may instead respond to understatement. Take a piece of paper, turn it into parchment (dip it in tea, burn the edges), and have an art student print the titles of a few fine books covering related areas like art, weaponry, and cookery. If the student can print in calligraphy and illuminate letters, all the better. When this task is completed, remove one shelf and set up the document and the listed books right in the stacks. Effective and simple, this display dramatically alerts young adults to the variety of resources available on the Middle Ages.

Displays and bulletin boards work as lures. They not only bring young adults into the library, but they also tempt them to read many fine books. If these suggestions prove satisfying, teenagers will return for more of the same. These payoffs justify the time and effort that goes into creating effective exhibits.

Other programming activities, like coordinating young adult advisory committees, inviting speakers, and conducting telephone conference calls with authors, afford librarians additional chances to recommend related reading material. Our stance, that young adults will profit by reading many books from a variety of genres, remains constant. We hope it emerges as an important one in all elements of library programming.

WEEDING

Selecting and sharing appropriate informational books in libraries makes up only two-thirds of the responsibilities toward these works. Equally as important is the process of weeding, or discarding those books that clutter a collection with outdated information. While individuals may treasure and revere particular timeworn, dog-eared, and well-loved volumes, professional librarians seriously evaluate each book they recommend to young adults in terms of currentness. Although there are no generally agreed upon criteria for estimating the shelf life of a book, it is agreed that obsolete material must be discarded from the library's collection.

Being out-of-date is a quality not restricted to informational books, and although date of publication may be significant—even crucial in some instances—in others it may be of little importance. All books are dated, although it often takes close examination to find this evidence.

Much of young adult fiction, especially that which deals with trendy issues and yesterday's popular culture, is especially vulnerable to dating because the stories, descriptions, and values are meaningless to today's readers.

Further evidence that older novels may not be appropriate for modern readers comes from the necessity to revise many of these titles. In updating series books, like *Nancy Drew* and *The Hardy Boys*, not only have reading levels been lowered, but archaic expressions have been eliminated; Nancy has lost her yellow roadster in favor of a sleek new convertible; and criminals, who were originally from East European countries, are presently not ethnically identifiable.

Yet there are those works of fiction that speak to generation after generation of young adult readers. In 1981 Barbara Samuels polled secondary English teachers in order to identify their students' favorite novels. The one title chosen overwhelmingly was S. E. Hinton's *The Outsiders*, a book over twenty years old at the time of Samuels's study. The second most favored book was *The Pigman*, first published in 1968. These two books have defied dating not only with students, but also with teachers. Both novels appear among the ten most frequently taught books in secondary school classes[22] and in college course offerings in adolescent literature.[23]

Similarly, certain informational books retain their popularity with young adults. Field guides to various plants and animals are informational works that not only continue to appeal, but also enjoy multiple printings. For example, *A Field Guide to the Mammals* has proven so popular that reprints in 1964 and 1976 were required just to keep the book in stock.

Reprinting is not done lightly by publishing houses, and collective decisions to reissue a book are made by marketing directors, editors, and production managers. According to Mimi Kayden, associate publisher and marketing director at E. P. Dutton, guaranteed sales from 1,000 to 1,500 copies of a book a year are necessary before a publishing house will reprint a hardcover title.[24]

The mean publication date of the most frequently circulated informational titles chosen by junior high students in our study predated the survey by ten years. After reading each volume, we concluded that only ten percent of these books should be considered out-of-date. Despite the value of some older works, however, informational books are unquestionably subject to dating. Book formats, methods of presentation, attitudes, and knowledge all change.

In a 1985 address to the American Library Association, James Cross Giblin described four major alterations in informational books over the past ten years. First of all, new titles often focus on one segment or aspect of the subject, a device that is intended to lead youngsters to generalizations about the whole. Second, text is more concise and tightly written, and fictionalization is allowed to bring facts into focus. Third, authors and publishers consider illustrations from the onset of book development, trying to fuse the two into a unified whole. And last, visual appeal is considered. Type size is often larger than the utilitarian nine point; trim size is more generous than the minimal margins common just ten years ago, and page formatting, which places illustrations and text together, is an integral part of design.

Information also changes, and facts must reflect recent knowledge. New knowledge compelled Alan Charig to include a chapter in his 1985 book, *A New Look at the Dinosaurs*, debating the issue of whether these animals were warm-blooded or cold-blooded, while such information was not available to noted paleontologist William Scheele when he wrote about prehistoric life over thirty years ago. The Mesozoic Era has not changed, but knowledge of it has. Contemporary authors must remain up-to-date even on subjects millions of years old.

Some inaccuracies appearing in out-of-date books are potentially dangerous. Books concerning drug use published a scant five years ago typically focus on the horrors of heroin. At the time of their publication, data about cocaine indicated less serious addiction; crack had not yet hit the streets. With what we know about the widespread use of cocaine among today's teenagers, older works about substance abuse that downplay this specific addiction are now obsolete. Similarly, books concerning teenage sexuality are particularly subject to dating. Advice to teenagers contemplating sexual relationships must still address physiological changes during adolescence; emotional, social, and physical pressures that influence decisions to have sex; and alternatives for contraception. But books published before the AIDS epidemic that cover these issues and do not suggest proper protection with condoms during sexual intercourse are indefensible in a library collection.

Problems may also occur with many older chemistry books. Warnings, even those displayed prominently within the text, fail to provide adequate safety precautions. Equally as disturbing, many of these books suggest that young adults use dangerous chemicals to carry out their experiments. As Pat Manning, children's librarian at the Eastchester Public Library in New York, and Alan R. Newman, a researcher in the Division of Environmental Chemistry at the Johns Hopkins University in Baltimore, clearly state the problem: "The most dangerous experiments are those in which the child is exposed to fumes or chemicals that are toxic, carcinogenic, mutagenic, or teratogenic. Even in that ideal well-ventilated room there is no protection against these agents. While a burn may be serious and/or disfiguring, and a missing finger traumatic, the threat of death, or cancer, or genetic distortion lying in wait in one's future is worse."[25]

Other areas, like the geography of the Middle East and Africa or knowledge of the galaxy, change rapidly, and although books will never offer as current information as periodicals will, they frequently provide appropriate explications for young adults. The importance of their becoming dated may have to balance the need not to ignore certain topics. The increased availability of online databases, however, will alleviate this problem. Access to huge informational retrieval systems like DIALOG, speedy document transmission through fascimile machines, and improved interlibrary loan facilities, are already lessening the research dependence on single books and those few periodicals indexed in *Abridged Reader's Guide*.

In an honest attempt to address the problems of dating, authors and publishers frequently resort to the revision of popular editions rather than the development of entirely new works. Revisions are not undertaken lightly. Before a revision is attempted, the original edition must have registered some degree of popularity in order to justify the costs, and information in that particular subject matter must not only still be useful or popular, but also be outdated.

Patricia Lauber's *Journey to the Planets* provides an example of this process. The original edition, published in 1982, lost its currentness as *Voyager 2* ventured further and further into our universe and transmitted additional data back to earth. Aware of the potential for new knowledge when writing the book, Lauber not only qualifies her statements with such phrases as "at the present time," but she also warns her readers than in the future they will have to consult new sources:

> At the present time, Neptune and Uranus are thought to be near-twins. They are almost the same size: Uranus is slightly bigger, but Neptune has greater mass. Both are thought to have deep atmospheres of hydrogen and helium. Methane clouds give them their greenish color. One odd difference between them is that Neptune gives off more heat than it receives from the sun, but Uranus does not. If *Voyager 2* lasts that long, it will send back the first close-up views of Uranus in 1986 and Neptune in 1989, and knowledge of these planets will take a great leap forward.[26]

On January 28, 1986, coincidentally the day the space shuttle Challenger exploded, *Voyager 2* began transmitting photographs of Uranus and its accompanying moons and rings. By August 1986, *National Geographic* had published a particularly accessible and well-written article concerning the new discoveries and possible theories generated by observations of the photographs.[27] Other articles in various journals followed. Even with these resources available, Lauber decided to revise her own work, updating it to include the new information about Uranus. This decision was made with the full knowledge that three years later, in 1989, when *Voyager 2* approached the planet Neptune, she would again face the same decision about revisions.

Librarians are in a quandary. Should they retain the first publication and update it with the various articles written about *Voyager 2*, or should they discard the older work and purchase the new edition, aware that it will outdate itself before the year is over? We suggest the latter course for several reasons. Although the information available in the 1988 edition is available elsewhere, it is not presented within the context and framework of the original publication. Lauber integrates new observations about Uranus with those of previously mentioned planets in our universe, comparing its black, rock rings and accompanying shepherd moons to the rings and moons of Saturn, for example. New sources can serve only as an appendage to this base, failing to provide a single, coherent narrative. Even though the second edition will also be rendered obsolete by new information, it is still the most superior form of presentation available to students.

Not only does our knowledge of facts change, but shifts also occur in the manner in which they are presented. Remaining contemporaneous requires more than just staying abreast of subject matter. Sound pedagogy should also be incorporated in informational books. For example, books showing scientific experiments were once modeled after cookbooks, merely presenting young readers with a set of directions to follow in order to illustrate a preset conclusion. Today, the best of these publications prompt readers to observe results, question findings, and begin to generate the principles involved in the process. Books like Vicki Cobb's *The Secret Life of Cosmetics: A Science Experiment Book*, which stress the process of discovery, are far superior to those selections that tell the reader what the experiment is, how to conduct it, what the results must be, and how to interpret them. (Not incidentally, Vicki Cobb's books are specifically recommended by Manning and Newman because she uses common household ingredients for her experiments. Indeed, the most exotic substances called for in this work are Epsom salts, beeswax, and an Ex-Lax tablet.)

Cobb introduces five divisions of cosmetics—soap and toothpaste, lotions and creams, fragrances, hair products, and makeup—first, by providing an anecdotal, historical background and second, through experiments that demonstrate properties, effectiveness, and even the composition of these products for which teenagers collectively shell out millions of dollars each year. Appropriate experiments address questions such as, How effective is toothpaste? What is the staying power of perfume? and How do you make cold cream? Cobb stresses careful observation by further questioning the readers during their procedures. Although discussions of the activities are geared toward answering the initial hypothesis, they are carefully constructed to allow the reader opportunities to draw conclusions. Suggested related activities for each experiment expand the opportunities for learning.

This charge to lead readers into the process of a discipline forms the precept of Henry Legard and Andrew Singer's *Elementary BASIC*. They choose Sherlock Holmes and John D. Watson to demonstrate the analytical reasoning necessary to program a computer in BASIC. Their original, tantalizing premise is that Henry Legard has inherited an old trunk filled with Watson's manuscripts which describe Holmes fascination with Charles Babbage's analytical machine as a tool for solving particular cases. Watson decided not to publish the details of these crimes and the unusual solutions during this lifetime, the authors say, because he felt that the people of nineteenth-century England wouldn't have the background to understand the workings of Babbage's invention. but he hoped htat some future generation would. As readers follow Holmes and Watson developing algorithms, defining clues, entering data, and instructing the analytical machine to manipulate that information, they work through the process of designing and writing a computer program.

There is also a process of discovery in the social sciences. As Jean Fritz points out, "One of the purposes in presenting the past is to develop the *watcher* in children, for the living of life and the watching of life are bound by one cord."[28] William Finnegan reveals this process of watching in *Crossing the Line*. In this personal account, the author recreates a year spent in South Africa teaching English and then traveling through the country. He arrives in 1980, looks at the political and social situation, and formulates suggestions for change. The longer he stays in South Africa, however, the more he realizes that neither his first impressions nor his initial conclusions are appropriate. Throughout the year, Finnegan repeats the process of sharing his ideas and the ways in which he generates them. In the epilogue, he writes about leaving South Africa with an enriched view of the world. When readers turn the last page and leave his book, they may also have a procedural model for enriching their own views of the world, for they've had the opportunities to vicariously engage in Finnegan's observational research.

Social perceptions change, and arcane attitudes will also date a book. All books contain value systems. Sometimes readers are oblivious to these attitudes if they conform to mainstream values, but as time passes and points of view shift, the book remains static, and thus becomes outmoded. What readers presently consider racial slurs, sexual stereotyping, and patronizing attitudes to Third World countries passed unnoticed in books published for young adults just a few years ago.

Language also dates informational books, particularly those volumes in which authors adopt a conversational tone. The hallmark of such works is typically those trendy expressions as fresh as the slang heard on any schoolyard. But jargon changes, and when this language becomes outmoded, the author's position shifts from that of someone who knows the score to that of someone who doesn't.

In short, while certain titles of both fiction and nonfiction are subject to early obsolescence, others are not. Publication date alone does not determine whether a particular work should be discarded. Judgments about weeding particular informational books need to include considerations of factual accuracy, format, attitudes, language, and methods of presentation. Consequently, decisions about the appropriateness of books remain subjective and can only be made on an individual basis.

READING GUIDANCE

Although teachers and librarians engage in group booktalking activities and reading aloud, set up displays and special events, and distribute special bibliographies and annual lists of books, the heart of any literary program remains the personal reading recommendations given to individual young adults. If those book suggestions prove appropriate, then adolescents will return for more. If they don't, then teenagers will either look to someone else for advice or they will reject reading altogether.

The initial hooks used to pull young adults into the literary world often come from mass-market and popular reading suggestions. To continue offering various combinations of the same base, however, fails to encourage growth and quickly delivers the message that reading is characteristic of a young child's activity. Adolescence itself marks a period of physical, social, and intellectual maturity. The books recommended to individual teenagers also need to reflect increasing sophistication, or young adults will outgrow them.

This practice of gradually offering more intricate works from within the same genre is frequently referred to as the concept of reading ladders. Traditionally, it characterizes a common strategy used when recommending works of fiction. Teachers and librarians who encounter younger teenagers passing through that "unconscious delight" stage with such mystery series as *Alfred Hitchcock and the Three Investigators, Nancy Drew,* and the *Hardy Boys*, typically begin recommending more sophisticated works: Joan Lowery Nixon's *The Séance,* Lois Duncan's *Killing Mr. Griffin,* Mary Higgins Clark's *Where Are the Children?,* Avi's *Wolf Rider,* Philip Finch's *In a Place Dark and Secret,* Elaine Konigsburg's *Father's Arcane Daughter,* Susan Hill's *The Woman in Black,* and Josephine Tey's *The Daughter of Time.* The progression representing a growing sophistication in plot, theme, and language from Carolyn Keene to Josephine Tey is neither direct nor swift, but instead takes place over several years, often in combination with other reading ladders representing additional subjects and genres.

Seldom, however, does this concept expand to include nonfiction. Yet, like all literary forms, nonfiction contains a variety of works reflecting similar gradations. Friends, current events, family situations, classroom discussions, new books, and popular movies all influence adolescent reading preferences. When young adults first become interested in a subject, they typically want to read a general introduction covering surface facts and the language particular to the topic. After exhausting that base, many require books that address how knowledge is structured: the process of research, the collection of data, and a rudimentary understanding of the pattern of the discipline. Finally, some young adults will become immersed in a field, and their books should lead them to analyze collected data and draw conclusions from it. The following discussion will move through this progression using the subject of computers as the base for a loosely constructed reading ladder.

A goodly number of computer overview books start historically, with the development of the analytical machine, and move chronologically to the present. Typically they examine different brands of computers, detail peripheral equipment, explore potential uses in home and society, and suggest careers to pursue. Information extends beyond the covers with recommended reading lists of both books and magazines as well as the names and addresses of various user clubs. Enthusiastic and informative, they impart a sense of camaraderie among those who share the reader's hobby.

Not every such book is appropriate for every teenager interested in computers. Individual recommendations will vary depending on a particular young adult's age, background of experience, and reading proficiency. Suggestions for this level of reading include Joseph Deken's *The Electronic Cottage*, Fred D'Ignazio's *Messner's Introduction to the Computer*, Catherine O'Neill's *Computers, Those Amazing Machines*, David Rothman's *The Silicon Jungle*, and Don Slater's *Information Technology*. Not to be neglected at this point in a teenager's reading are biographies such as David Ritchie's *The Computer Pioneers: The Making of the Modern Computer* and Jeffrey S. Young's *Steve Jobs: The Journey is the Reward*. Fiction like Monica Hughes' *The Dream Catcher*, Orson Scott Card's *Ender's Game*, Ellen W. Leroe's *Robot Romance*, and Whitley Strieber and James Kunetka's *Nature's End: The Consequences of the Twentieth Century*, will also appeal to various young adults reading widely about computer science. Some teenagers requesting more specificity at this level will want works on robots, artificial intelligence, computer ethics, or specific program utilities. Consequently, volumes like Richard Forsyth's *Machines that Think*, Robin McKie's *Robots*, Marvin Minsky's collection of essays on *Robotics*, Dorothy B. Francis' *Computer Crime*, Christopher Lampton's *CD-ROMs* and Elayne Engelman Schulman's *Data Bases* will begin to satisfy these related needs.

Occasionally a young adult will pick up the special language associated with computers through reading many of the titles mentioned above. Those who haven't, and don't want to be embarrassed by referring to the peeks and pokes as a number chart, pronouncing ASCII as ash-two, or expecting hard copy to be a strenuous process will use specialized computer dictionaries to fill in their lexical gaps. Patricia Coniffe's *Computer Dictionary*, Bantam Books' *The Illustrated Computer Dictionary,* and *Webster's New World Compact Dictionary of Computer Terms* indicate the range of available tools appropriate for the youngest to the most mature teenager.

Joke books establish the discourse for playing with this newly acquired language. Riddles from Bishop's *Hello Mr. Chips* and Keller's *Ohm on the Range* such as "What did everyone say when the science teacher crossed a computer with a skunk?" (CPU); "What kind of display terminal do sailors use?" (A sea-R-T); or, "What do you call a wristwatch worn in the twenty-first century?" (a future-wrist-tick) not only provide opportunities for younger teenagers to manipulate their new vocabularies, but also expand the scope of their reading interests.

As young adults begin to read widely at this introductory level, teachers and librarians can gradually make recommendations of more sophisticated titles about computer science. Books about programming that stress the copying of programs over the invention of new ones fit comfortably into this level. David Ahl's *Basic Computer Games* and *More Basic Computer Games* provide novices with working programs to enter and save on their own systems. Young adults typing these routines learn important conventions of the discipline: lines must be numbered, zeroes have a slash through them, and l's and 1s can't be typed interchangeably. Furthermore, teenagers can begin to see patterns which they may want to incorporate into their own programs or use when evaluating commercial software. In other words, tedious exercises involving drill and practice, almost universally rejected in other contexts, are eagerly sought after by computer enthusiasts who often use them to acquire incidental but highly useful knowledge. Young adults at this stage who are interested in artificial intelligence may also enjoy Dorothy Hinshaw Patent's *The Quest for Artificial Intelligence,* which explores the concept of intelligence and how scientists attempt to duplicate it.

Programming books typically address teenagers at two different levels of exploration in computer science. For example, readers will determine their own uses for the BASIC routines presented in Kate Petty's *Pictures*. Some will copy the programs and use them without modification, while others will let them serve as a framework for their own original designs. Similar works like Christopher Lampton's *Programming in BASIC*, Roz Ault's *BASIC Programming for Kids*, and Henry Legard and Andrew Singer's *Elementary BASIC* provide the reader with the option of reproducing the programs as directed or of moving beyond the existing subroutines.

Learning to program a computer seems to begin the process of understanding how these machines work. This process begins with the sequential, deliberate instruction offered through many programming books. Once young adults acquire these skills, they may want to move further into programming or they may be content to become well-versed in the existing software on the market. Those who want to pursue programming will begin the process of immersion in the field, and demand increasingly more challenging programming languages and problems. Richard C. Adams' *Science with Computers* introduces problem solving and encourages young adults to experiment on their own. Some teenagers may also want to build their own computers, and will discover both sensible advice and solid direction in books like Irwin Math's *Bits and Pieces*. Whatever their particular interests, these young adults will require more complex books to nurture them.

As was noted in Chapter 5, the line frequently blurs between those books that offer an introduction, suggest a process, or provide immersion in a field. One such book is Michael Crichton's *Electronic Life*, which offers an overview for the novice, word play for the language enthusiast, programs for the copier, and programming strategies for the more sophisticated user. Young adults may choose not to explore a topic in-depth, and instead content themselves to reading numerous books about related content. If so, then librarians and teachers will want to respect those decisions. They can suggest more complex works, but should never force them on potential readers.

We began this book with a discussion of teenagers and their preference for reading informational books. These young adult reading interests called our attention to this exciting part of young adult literature. So it seemed fitting to end this book with a discussion of effective methods for using informational books with adolescents. Informational books offer teachers and librarians a chance to get youngsters to think about important issues from varying viewpoints, to hear quality literature read aloud, and to be asked meaningful questions about the books they've read. Booktalking informational books, developing displays that highlight new titles in this genre, and creating bibliographies that call attention to various nonfiction titles are all important techniques that help tap the reading interests of today's adolescents.

NOTES

1. Vacca, Richard T. and Vacca, Jo Anne L. (1989). *Content Area Reading*. Third ed. Glenview, IL: Scott Foresman, pp. 7–8.

2. Vaughan, Joseph L. and Estes, Thomas H. (1986). *Reading and Reasoning beyond the Primary Grades*. Newton, MA: Allyn & Bacon, p. 180.

3. Edelman, Bernard, editor (1985). *Dear America: Letters Home from Vietnam*. New York: W. W. Norton, p. 291

4. Edelman, Bernard, editor (1985), p. 137.

5. Edelman, Bernard, editor (1985), p. 214.

6. Greene, Bob (1989). *Homecoming: When the Soldiers Returned from Vietnam*. New York: G. P. Putnam's Sons, p. 59.

7. *Becoming a Nation of Readers: The Report of the Commission on Reading.* (1985). Champaign-Urbana, IL: Center for the Study of Reading, p. 23.

8. Jett-Simpson, Mary (1980). Students' Atitudes toward Reading Motivational Activities. Paper presented at the 70th annual conference of the National Association of Teachers of English. Cincinnati, Ohio, November 23, 1980, p. 5.

9. Carlsen, G. Robert and Sherrill, Anne (1988). *Voices of Readers: How We Come to Love Books.* Urbana, IL: National Council of the Teachers of English, pp. 146–147. Copyright © 1988 by The National Council of Teachers of English. Reprinted with permission.

10. Trelease, Jim (1989). *The New Read-Aloud Handbook.* Second rev. ed. New York: Penguin, pp. 13–14.

11. Trelease, Jim (1989), p. 152.

12. Peck, Richard (1978). Ten Questions to Ask about a Novel. *ALAN Newsletter, 5*, p. 7.

13. Chelton, Mary K. (1976). Booktalking: You Can Do It. *School Library Journal, 22*, p. 39.

14. Rochman, Hazel (1987). *Tales of Love and Terror: Booktalking the Classics.* Chicago: American Library Association, p. 29.

15. Garraty, John A. (1989). *1,001 Things Everyone Should Know about American History.* New York: Doubleday, p. 49.

16. Garraty, John A. (1989), p. 105.

17. Garraty, John A. (1989), p. 19.

18. Garraty, John A. (1989), p. 132.

19. Bodanis, David (1986). *The Secret House: 24 Hours in the Strange and Unexpected World in Which We Live Our Nights and Days.* New York: Simon & Schuster, p. 15.

20. Rochman, Hazel (1987). *Tales of Love and Terror: Booktalking the Classics.* Chicago: American Library Association, p. 27.

21. Meltzer, Milton (1987). *The American Revolutionaries: A History in Their Own Words, 1750–1800.* New York: Thomas Y. Crowell, p. 6.

22. Samuels, Barbara G. (1981). A National Survey to Determine the Status of the Young Adult Novel in the Secondary School English Classroom. Unpublished doctoral dissertation, University of Houston.

23. Abrahamson, Richard F. (1981). How Adolescent Literature Is Taught in American Colleges and Universities: The Results of a National Survey. *English Education, 13*, pp. 224–229.

24. Kayden, Mimi (1982). In Print or Out of Print? The Continuing Problem. *Top of the News, 38*, pp. 236–239.

25. Manning, Pat and Newman, Alan R. (1986). Safety Isn't Always First: A Disturbing Look at Chemistry Books. *School Library Journal, 33*, p. 102.

26. Lauber, Patricia (1972). *Journey to the Planets.* New York: Crown, p. 83.

27. Gore, Rick (1986). Uranus: *Voyager* Visits a Dark Planet. *National Geographic, 170*, pp. 179–195.

28. Fritz, Jean (1981). "The Very Truth." In Betsy Hearne and Marilyn Kaye, *Celebrating Children's Books.* New York: Lothrop, Lee & Shepard, p. 86.

Bibliography

Abrahamson, Richard F. (1981). How Adolescent Literature Is Taught in American Colleges and Universities: The Results of a National Survey. *English Education, 13,* 224–229.

Adams, Richard C. (1987). *Science with Computers.* New York: Franklin Watts/Experimental Science Series.

Adamson, Linda G. (1985). And Who Taught You Children's Literature? *The Horn Book, 61,* 631-632.

Adler, Irving (1967). The Prose Imagination. *School Library Journal, 13,* 22–23.

Ahl, David (1978). *Basic Computer Games.* Morristown, NJ: Creative Computing Press.

Ahl, David (1979). *More Basic Computer Games.* New York: Workman.

Aldiss, Brian W. with David Wingrove (1986). *Trillion Year Spree: The History of Science Fiction.* New York: Atheneum.

Alm, Julie N. (1978). "Young Adult Favorites: Reading Profiles from Nine Hawaii High Schools." In Jana Varlejs, *Young Adult Literature in the Seventies.* Metuchen, NJ: Scarecrow Press.

Ames, Lee J. (1977). *Draw 50 Airplanes, Aircraft and Spacecraft.* Garden City, NY: Doubleday.

Ames, Lee J. (1978). *Draw 50 Famous Faces.* Garden City, NY: Doubleday.

Ames, Lee J. (1981). *Draw 50 Dogs.* Garden City, NY: Doubleday.

Ames, Lee J. (1986). *Draw 50 Cars, Trucks, and Motorcycles.* Garden City, NY: Doubleday.

Anson, Robert Sam (1987). *Best Intentions: The Education and Killing of Edmund Perry.* New York: Random House.

Ardley, Neil (1983). *Computers.* New York: Warwick Press.

Ardley, Neil (1989). *Music.* New York: Knopf/An Eyewitness Book.

Arnosky, Jim (1986). *Flies in the Water, Fish in the Air.* New York: Lothrop Lee & Shepard.

Arthur, Alex (1989). *Shell.* New York: Knopf/An Eyewitness Book.

Ashabranner, Brent (1988). *Always to Remember: The Story of the Vietnam Veterans Memorial.* New York: Dodd, Mead.

Ashabranner, Brent (1988). Did You Really Write That for Children? *The Horn Book, 64,* 749-754.

Ashabranner, Brent and Ashabranner, Melissa (1987). *Into a Strange Land: Unaccompanied Refugee Youth in America.* New York: G.P. Putnam's Sons.

Ault, Roz (1983). *BASIC Programming for Kids.* Boston: Houghton Mifflin.

Avi (1986). Review the Reviewers? *School Library Journal, 32,* #8, 114-115.

Avi (1986). *Wolf Rider: A Tale of Terror.* New York: Bradbury Press.

Bacon, Betty (1984). "The Art of Nonfiction." In Pamela Petrick Barron and Jennifer Q. Burley, *Jump over the Moon: Selected Professional Readings*. New York: Holt, Rinehart & Winston, 195–204.

"Barbara Tuchman" (1989). *The Dallas Morning News*, February 7, Section A, 10.

Barnaby, Ralph S. (1968). *How to Make and Fly Paper Airplanes*. New York: Four Winds.

Baskin, Barbara and Harris, Karen (1980). *Books for the Gifted Child*. New York: R. R. Bowker.

Becoming a Nation of Readers: The Report of the Commission on Reading (1985). Champaign-Urbana, IL: Center for the Study of Reading.

Benedict, Helen (1987). *Safe, Strong, & Streetwise*. Boston: Joy Street Books.

Berger, Melvin (1989). *The Science of Music*. New York: Thomas Y. Crowell.

Bethancourt, T. Ernesto (1976). *The Dog Days of Arthur Cane*. New York: Holiday House.

Bishop, Ann (1982). *Hello Mr. Chips*. New York: E. P. Dutton.

Blair, Judith R. (1974). The Status of Non-fiction in the Reading Interests of Second, Third and Fourth Graders. MEd Thesis: Rutgers University, ED095481.

Blumberg, Rhoda (1976). *Sharks*. New York: Franklin Watts.

Bodanis, David (1986). *The Secret House: Twenty-Four Hours in the Strange and Unexpected World in Which We Spend Our Nights and Days*. New York: Simon & Schuster.

Bodart, Joni (1985). *Booktalk! 2: Booktalking for All Ages and Audiences*. New York: Wilson.

Bolognese, Don (1977). *Drawing Horses and Foals*. New York: Franklin Watts.

Bolognese, Don (1977). *Drawing Spaceships and Other Spacecraft*. New York: Franklin Watts.

Boyd, Brendan and Garrett, Robert (1989). *Hoops: Behind the Scenes with the Boston Celtics*. Boston: Little, Brown.

Boyne, Walter (1988). *The Smithsonian Book of Flight for Young People*. New York: Atheneum.

Braymer, Marjorie (1983). *Atlantis: The Biography of a Legend*. New York: Atheneum/A Margaret K. McElderry Book.

Brooks, Bruce (1986). *Midnight Hour Encores*. New York: Harper & Row.

Bunting, Eve (1982). *The Great White Shark*. New York: Julian Messner.

Burchard, Sue (1985). *The Statue of Liberty: Birth to Rebirth*. New York: Harcourt Brace Jovanovich.

Burger, Carl (1982). *All About Dogs*. Eau Claire, WI: E. M. Hale.

Burnford, Sheila (1961). *The Incredible Journey*. Boston: Little, Brown.

Burnford, Sheila (1975). *Bel Ria*. Boston: Little, Brown.

Burnie, David (1988). *Tree*. New York: Alfred A. Knopf/An Eyewitness Book.

Butterworth, W. E. (1983). *A Member of the Family*. New York: Four Winds.

Callahan, Steven (1986). *Adrift: Seventy-Six Days Lost at Sea*. Boston: Houghton Mifflin.

Campbell, Patty, Davis, Pat, and Quinn, Jerry (1978). "We Got There . . . It Was Worth the Trip!" In Jana Varlejs, *Young Adult Literature in the Seventies*. Metuchen, NJ: Scarecrow Press, 179–185.

Card, Orson Scott (1985). *Ender's Game*. New York: TOR Books.

Carlsen, G. Robert (1980). *Books and the Teenage Reader,* Second Revised Edition. New York: Bantam.

Carlsen, G. Robert, and Sherrill, Anne (1988). *Voices of Readers: How We Come to Love Books*. Urbana, IL: National Council of the Teachers of English.

Carr, Jo (1982). *Beyond Fact: Nonfiction for Children and Young People.* Chicago: American Library Association.

Carter, Betty (1982). Leisure Reading Habits of Gifted Students in a Suburban Junior High School. *Top of the News, 38,* 312–317.

Carter, Betty (1987). A Content Analysis of the Most Frequently Circulated Information Books in Three Junior High Libraries. Unpublished doctoral dissertation, University of Houston.

Carter, Betty and Harris, Karen (1982). What Junior High Students Like In Books. *Journal of Reading, 26,* 42–46.

Carter, Samuel, III (1971). *The Happy Dolphins.* New York: G. P. Putnam's Sons.

Charig, Alan (1985). *A New Look at the Dinosaurs.* New York: Facts on File.

Chatton, Barbara (1985). Using Young Adult Literature in the Content Areas. *The ALAN Review, 13,* 49-52.

Chelton, Mary K. (1976). Booktalking: You Can Do It. *School Library Journal, 22,* 39–43.

Children's Choices (1978). *The Reading Teacher, 32,* 42–46.

Children's Choices (1979). *The Reading Teacher, 33,* 47–52.

Children's Choices for 1980 (1980). *The Reading Teacher, 34,* 52–56.

Children's Choices for 1981 (1981). *The Reading Teacher, 35,* 68–72.

Children's Choices for 1982 (1982). *The Reading Teacher, 36,* 75–79.

Children's Choices for 1983 (1983). *The Reading Teacher, 37,* 65–66.

Children's Choices for 1984 (1984). *The Reading Teacher, 38,* 71–75.

Childress, Glenda (1985). Gender Gap in the Library: Different Choices for Boys and Girls. *Top of the News, 42,* 69–73.

Clark, Mary Higgins (1976). *Where Are the Children?* New York: Dell.

Classroom Choices (1975). *The Reading Teacher, 29,* 129–132.

Classroom Choices (1976). *The Reading Teacher, 30,* 58–63.

Classroom Choices (1977). *The Reading Teacher, 31,* 18–23.

Cobb, Vicki (1985). *The Secret Life of Cosmetics: A Science Experiment Book.* New York: J. B. Lippincott.

Cohen, Susan and Cohen, Daniel (1985). *A Six-Pack and a Fake I.D.: Teens Look at the Drinking Question.* New York: M. Evans.

Collier, James Lincoln and Collier, Christopher (1974). *My Brother Sam Is Dead.* New York: Four Winds.

Conniffe, Patricia (1984). *The Computer Dictionary.* New York: Scholastic.

Conover, Ted (1987). *Coyotes: A Journey through the Secret World of America's Illegal Aliens.* New York: Random House/Vintage.

Cook, Fred J. (1980). *The Ku Klux Klan: America's Recurring Nightmare.* New York: Julian Messner.

Coombs, Charles (1988). *Soaring: Where Hawks and Eagles Fly.* New York: Henry Holt.

Cooper, Heather and David Pelham (1985). *The Universe: A Three Dimensional Study.* New York: Random House.

Corbeil, Jean-Claude (1986). *The Facts on File Visual Dictionary.* New York: Facts on File.

Cormier, Robert (1974). *The Chocolate War.* New York: Pantheon.

Crichton, Michael (1969). *The Andromeda Strain.* New York: Alfred A. Knopf.

Crichton, Michael (1983). *Electronic Life.* New York: Alfred A. Knopf.

Crichton, Michael (1987). *Sphere.* New York: Alfred A. Knopf.

Crutcher, Chris (1986). *Stotan!* New York: Greenwillow Books.

Curry, Jane Louise (1987). *Me, Myself and I: A Tale of Time Travel.* New York: Margaret K. McElderry.

Darcy, Laura and Boston, Louise, compilers (1983). *Webster's New World Compact Dictionary of Computer Terms.* New York: Simon & Schuster.

Deken, Joseph (1983). *The Electronic Cottage.* New York: Bantam Books.

Dewey, Melvil (1979). *Dewey Decimal Classification and Relative Index.* Vol. 1.

Dewey, Melvil (1979). *Dewey Decimal Classification and Relative Index.* Vol. 2, *Schedules.*

D'Ignazio, Fred (1983). *Invent Your Own Computer Games.* New York: Franklin Watts.

D'Ignazio, Fred (1983). *Messner's Introduction to the Computer.* New York: Julian Messner.

Dingerkus, Guido (1985). *The Shark Watchers' Guide.* New York: Julian Messner.

Dolan, Edward F. (1989). *MIA: Missing in Action: A Vietnam Drama.* New York: Franklin Watts.

Dostert, Pierre Etienne (1988). *Africa 1988.* 23rd Annual Edition. Washington, DC: Stryker-Post Publications.

Dostert, Pierre Etienne (1988). *Latin America 1988.* 22nd Annual Edition. Washington, DC: Stryker-Post Publications.

Drimmer, Frederick (1988). *Born Different: The Amazing Stories of Some Very Special People.* New York: Atheneum.

Druse, Judy (1989). Booktalking for Physics Classes? *Noteworthy, 2,* 3 and 6.

Duncan, Lois (1978). *Killing Mr. Griffin.* Boston: Little, Brown.

Durrell, Gerald and Durrell, Lee (1983). *The Amateur Naturalist.* New York: Alfred A. Knopf.

Edelman, Bernard, editor (1985). *Dear America: Letters Home from Vietnam.* New York: W. W. Norton.

Eisley, Loren (1957). *The Immense Journey.* New York: Time.

Ellis, W. Geiger (1987). To Tell The Truth or at Least a Little Nonfiction. *ALAN Review, 14,* 39–40.

Feldbaum, Carl B., and Bee, Ronald J. (1988). *Looking the Tiger in the Eye.* New York: Harper & Row.

Ferris, Timothy (1984). *Spaceshots: The Beauty of Nature Beyond Earth.* New York: Pantheon Books.

Finch, Phillip (1985). *In a Place Dark and Secret.* New York: Franklin Watts.

Fine, John Christopher (1988). *The Hunger Road.* New York: Atheneum.

Finnegan, William. *Crossing the Line: A Year in the Land of Apartheid.* New York: Harper & Row.

Fisher, David E. (1988). *The Origin and Evolution of Our Own Particular Universe.* New York: Atheneum.

Fisher, Margery (1972). *Matters of Fact: Aspects of Non-fiction for Children.* New York: Thomas Y. Crowell.

Fisher, Maxine P. (1986). *Recent Revolutions in Anthropology.* New York: Franklin Watts/A Science Impact Book.

Forbes, Esther (1943). *Johnny Tremain.* Boston: Houghton Mifflin.

Ford, Dennis (1989). Review of Walter Boyne's *The Smithsonian Book of Flight for Young People in School Library Journal, 35,* 96.

Forsyth, Richard (1986). *Machines that Think.* New York: Warwick Press/Science in Action.

Francis, Dorothy B (1987). *Computer Crime.* New York: E. P. Dutton/Lodestar Books.

Freedman, Russell (1983). *Children of the Wild West.* New York: Clarion Books.

Freedman, Russell (1987). *Indian Chiefs.* New York: Holiday House.

Freedman, Russell (1987). *Lincoln: A Photobiography.* New York: Clarion Books.

Freedman, Russell (1988). *Buffalo Hunt.* New York: Holiday House.

Fritz, Jean (1981). "The Very Truth." In Betsy Hearne and Marilyn Kaye, *Celebrating Children's Books.* New York: Lothrop, Lee & Shepard, 81–86.

Fritz, Jean (1988). Biography: Readability Plus Responsibility. *The Horn Book, 64,* 759–760.

Fritz, Jean (1988). *China's Long March: 6,000 Miles of Danger.* New York: G. P. Putnam's Sons.

Frost, Robert (1969). *The Poetry of Robert Frost.* Edited by Edward Connery Lathem. New York: Holt, Rinehart and Winston.

Gallant, Roy A. (1986). *Private Lives of the Stars.* New York: Macmillan.

Garraty, John A. (1989). *1,000 Things Everyone Should Know about American History.* New York: Doubleday.

Gelman, Rita Golden (1988). *Inside Nicaragua: Young People's Dreams and Fears.* New York: Franklin Watts.

Giblin, James Cross (1988). *Let There Be Light: A Book about Windows.* New York: Thomas Y. Crowell.

Gioglio, Gerald R. (1989). *Days of Decision: An Oral History of Conscientious Objectors in the Military during the Vietnam War.* Trenton, NJ: The Broken Rifle Press.

Gipson, Fred (1956). *Old Yeller.* New York: Harper & Row.

Glenn, Mel (1982). *Class Dismissed!* New York: Clarion Books.

Goldberg, Jeff (1989). *Anatomy of a Scientific Discovery.* New York: Bantam Books.

Gore, Rick (1986). Uranus: *Voyager* Visits a Dark Planet. *National Geographic, 170,* 179–195.

Greene, Bob (1989). *Homecoming: When the Soldiers Returned from Vietnam.* New York: G. P. Putnam's Sons.

Guinness Book of World Records (1989). New York: Bantam Books.

Gustafson, Anita (1985). *Guilty or Innocent?* New York: Holt, Rinehart & Winston.

Hammond, Tim (1988). *Sports.* New York: Alfred A. Knopf/An Eyewitness Book.

Harris, Bill (1979). *Texas.* New York: Mayflower Books.

Harrison, Hal H. (1971). *The World of the Snake.* New York: J. B. Lippincott.

Hartmann, William K. (1987). *Cycles of Fire: Stars, Galaxies and the Wonder of Deep Space.* New York: Workman.

Haskins, James (1987). *Black Music in America: A History Through Its People.* New York: Thomas Y. Crowell.

Haskins, James and Benson, Kathleen (1988). *The 60's Reader.* New York: Viking Kestrel.

Heckman, Philip (1986). *The Magic of Holography.* New York: Atheneum.

Hentoff, Nat (1988). *American Heroes: In and Out of School.* New York: Delacorte Press.

Heppenheimer, T. A. (1985). "Man Makes Man." In Marvin Minsky, *Robotics.* Garden City, NY: Anchor Press/Doubleday, 28–69.

Herda, D. J. (1982). *Dirt Bike Racing.* New York: Julian Messner.

Hermes, Patricia (1985). *A Solitary Secret.* San Diego, CA: Harcourt Brace Jovanovich.

Hill, Helen, Perkins, Agnes, and Helbig, Althea, selectors (1977). *Straight On Till Morning: Poems of the Imaginary World.* New York: Thomas Y. Crowell.

Hill, Susan (1986). *The Woman in Black.* New York: David R. Godine.

Hinton, S. E. (1962). *The Outsiders.* New York: Viking Press.

Hofsinde, Robert (1960). Brother of the Indian. *Horn Book, 36,* 16–21.

Hughes, Monica (1986). *The Dream Catcher.* New York: Atheneum/Argo.

Hyde, Margaret O. and Outwater, Alice D. (1978). *Addictions: Gambling, Smoking, Cocaine Use and Others.* New York: McGraw Hill.

Ifrah, Georges (1985). *From One to Zero: A Universal History of Numbers.* New York: Viking.

The Illustrated Computer Dictionary. (1983). New York: Bantam Books.

Isaacson, Philip M. (1989). *Round Buildings, Squre Buildings, & Buildings that Wiggle Like a Fish.* New York: Alfred A. Knopf/A Borzoi Book.

Jacobson, Morris K. and Emerson, William K. (1977). *Wonders of Starfish.* New York: Dodd, Mead.

Jaspersohn, William (1983). *Magazine: Behind the Scenes at Sports Illustrated.* Boston: Little, Brown.

Jespersen, James and Fitz-Randolph, Jane (1987). *From Quarks to Quasars: A Tour of the Universe.* New York: Atheneum.

Jett-Simpson, Mary (1980). Students' Atitudes toward Reading Motivational Activities. Paper presented at the 70th annual conference of the National Association of Teachers of English. Cincinatti, Ohio, November 23, 1980.

Jordan, Arthur M. (1921). *Children's Interests in Reading.* New York: Teachers College, Columbia University.

Karlin, Robert (1962). Library-Book Borrowing vs. Library-Book Reading. *The Reading Teacher, 16,* 77–81.

Katz, William Loren and Crawford, Mark (1989). *The Lincoln Brigade: A Picture History.* New York: Atheneum.

Kayden, Mimi (1982). In Print or Out of Print? The Continuing Problem. *Top of the News, 38,* 236–239.

Keller, Charles (1982). *Ohm on the Range.* Englewood Cliffs, NJ: Prentice-Hall.

Kiefer, Irene (1984). *Nuclear Energy at the Crossroads.* New York: Atheneum.

Kimmel, Margaret Mary and Segel, Elizabeth (1988). *For Reading Out Loud!* New York: Delacorte.

King, Martin Luther, Jr. (1964). *Why We Can't Wait.* New York: New American Library.

Knight, David C. (1983). *Robotics: Past, Present & Future.* New York: William Morrow.

Knowles, John (1980). *A Separate Peace.* New York: Dell.

Kolodny, Nancy J., Kolodny, Robert C., and Bratter, Thomas E. (1986). *Smart Choices.* Boston: Little, Brown.

Konigsburg, Elaine (1976). *Father's Arcane Daughter.* New York: Atheneum.

Krasnoff, Barbara (1982). *Robots: Reel to Real.* New York: Arco Publishing.

Kuklin, Susan (1989). *Fighting Back: What Some People Are Doing about AIDS.* New York: G. P. Putnam's Sons.

Lampton, Christopher (1983). *Programming in BASIC.* New York: Franklin Watts.

Lampton, Christopher (1986). *Mass Extinctions: One Theory of Why the Dinosaurs Vanished.* New York: Franklin Watts/An Impact Book.

Lampton, Christopher (1987). *CD-ROMs.* New York: Franklin Watts/A First Book.

Langone, John (1986). *Dead End: A Book about Suicide.* New York: Little, Brown.

Lauber, Patricia (1982). *Journey to the Planets.* New York: Crown Publishers.

Lauber, Patricia (1987). *Journey to the Planets.* Rev. ed. New York: Crown Publishers.

Lasky, Kathryn (1985). Reflections on Nonfiction. *The Horn Book, 61,* 527–532.

Lawson, Don (1986). *An Album of the Vietnam War.* New York: Franklin Watts.

Lawson, Don (1989). *The Abraham Lincoln Brigade: Americans Fighting Facism in the Spanish Civil War.* New York: Thomas Y. Crowell.

Lederer, Richard (1987). *Anguished English.* Charleston, SC: Wyrick.

Legard, Henry and Singer, Andrew (1982). *Elementary BASIC.* New York: Random House.

Leroe, Ellen W. (1985). *Robot Romance.* New York: Harper & Row.

LeShan, Eda (1985). The Pleasure Principle: A Lively Look at the New Nonfiction. Program presented by the Children's Book Council/ALA Joint Committee at the American Library Association's 104th Annual Conference, Chicago, Illinois.

Mabie, Margot C. J. (1985). *Vietnam: There and Here.* New York: Holt, Rinehart & Winston.

Mabie, Margot C. J. (1987). *The Constitution: Reflections of a Changing Nation.* New York: Henry Holt.

Macaulay, David (1979). *Motel of the Mysteries.* Boston: Houghton Mifflin.

Macaulay, David (1980). *Unbuilding.* Boston: Houghton Mifflin.

Macaulay, David (1983). *Mill.* Boston: Houghton Mifflin.

Macaulay, David (1985). *Pyramid.* Boston: Houghton Mifflin.

Macaulay, David (1988). *The Way Things Work.* Boston: Houghton Mifflin.

Manchel, Frank (1982). *An Album of Great Science Fiction Films.* New York: Franklin Watts.

Manning, Pat and Newman, Alan R. (1986). Safety Isn't Always First: A Disturbing Look at Chemistry Books. *School Library Journal, 33,* 99–102.

Marrin, Albert (1985). *1812: The War Nobody Won.* New York: Atheneum.

Marrin, Albert (1986). *The Yanks Are Coming: The United States in the First World War.* New York: Atheneum.

Math, Irwin (1984). *Bits and Pieces: Understanding and Building Computer Devices.* New York: Charles Scribner's Sons.

McGowen, Tom (1981). *Encyclopedia of Legendary Creatures.* Chicago: Rand McNally.

McKenna, Michael C. (1986). Reading Interests of Remedial Secondary School Students. *Journal of Reading, 29,* 346–351.

McKie, Robin (1986). *Robots.* New York: Franklin Watts/Modern Technology.

McWhirter, Norris and McWhirter, Ross, editors (1975). *The Guinness Book of Amazing Achievements.* New York: Sterling.

McWhirter, Norris and McWhirter, Ross, editors (1989). *The Guinness Book of World Records.* New York: Sterling.

Meigs, Cornelia, Nesbitt, Elizabeth, Eaton, Anne Thaxter, and Viguers, Ruth Hill (1969). *A Critical History of Children's Literature.* Rev. ed. New York: Macmillan, 101.

Meltzer, Milton (1976). Where Do All the Prizes Go? The Case for Nonfiction. *The Horn Book, 52,* 17-23.

Meltzer, Milton (1982). *The Truth about the Ku Klux Klan.* New York: Franklin Watts.

Meltzer, Milton (1982). "Who's Neutral?" In Jo Carr, *Beyond Fact.* Chicago: American Library Association, 103–109.

Meltzer, Milton (1985). *Ain't Gonna Study War No More: The Story of America's Peaceseekers.* New York: Thomas Y. Crowell.

Meltzer, Milton (1987). *The American Revolutionaries: A History in Their Own Words.* New York: Thomas Y. Crowell.

Meltzer, Milton (1988). *Rescue: The Story of How Gentiles Saved Jews in the Holocaust.* New York: Harper & Row.

Meltzer, Milton (1989). *Voices from the Civil War.* New York: Thomas Y. Crowell.

Mercer, Charles (1985). *Statue of Liberty.* New York: G. P. Putnam's Sons.

Merriman, Nick (1989). *Early Humans.* New York: Alfred A. Knopf/An Eyewitness Book.

Messina, Lincoln E. (1979). The Relationship of the Expressed Reading Interests of Fourth Grade Students to their Free Selection at Library Book Choices. M.D. Thesis: Kean College at New Jersey. ED169505.

Meyer, Carolyn (1986). *Voices of South Africa: Growing Up in a Troubled Land.* San Diego, CA: Harcourt Brace Jovanovich.

Meyer, Carolyn and Gallenkamp, Charles (1985). *The Mystery of the Ancient Maya*. New York: Atheneum/A Margaret K. McElderry Book.

Miller, Jonathan and Pellham, David (1983). *The Human Body*. New York: Viking Press.

Miller, Jonathan and Pellham, David (1984). *The Facts of Life*. New York: Viking Press.

Milne, Lorus J. and Milne, Margery (1987). *A Shovelful of Earth*. New York: Henry Holt.

Minsky, Marvin, editor (1985). *Robotics*. Garden City, NY: Doubleday/Omni Press Books.

Moll, Richard (1985). *The Public Ivys: A Guide to America's Best Public Undergraduate Colleges and Universities*. New York: Viking.

Montague-Smith, Patrick (1984). *The Royal Family Pop-up Book*. New York: Bounty Books.

Moore, Janet Gaylord (1968). *The Many Ways of Seeing*. New York: World Publishing.

Moore, Patrick (1983). *The Space Shuttle Action Book*. New York: Random House.

Moulton, Priscilla Landis (1966). An Experiment in Cooperative Reviewing by Scientists and Librarians. *The Horn Book, 42*, 345–349.

Mowat, Farley (1979). *Never Cry Wolf*. New York: Bantam Books.

Murphy, Jim (1978). *Weird & Wacky Inventions*. New York: Crown Publishers.

Murphy, Jim (1986). *Guess Again: More Weird & Wacky Inventions*. New York: Bradbury.

National Geographic Book of Mammals, Volume 1 (1981). Washington, DC: National Geographic Society.

National Geographic Book of Mammals, Volume 2 (1981). Washington, DC: National Geographic Society.

Nicholls, Peter (1984). *The World of Fantastic Films: An Illustrated Survey*. New York: Dodd, Mead.

Nichols, Cathleen Armstrong (1984). Reading Preferences of Remedial Ninth, Tenth, Eleventh and Twelfth Grade Students from California. Unpublished doctoral dissertation, Brigham Young University.

Nilsen, Alleen Pace and Donelson, Kenneth L. (1985). *Literature for Today's Young Adults*. Glenview, IL: Scott Foresman.

Nixon, Joan Lowery (1980). *The Séance*. San Diego, CA: Harcourt Brace Jovanovich.

Norvell, George. (1973). *The Reading Interests of Young People*. East Lansing, MI: Michigan State University Press.

Nourse, Alan E. (1986). *AIDS*. New York: Franklin Watts.

Nourse, Alan E. (1989). *AIDS*. Rev. ed. New York: Franklin Watts.

Nugent, Susan M. (1983). The Evolution of a Syllabus: Adolescent Literature. *The ALAN Review, 10*, 72-29.

Oliver, James A. (1964). *Snakes in Fact and Fiction*. New York: Macmillan.

O'Neill, Catherine (1985). *Computers: Those Amazing Machines*. Washington, DC: National Geographic Society.

Palmer, Laura (1987). *Shrapnel in the Heart: Letters and Remembrances from the Vietnam Veterans Memorial*. New York: Random House.

Parker, Steve (1988). *Pond & River*. New York: Alfred A. Knopf/An Eyewitness Book.

Parker, Steve (1989). *Mammal*. New York: Alfred A. Knopf/An Eyewitness Book.

Parnell, Peter (1984). *The Daywatchers*. New York: Macmillan.

Patent, Dorothy Hinshaw (1986). *The Quest for Artificial Intelligence*. San Diego, CA: Harcourt Brace Jovanovich.

Paterson, Donald G. and Tinker, Miles A. (1940). *How to Make Type Readable*. New York: Harper & Row.

Peck, Richard (1978). Ten Questions to Ask about a Novel. *ALAN Newsletter, 5*, 1 & 7.

Perl, Lila (1975). *Slumps, Grunts and Snickerdoodles: What Colonial America Ate and Why.* New York: Clarion Books.

Peters, David (1986). *Giants of Land, Sea & Air: Past & Present.* New York: Alfred A. Knopf; San Francisco: Sierra Club Books/A Borzoi Book.

Petty, Kate (1986). *Pictures.* New York: Gloucester Press/Micro Fun.

The Pleasure Principle: A Lively Look at the New Nonfiction. (1985). Program presented by the Children's Book Council/ALA Joint Committee at the American Library Association's 104th Annual Conference, Chicago, Illinois.

Plotz, Helen, compiler (1955). *Imagination's Other Place: Poems of Science and Mathematics.* New York: Thomas Y. Crowell.

Podendorf, Illa (1984). "Characteristics of Good Science Materials for Young Readers." In Pamela Petrick Barron and Jennifer Q. Burley, *Jump over the Moon: Selected Professional Readings.* New York: Holt, Rinehart & Winston, 214–219.

Poynter, Margaret and Klein, Michael J. (1984). *Cosmic Quest: Searching for Intelligent Life among the Stars.* New York: Atheneum.

Pringle, Laurence (1981). "Science Done Here." In Betsy Hearne and Marilyn Kaye, *Celebrating Children's Books.* New York: Lothrop, Lee & Shepard, 108–115.

Pringle, Laurence (1985). *Nuclear War: From Hiroshima to Nuclear Winter.* Hillside, NJ: Enslow.

Pringle, Laurence (1986). *Throwing Things Away: From Middens to Resource Recovery.* New York: Thomas Y. Crowell.

Probst, Robert E. (1986). "Adolescent Literature and the English Curriculum." *English Journal, 75,* 26–30.

Purves, Alan C. and Beach, Richard (1972). *Literature and the Reader: Research in Response to Literature, Reading Interests and the Teaching of Literature.* Urbana, IL: National Council of the Teachers of English.

Purves, Alan C. and Monson, Dianne L. (1984). *Experiencing Children's Literature.* Glenview, IL: Scott, Foresman.

Rahn, Joan Elma (1983). *Keeping Warm, Keeping Cool.* New York: Atheneum.

Rawls, Wilson (1961). *Where the Red Fern Grows.* Garden City, NY: Doubleday.

Reed, Don C. (1986). *Sevengill: The Shark and Me.* New York: Alfred A. Knopf/Sierra Club Books.

Reed, Don C. (1989). *The Dolphins and Me.* Boston: Sierra Club Books/Little, Brown.

Richards, Herbert (1982). *The T. F. H. Book of Puppies.* Neptune City, NJ: T. F. H.

Riis, Jacob A. (1957). *How the Other Half Lives.* New York: Hill and Wang.

Ritchie, David (1986). *The Computer Pioneers: The Making of the Modern Computer.* New York: Simon & Schuster.

Rochman, Hazel (1986). The YA Connection: Footnotes and Critical Thinking. *Booklist, 82,* 639.

Rochman, Hazel (1987). *Tales of Love and Terror: Booktalking the Classics.* Chicago: American Library Association.

Rochman, Hazel (1989). Booktalking: Going Global. *Horn Book, 65,* 30–35.

Rogasky, Barbara (1988). *Smoke and Ashes: The Story of the Holocaust.* New York: Holiday House.

Ross, Patricia (1971). *Mexico.* Grand Rapids, MI: Fideler.

Rothman, David H. (1985). *The Silicon Jungle.* New York: Ballantine Books.

Rudman, Herbert C. (1955). The Informational Needs and Reading Interests of Children in Grades IV through VII. *Elementary School Journal, 55,* 502–512.

Sagan, Carl (1980). *Cosmos.* New York: Random House.

St. George, Judith (1989). *Panama Canal: Gateway to the World.* New York: G. P. Putnam's Sons.

Salzberg, Charles (1987). *From Set Shot to Slam Dunk: The Glory Days of Basketball in the Words of Those Who Played It.* New York: E. P. Dutton.

Sandler, Martin (1979). *The Story of American Photography.* Boston: Little, Brown.

Samson, John G. (1979). *The Pond: The Life of the Aquatic Plants, Insects, Fish, Amphibians, Reptiles, Mammals and Birds that Inhabit the Pond and Its Surrounding Hillside and Swamp.* New York: Alfred A. Knopf.

Samuels, Barbara G. (1981). A National Survey to Determine the Status of the Young Adult Novel in the Secondary School English Classroom. Unpublished doctoral dissertation, University of Houston.

Samuels, Barbara G. (1989). Young Adults' Choices: Why Do Students 'Really Like' Particular Books? *Journal of Reading, 32,* 714–719.

Sattler, Helen Roney (1981). *Dinosaurs of North America.* New York: Lothrop, Lee & Shepard.

Sattler, Helen Roney (1986). *Sharks, the Super Fish.* New York: Lothrop, Lee & Shepard.

Sayer, Angela (1980). *Crescent Color Guide to Dogs.* New York: Crescent Books.

Sayer, Angela (1981). *Crescent Color Guide to Puppies.* New York: Crescent Books.

Schaller, George and Schaller, Kay (1977). *Wonders of Lions.* New York: Dodd, Mead.

Schulman, Elayne Engelman (1987). *Data Bases for Beginners.* New York: Franklin Watts/A Computer Literacy Skills Book.

Schulman, Elayne Engelman and Page, Richard R. (1987). *Spreadsheets for Beginners.* New York: Franklin Watts/A Computer Literacy Skills Book.

Scott, Elaine (1985). *Stocks and Bonds, Profits and Losses: A Quick Look at Financial Markets.* New York: Franklin Watts.

Shilts, Randy (1987). *And the Band Played On: Politics, People, and the AIDS Epidemic.* New York: St. Martin's.

Silverstein, Alvin and Silverstein, Virginia (1986). *AIDS: Deadly Threat.* Hillside, NJ: Enslow.

Silverstein, Herma (1989). *Teenage and Pregnant: What You Can Do.* Englewood Cliffs, NJ: Julian Messner.

Simon, Seymour (1971). *The Paper Airplane Book.* New York: Viking.

Simon, Seymour (1988). New Visions: Science Books Are the Real Thing. Paper presented at the Thirty-Third Annual Convention of the International Reading Association, Toronto, Canada.

Slater, Don (1986). *Information Technology.* New York: Franklin Watts/Modern Technology.

Soares, Anthony T. (1963). Salient Elements of Recreational Reading of Junior High School Students. *Elementary English, 40,* 843–845.

Soares, Anthony T. and Simpson, Ray H. (1967). Interest in Recreational Reading of Junior High Students. *Journal of Reading, 11,* 14–21.

Stanchfield, Jo M. (1962). Boys' Reading Interests as Revealed through Personal Conferences. *The Reading Teacher, 16,* 41–44.

Strang, Ruth (1946). Reading Interest, 1946. *English Journal, 35,* 477–482.

Stewig, John Warren (1980). *Children and Literature.* Chicago: Rand McNally, 479–516.

Street, James (1954). *Good-bye My Lady.* New York: J. B. Lippincott.

Strieber, Whitley and Kunetka, James (1986). *Nature's End: The Consequences of the Twentieth Century.* New York: Warner Books.

Strunk, William, Jr. and White, E. B. (1972). *The Elements of Style.* Second ed. New York: Macmillan.

Sullivan, Jack, editor (1986). *The Penguin Encyclopedia of Horror and the Supernatural.* New York: Viking.

Superman from the 30's to the 80's (1983). New York: Crown Publishers.

Sutton, Roger (1987). In the YA Corner: Matchmaker, Matchmaker. *School Library Journal, 33,* 40.

Sutton, Roger (1988). Review of *Let There Be Light: A Book about Windows.* In *The Bulletin of the Center for Children's Books, 42,* 71.

Taft, David (1986). *Computer Programming.* New York: Warwick Press/Science in Action.

Tchudi, Stephen N. (1986). *Soda Poppery: The History of Soft Drinks in America.* New York: Charles Scribner's Sons.

Tey, Josephine (1951). *The Daughter of Time.* New York: Collier Books.

Trefil, James S. (1981). *Living in Space.* New York: Charles Scribner's Sons.

Trelease, Jim (1985). *The Read-Aloud Handbook.* New York: Viking Penguin.

Trelease, Jim (1989). *The New Read-Aloud Handbook.* Second rev. ed. New York: Penguin.

Tuchman, Barbara W. (1981). *Practicing History: Selected Essays.* New York: Alfred A. Knopf.

Turner, Tina with Loder, Kurt. (1986). *I, Tina.* New York: William Morrow.

Vacca, Richard T. (1981). *Teaching Reading in the Content Areas.* Boston: Little, Brown.

Vacca, Richard T. and Vacca, Jo Anne L. (1989). *Content Area Reading.* Third ed. Glenview, IL: Scott Foresman.

Vaughan, Joseph L., and Estes, Thomas H. (1986). *Reading and Reasoning Beyond the Primary Grades.* Newton, MA: Allyn & Bacon.

Voss, Jacqueline and Gale, Jay (1986). *A Young Woman's Guide to Sex.* New York: Henry Holt.

Watson, Lyall (1987). *The Dreams of Dragons.* New York: William Morrow.

Weiss, Ann E. (1988). *Lies, Deception and Truth.* Boston: Houghton Mifflin.

Whalley, Paul (1989). *Butterfly & Moth.* New York: Alfred A. Knopf/An Eyewitness Book.

White, Kay (1976). *The Wonderful World of Dogs.* New York: Hamlyn Publishing Group.

Whitehead, Robert J. (1984). *A Guide to Selecting Books for Children.* Metuchen, NJ: Scarecrow Press.

Wilford, John Noble (1986). *The Riddle of the Dinosaur.* New York: Alfred A. Knopf.

Wilson, Patricia J. and Kimzey, Ann C. (1987). *Happenings: Developing Successful Programs for School Libraries.* Littleton, CO: Libraries Unlimited.

Wirths, Claudine G. and Bowman-Kruhm, Mary (1987). *I Hate School: How to Hang In and When to Drop Out.* New York: Thomas Y. Crowell.

Wood, Leonard A. (1986). How Teenage Book Tastes Change. *Publishers Weekly,* August 22, 39.

Young Adults' Choices 1987 (1987). *Journal of Reading, 31,* 34–43.

Young Adults' Choices 1988 (1988). *Journal of Reading, 32,* 100–107.

Young, Jeffrey S. (1988). *Steve Jobs: The Journey Is the Reward.* Glenview, IL: Scott Foresman.

Young, Louise B. (1984). *The Blue Planet.* New York: New American Library/Meredian Books.

Zerman, Melvyn Bernard (1986). *Taking on the Press: Constitutional Rights in Conflict.* New York: Harper & Row.

Zindel, Paul (1968). *The Pigman.* New York: Harper & Row.

Zvirin, Stephanie (1989). Review of Edward F. Dolan's *MIA: Missing In Action: A Vietnam Drama.* In *Booklist, 85,* 1536.

Index

by Linda Webster

BETTY CARTER

Betty Carter, a former junior high reading teacher and school librarian, teaches young adult and children's literature at Texas Woman's University in the School of Library and Information Studies. She is the co-author of two educational computer programs, the present editor of the *Journal of Reading's* software review column, and is currently editing *Reading Education in Texas*. In addition, Dr. Carter was a member, and past chair, of the American Library Association's Best Books for Young Adults committee.

RICHARD F. ABRAHAMSON

Richard F. Abrahamson, past president of NCTE's Assembly on Adolescent Literature, teaches young adult and children's literature at the University of Houston in the College of Education. At present, Dr. Abrahamson is a member of the editorial board of the National Council of the Teachers of English and the editorial advisory board for *The Reading Teacher*. He is well known for his columns on young adult literature that have appeared in both *English Journal* and the *Journal of Reading*, and is a winner of the Educational Press Association Award for excellence in educational journalism.

Together Betty Carter and Richard Abrahamson co-edited the 1988 edition of *Books for You: A Booklist for Senior High Students* for the National Council of the Teachers of English.